Prophetic Discourse in a Crisis of Exile

Biblical Hermeneutics Rediscovered

The Series as the name suggests will focus on Biblical Hermeneutics, i.e., literary works concerned with methods of interpreting the Old and New Testaments of the Bible via different stream of topics like Literature and Poetry, Indigenous Philosophizing, Ethical response towards Ecology, Health and Healing, Science and Technology, Feminist Theology, Sociological approach towards Human Rights, Law and Politics, Arts, History of Ideas, Ancient Civilizations, Cultural Contiguity, Religious Cosmologies and Mysticism, Appraisal of various Theologians, World Peace and Harmony, Global Capitalism, Network Marketing, Cybertheology, Population and Demographics, Epigraphic Studies, Contextualized Education, and many others. We welcome a Mss. on any topic/s mentioned, whether they are original works, scholarly monographs, collections of conference papers, revised dissertations, or translations of historical documents. Through the Series we, the Publishers, are striving to put forward published works that may help Institutions, Academic Bodies, Researchers, Scholars and the World at large in furthering their respective knowledge and understanding on the concerned subject. We welcome your comments on our efforts and further suggestions on how we can enshrine new ray of analysing and explaining the written Texts through our upcoming books.

Biblical Hermeneutics Rediscovered - 27

Prophetic Discourse in a Crisis of Exile

Purity and Group Identity in the Book of Ezekiel

B. Lalnunzira

Christian World Imprints

First Published in 2020 by

Christian World Imprints
Christian Publishing & Books from India
C-3, Wazirpur Industrial Area
Delhi-110052
cwidelhi2017@gmail.com
www.ChristianWorldImprints.com
Phone: +91 11 41526079

ISBN: 978-93-5148-449-3 (HB)
ISBN: 978-93-5148-450-9 (PB)

Printed in India.

Contents

Foreword

It is a great joy and a special privilege for me to introduce the work of my colleague Rev. Dr. B. Lalnunzira. I am delighted to learn that his doctoral dissertation has got a book form entitled *Prophetic Discourse in a Crisis of Exile*. Identity is a loaded term used to define an individual or a group. While inhabitants of our planet are all connected as if we are now in a global village, individuals and groups define themselves differently. This may be termed as identity. Description of identity is governed by various characteristics. Biblical literature is also marked by identification of the people of God and other groups with attribution of traits. The issue of identification of oneself and others in the Bible needs to be examined to understand how Biblical literature evolved in various contexts.

The author of this book brings into light the issue of identity in the context of Babylonian exile and how prophet Ezekiel interprets purity as a mark of identity. He shows that in a crisis of exile, prophetic discourse on purity and identity played a crucial role for the people of Israel. I am sure that the readers of this book will understand how Biblical authors delineate challenging messages in their own time. I congratulate the author for his research on this important issue and for bringing out this book.

Rev. Dr. B. Lalnunzira was my student when he did his BTh in Aizawl Theological College (ATC), Aizawl. After some years of pastoral experience, he joined the teaching faculty of ATC in 2007. He was deputed to Bishop's College, Kolkata and then pursued his doctoral studies abroad. After earning his PhD degree in Biblical Studies, he has been part of the ATC faculty since June 2016 and he is now my colleague. As a student, I found him outstanding, hardworking and well versed with biblical languages, and he has turned out now to be a mature and gifted scholar. It's very appropriate that this book comes out from such a person. I strongly believe that this book will be of great use for the biblical students, scholars and Christian ministers. I hope that more scholarly books will come out of the author's hands in the future.

Durtlang, Mizoram
26th May 2020

Rev. Prof. Vanlalnghaka Ralte
Principal
Aizawl Theological College

Acknowledgements

This book is an outcome of my doctoral programme at the Graduate Theological Union, Berkeley, CA (USA). First of all, I thank my supervisor Prof. Gina Hens-Piazza without whose help this project will not come to exist in this manner. It is an immense pleasure for me to express my gratitude to my supervisor during my doctoral studies. I also express my heartfelt thanks to institutions, teachers, friends, and my family without whose love and support this book would not be existed. Though not possible to list them all, I cannot avoid mentioning some of them.

First, I thank Mizoram Presbyterian Church Synod (Presbyterian Church of India), who allowed me to pursue on my doctoral studies in a deputation. I thank for the prayers and supports of the Church where I am a minister. Second, I am thankful to the Council for World Mission (CWM), who supported my studies with a scholarship grant. I am thankful to the leaders and office staffs of the CWM for their warm and hospitable care. I am also very grateful to St John's Presbyterian Church at Berkeley who had been our family and support. St John's contributed a lot for my doctoral studies. We received enormous support financially, emotionally and spiritually from St John's.

There are many people whose contributions to my life and my studies could not be left unmentioned. First, I am very thankful to my advisor Prof. Gina Hens-Piazza who was my first and final teacher at the GTU, who has helped me achieving my goal of studies. I am so thankful for her constant support and able supervision in shaping my dissertation. I am also very thankful to my committee – Dr. Aaron Brody (Pacific School of Religion) and Prof. Ann Swidler (University of California at Berkeley) for their understanding and untiring help. I am also thankful to Dr. Annette Schellenberg, my former advisor and teacher. It is her initial thought that helped me shaping my dissertation. I am very thankful to many friends who helped me editing my manuscripts. For an international student like me, English editing is a big chunk and the help of Rev. Bob Mackenzie (parish associate at St John's Presbyterian church at Berkeley) and Sarah Johnson from St John's, will never be forgotten.

My family lived at Berkeley Presbyterian Mission Homes for more than five years. The Mission Homes contributed a lot for my studies by providing a house and creating access to meet friends and scholars of various backgrounds. I am very thankful to the GTU and its member schools for educating me in various capacities. I am indebted to the GTU for the enormous insights I get through her academic excellence.

Finally, the support of my family – Rami (my wife), Chhani and Zuali (our daughters) are very crucial in my journey of writing dissertation. Their sacrifice and endless help enabled me to go this far. Rami you are my best partner and support in my entire life. Above all, God is so good to me. It is the grace of God, and strengthening power that enabled me to finish this project. Glory be to him!

I dedicate this humble work to my father B. Lalnghaka (L) who ascended to eternal peace in November 2011 while I was at the stage of my course work. I will not meet him again here on earth; but I will meet him someday to share my experience of joy in this work.

I am also grateful to Rev. Prof. Vanlalnghaka Ralte, principal of Aizawl Theological College and secretary of Theological Education Board of the Mizoram Presbyterian Church, who kindly wrote the forward for this book. He has been my support in this endeavor. His constant encouragement in my theological pursuit is commendable.

I am so thankful to the staff of Christian World Imprints who earnestly labour for the publication of this book. I am grateful to Mr. Sudhanshu Kanda for his support and coordination of the work.

Abbreviations

AB	Anchor Bible
ABD	Anchor Bible Dictionary
ABSS	Archaeology and Biblical Studies Series
AnBib	Analecta Biblica
ANET	Ancient Near Eastern Texts Relating to the Old Testament
AOTC	Abingdon Old Testament Commentaries
ASTI	Annual of Swedish Theological Institute
ASV	American Standard Version
AV	Authorized Version
BDB	F. Brown, S.R. Driver, and C. A. Briggs. *A Hebrew and English Lexicon of the Old Testament.*
BETL	Bibliotheca Ephemeridum Theologicarum Lovaniensium
BHS	Biblia Hebraica Stuttgartensia
BJS	Biblical and Judaic Studies
BZAW	Beihefte zur Zeitschrift fur die Alttestamentliche Wissenschaft
CBQ	Catholic Biblical Quarterly
FAT	Forschungen zum Alten Testament
FOTL	Forms of the Old Testament Literature
FRLANT	Forchungen zur Religion und Literatur des Alten und Newuen Testaments
FZB	Forschung zur Bibel
H	Holiness Code
HALOT	Hebrew and Aramaic Lexicon of the Old Testament
HBM	Hebrew Bible Monograph
HBS	Herders Biblische Studien
HSM	Harvard Semitic Monographs
HSS	Harvard Semitic Studies

HUCA	Hebrew Union College Annual
IB	Interpreter's Bible
ICC	International Critical Commentary
Ind	Indiana
ITC	International Theological Commentary
JB	Jerusalem Bible
JBL	Journal of Biblical Literature
JSOT	Journal for the Study of the Old Testament
JSOTSup	Journal for the Study of the Old Testament Supplement Series
LHB	Library of Hebrew Bible
LSTS	Library of Second Temple Studies
MT	Masoretic Text
NAB	New American Bible
NAC	New American Commentary
NASB	New American Standard Bible
NCB	New Century Bible
NEB	New English Bible
NIB	New Interpreter's Bible
NIBC	New International Bible Commentary
NICOT	New International Commentary of the Old Testament
NIDB	New Interpreter's Dictionary of the Bible
NIDOTTE	New International Dictionary of Old Testament Theology & Exegesis
NIV	New International Version
NJB	New Jerusalem Bible
NRSV	New Revised Standard Version
OTE	Old Testament Essays
OTL	Old Testament Library
OTS	Old Testament Studies
P	Priestly Source
PTMS	Princeton Theological Monograph Series
REB	Revised English Bible
RJSS	Routledge Jewish Studies Series
SBL	Society of Biblical Literature
SBLDS	Society of Biblical Literature Dissertation Series
SJLA	Studies in Judaism and Late Antiquity
SJOT	Scandinavian Journal of the Old Testament
SSSP	Springer Series in Social Psychology
TAD	Textbook of Aramaic Documents from Ancient Egypt
TDNT	Theological Dictionary of the New Testament

TDOT	Theological Dictionary of the Old Testament
TLOT	Theological Lexicon of the Old Testament
TOTC	Tyndale Old Testament Commentaries
VTSup	Vetus Testamentum Supplements
WBC	Word Biblical Commentary
ZAW	Zeitschrift fur die Alttestamentliche Wissenschaft

Introduction

1. Why Purity and Identity Matters for Ezekiel

The book of Ezekiel contains a number of references to purity.[1] In many instances, Israel's history and current situation is explained in relation to issues of purity and impurity. Noteworthy, in particular, is that in Ezekiel the concept of purity is frequently used in connection with groups of Israelites, be it the people in the exile or those who remained in Judah (or Jerusalem). Scholars normally study the concept of purity focusing on the priestly writings of the Pentateuch while the book of Ezekiel does not get that much attention. Those who study purity issues in the book of Ezekiel normally do not consider how it might have used in relation to larger social issues. This book looks at the concept of purity in Ezekiel and how it is used in connection with group identification. It can be assumed that in the book of Ezekiel the concept of purity/impurity plays a fundamental role in the construction of identity. It is important to explore how the priestly group(s) of the exilic age that authored the book of Ezekiel utilized the priestly purity system to define who constitutes the true Israel and who does not.

From the time of deportations starting at the beginning of sixth century BCE, Israel lived a double existence. Part of the population lived in Judah and another part in the diaspora outside the land. Biblical sources, such as Jeremiah, Ezekiel, and Ezra-Nehemiah, indicate that lines were drawn between disparate socio-religious groups, and that polemic stances evolved in the exilic and early post exilic period (Jer 24:4-10; Ezek 33:24; Ezra 9:1-2; Neh 9:2-3). Group conflicts between the disparate groups created desires to restructure and refine cultural/religious and kinship-based standards of identity, responding to the conditions of

1 The term טהר (pure/clean) occurs 16 times, and the root טמא (impure/unclean) occurs 44 times in the book. There are also related terms to purity such as קדש (holy) and חלל (profane), used frequently in the book. These terms are used interchangeably in many instances. See Jacob Neusner, *The Idea of Purity in Ancient Judaism* (Leiden: Brill, 1973), 18, 26.

exile that were endangering Israel's identity and continued existence. Identifying 'who is the true Israel' was contested during this period, as we know primarily from the literature of the exilic period.[2]

In the study of the book of Ezekiel, the scholarly consensus holds that the book reflects the period of the Babylonian exile; originally going back to the prophet Ezekiel, the book received its final form in the hand of a priestly group of the late exilic period. The tension between the exilic group and those remaining in Judah is mirrored in a quotation that Ezekiel places on the lips of those remain in Jerusalem: "They have gone far from YHWH; to us this land is given for a possession." (Ezek 11:15; 33:24). The book of Ezekiel, however, reflects a different view: Ezekiel and his editors clearly favor those in exile and delegitimize the claims of those who remain in Judah due to their impurity (eg. Ezek 33:25-29). Most important in their argument is the question, with which group YHWH is present. For example, according to Ezek 11:16, YHWH says, "I have been a sanctuary to them (the exilic group) for a little while in the countries where they have gone." The book shows that Ezekiel's primary concern is the impurity of the people, the land, and the temple; YHWH cannot dwell any longer in the temple (in Jerusalem) due to their religious apostasy and impurity (Ezek 8). YHWH's glory (*kābôd*) leaves Jerusalem and dwells among those who are exiled in Babylonia (Ezek 10). In the latter section of the book, a restoration of the exilic group to their homeland is envisioned as purification of the exiles (34:8-38; 37:1-28). In the last section of the book (Ezek 40-48), which was probably added at a late exilic date, a new temple community is envisioned. In this vision, the criteria of who will serve in the temple and who would be in the new community are determined by purity (44:1-16). These examples show that in Ezekiel there is a significant connection between purity and identity construction. There are a number of passages, which illustrate the discussion of this connection. Employing both exegetical and social scientific methods, this project selects five relevant passages to investigate how purity and group identity are connected in the book of Ezekiel.

2. The Research on Purity and Identity in Ezekiel

Earlier research on the idea of purity in the book of Ezekiel focuses broadly on a general understanding of purity and holiness. Tova Ganzel's work on *The Concept of Holiness in the Book of Ezekiel* focuses on the understanding of holiness and purity in relation to defilement and profanation. Ganzel insists that Israel's sins defiled the land of Israel and the temple. She also makes a claim that it desecrated

2 "Literature of the exilic period" here designates a large corpus of biblical literature authored or edited during the sixth century BCE. There is no consensus in the attribution of exilic literature. Books such as Jeremiah, Deutero-Isaiah, Lamentations, and Ezekiel are reflecting the exilic situations and are usually dated to the exile. See Rainer Albertz, *Israel in Exile: The History and Literature of the Sixth Century BCE,* trans. David Green (Atlanta: Society of Biblical Literature, 2003).

the Sabbath and God's name throughout their history, "essentially making them impure and unsanctified."[3] In his book *The Idea of Retribution in Ezekiel*, and in his article "*Profanation/ Sanctification and the Past, Present, and Future of Israel in the book of Ezekiel*," Ka Leung Wong demonstrates that in Ezekiel, "the history of Israel (her past, present, and future) revolves around the principle of purity/ impurity."[4] These broader perspectives provide an opportunity to explore the meaning and usage of purity in relation to Israel's history.

The publication of Dalit Rom-Shiloni entitled *Exclusive Inclusivity: Identity Conflicts Between the Exiles and the People who Remained (6th-5th Century)* enriches a study of Ezekiel in relation to group identification. Rom-Shiloni states that the sixth-fifth century BCE literature, including the book of Ezekiel show internal polemics between the Judean exiles in Babylonia. He demonstrates that the book of Ezekiel in its original and secondary/redactional form maintain ingroup/ outgroup split between the exiles and those who remained in the land. [5] The study illustrates the construction of group identity in the book of Ezekiel. However, it leaves out the connection between purity and formation of identity.

One of the finest examples of research on the use of purity in relation to group identity is found in Armin Sidlecki's MA Thesis: "Purity and Power: A Rhetorical Study of the Ideology of Purity and Defilement in the Book of Ezekiel." Sidlecki crafts his project within three phases: the defilement, the purification, and the restoration. He concludes that "Ezekiel synthesizes the preexisting notion of religious, political, and social purity with an ideology that was endorsed by his exilic counterpart in order to exclude those of the Jerusalemite in the exilic age."[6] For Sidlecki, Ezekiel's rhetoric and ideology of purity and power represents the bias view of the exilic group. This study paves a new direction for studying the idea of purity in relation to group identification. However, this project hinges on a rhetorical analysis, leaving out the social reality of the texts that influenced the book of Ezekiel. Moreover, it touches only few passages. This project addresses the

---

3 Tova Ganzel, "The Concept of Holiness in the Book of Ezekiel" (PhD Dissertation: Bar-Ilan University, Ramat-Gan, Israel, 2005). See English abstract of the thesis, 11. See also her article entitled, "The Defilement and Desecration of the Temple in Ezekiel," *Biblica* 89, no. 3 (2008): 369-379.

4 Ka Leung Wong, *The Idea of Retribution in the Book of Ezekiel* VTSup 87 (Leiden: Brill, 2001), 124. Also Ka Leung Wong, "Profanation/Sanctification and the Past Present and Future of Israel in the Book of Ezekiel," *JSOT* 28, no. 2 (2003): 210-239.

5 Dalit Rom-Shiloni, *Exclusive Inclusivity: Identity Conflict Between the Exiles and the People who Remained (6th-5th century BCE)* (New York: Bloomsbury, 2013). 197. See also Dalit Rom-Shiloni, "From Ezekiel to Ezra-Nehemiah: Shifts of Group Identities within Babylonian Exilic Ideology," in Judah and the Judeans in the Achaemenid Period: Negotiating Identity in an International Context, eds. Oded Lipschits, Gary Knoppers, and Manfred Oeming (Winona Lake, Ind: Eisenbrauns, 2011), 127-151.

6 Armin Siedlecki, "Purity and Power: A Rhetorical Study of the Ideology of Purity and Defilement in the book of Ezekiel" (MA Thesis: Wilfrid Laurier University, 1991), 126.

lacunae of the studies mentioned above by using both classical exegetical methods and social scientific methods to investigate how the purity system functions in the book of Ezekiel in connection with identity construction.

3. Methodology

The book consists of two main parts. The first deals with methodology, background study, and a study on the use of purity and its related concepts in the book of Ezekiel. As a background study, I investigate the socio-historical situations of the Israelites during the exilic age, intergroup relationship in that period, and group identification in the exilic literature. This is followed by a general survey on the use of purity in the book of Ezekiel, which introduces a discussion on purity and identity in Ezekiel. The second part consists of careful exegesis of the passages in Ezekiel that touches on the question of identity and employs the concept of purity/impurity. Exegetical studies focus on the final composition of the text and will address redaction-historical issues only when they are relevant to my question. Since this project also concerns the social structures behind the formation of the book of Ezekiel, special attention is given to the settings of each individual unit of Ezekiel's texts. To better understand the connection between purity and group identity in Ezekiel, in addition to classical historical-methods, social scientific theories are employed. By applying social identity theories, the book draws attention to questions of group identity, boundary mechanism in intergroup relationship, and the role of purity systems in group constructions.

In defining group identity, I employ theories of group identity in general, but particularly focus on the Social Identity Theory developed by Henri Tajfel and others. Social Identity Theory (SIT) was articulated in the 1970s by Henri Tajfel and since then developed by many others.[7] According to Tajfel, social identity

7 The works following Tajfel and Turner are mainly found in collection of articles in edited books. These are some of the well-known works among many: W. G. Austin and S. Worchel (eds), *The Social Psychology of Intergroup Relations* (Monterey, CA: Brooks/Cole, 1979); J. C. Turner, M. A. Hogg, P. J. Oakes, S. D. Reicher, and M. S. Wetherell (eds), *Rediscovering Social Group: A Self-Categorization Theory* (Oxford: Blackwell, 1987); J. M. Rabie, J. C. Schot, and L. Visser, "Social Identity Theory: A Conceptual and Empirical Critique from the Perspective of a Behavioural Interaction Model," in *European Journal of Social Psychology* 19 (1989): 171-202; Dominic Abrams and Michael Hogg (eds), *Social Identity Theory: Constructive and Critical Advances* (New York: Springer-Verlag, 1990); P. J. Oakes and S. A. Haslam (eds), *Stereotyping and Social Reality* (Oxford: Blackwell, 1994); W. Peter Robinson, *Social Groups and Identities: Developing the Legacy of Henri Tajfel* (Oxford: Butterworth-Heinemann, 1996); Stephen Worchel, J. Francois Morales, Dario Paez and Jean-Claude Deschamps (eds), *Social Identity: International Perspective* (London: Sage Publications, 1998); Naomi Ellemers, Russell Spears, and Bertijan Doosje (eds), *Social Identity Context, Commitment, Content* (Oxford: Blackwell, 1999); Dominic Abrams and Michael A. Hogg (eds), *Social Identity and Social Cognition* (Oxford: Blackwell, 1999); Michael Hogg and Dominic Abrams (eds), *Intergroup Relations* (Philadelphia, PA: Psychology Press, 2001); Michael A. Hogg and Deborah J. Terry (eds), Social Identity Processes in Organizational Contexts (Philadelphia, PA: Psychology Press,

is "that part of the individual's self concept which derives from their knowledge of their membership of a social group together with the value and emotional significance attached to it."[8] Tajfel and Turner maintain that, "people categorize themselves into groups in an attempt to establish a positive sense of value by distinguishing their groups (ingroup) from other groups (outgroup), in which boundaries serve as identity markers."[9] In intergroup conflicts, the tendency of the dominant group is to maintain and justify the status quo and create new categories of differentiation.[10] In short, social identity theory holds that group identify themselves and others in order to establish a positive sense of value in which boundary (group norms) serve as a distinguishing mark.

In addition to the works of Tajfel and Turner as a methodological point of reference, some other works on social and anthropological theories of group conflicts, group beliefs and ideology, and boundary construction in group relationships are reviewed. These include Muzafer Sheriff, Daniel-Bar Tal, Michael Walzer, Emile Durkheim, and Mary Douglas among others. There are several methods in the study of the role of purity regulations as boundary construction. Some relevant works are highlighted in this project. Some are worth examining as methodological framework as well. Following W. Robertson Smith's method of purity as symbolic system, Mary Douglas contributes to the understanding of Biblical purity system. Therefore, I employ her theories in this study. Douglas argues for a close correlation between purity ideas and concerns over social boundaries. According to her, "dirt (impurity) is matter out of place," and hence it offends against order.[11] Purity plays a role of classification or differentiation in group relationships.

2001); Richard D. Ashmore, Lee Jussim and David Wilder (eds), *Social Identity, Intergroup Conflict, and Conflict Reduction* (Oxford: Oxford University Press, 2001); Rupert Brown and Dora Capozza (eds), *Social Identities: Motivational, Emotional and Cultural Influences* (Hove, East Sussex: Psychology Press, 2006).

8 Henri Tajfel, "Introduction," in *Social Identity and Intergroup Relations*, ed. Henri Tajfel (Cambridge: Cambridge University Press, 1982), 2.

9 Henri Tajfel and John C. Turner, "The Social Identity Theory of Intergroup Behavior," in *Psychology of Intergroup Relation*, eds. W. G. Austin and S. Worchel (Monterey, CA: Brooks/Cole, 1986), 17.

10 Henri Tajfel and John C. Turner, "An Integrative Theory of Intergroup Conflict," in *Intergroup Relations*, eds. Michael Hogg and Dominic Abrams (Philadelphia, PA: Psychology Press, 2001), 98. See also Marilynn B. Brewer, "Intergroup Identification and Intergroup Conflict: When Does Ingroup Love Becomes Outgroup Hate?" in *Social Identity, Intergroup Conflict, and Conflict Reduction*, eds. Richard D. Ashmore, Lee Jussim and David Wilder (Oxford: Oxford University Press, 2000), 17-30.

11 Mary Douglas, *Purity and Danger: An Analysis of Concepts of Pollution and Taboo* (New York: Oxford University Press Inc., 1966), 35.

4. Overview of the Book

This book is designed with two parts. Part One consists of three chapters: theory, context and a general discussion on purity and identity in the book of Ezekiel. Part Two consists of exegeses of five passages that add to the analysis of purity and group identity.

Chapter one is a review of methodologies of sociological, anthropological, and psychological paradigms of group (social) identity. I will enlist the Social Identity Theory promoted by Tajfel and others to investigate how group identity is constructed in social interaction and relationship. Since identity is correlated with many other forms of social processes, I will also investigate the relationships between identity and conflicts, construction of ideology in group relationships, and how boundary works in group identification. In the latter part of my discussion, I will delve into theories of purity offered by social anthropologists and biblical scholars. This review will help to explain how purity systems function as boundary markers in intergroup relationships.

In chapter two, I brought out the socio-historical situations and intergroup relationships of the Israelites during the period of the exile and how group identification was developed through the literature of the era. My intention is to assess the dynamics of group relationship in this era. Using available primary and secondary sources, I will assess the life-situation of the communities of Israel who were in Judah, Babylonia, and Egypt. I will also investigate how these groups interacted, and how they identified themselves and others through literature. This chapter serves as a backdrop to examine how the book of Ezekiel, one of the exilic literatures, domesticates the concept of purity as an identity marker.

Chapter three discusses the idea of purity in the book of Ezekiel. My focus is on the basic idea of purity in the book of Ezekiel, and how purity languages are used in connection with group identity. I will briefly define terminologies of purity and their usages. My main discussion will focus on various types of purity/impurity and also look into the concept of purification in the book of Ezekiel. This study will form a basis for the next chapters in which I exegete relevant passages that discuss purity and identity.

Chapters four-seven consist of exegetical studies of selected passages. This section investigates five selected texts from the book of Ezekiel to explore how purity plays an important role in group identification. I study these passages in conversation with other relevant texts both in the book of Ezekiel and other books of the Hebrew Bible. The discussion is limited to four chapters representing four areas of discussions. Chapter four is an exegesis on Ezekiel 11:14-21 and 33:25-29. These texts are explicit identification of ingroup and outgroup. It is a comparison of the exiles and those who remained in Judah and Jerusalem during the exilic period. Chapter five illustrates the judgment of God on the homelanders found in Ezekiel 22:1-16. This chapter investigates how the book of Ezekiel rejects the inhabitants of Judah and Jerusalem as a consequence of their sins and impurities.

Chapter six explores how restoration and purification of the exiles are illustrated in Ezekiel 37:15-28. This chapter examines the symbolism of the two sticks that represent the diaspora communities of the northern and the southern kingdoms. The final chapter evaluates the portrayal of the new temple community found in Ezekiel 44:1-16. This chapter investigates how the rigorous legislation of the new community disqualifies certain groups of the community from membership and participation in the worship and service at the new temple. The book is concluded with the outcomes of the research and the implications of the study in the understanding of the book of Ezekiel in relation to purity and group identity.

5. The Approach on the Book of Ezekiel

The investigation in this book focuses on the final form of the texts while acknowledging redactional layers in the book. Hence, it is a synchronic-diachronic approach. The book of Ezekiel has been known to be one of the exilic literatures written by prophet Ezekiel who also experienced the exilic catastrophe (1:3; 29:17). Since the last century, scholars have been observing numerous repetitive doublets and illogical breaks in the text and thereby have suggested a late editorial compilation.[12] Scholars generally regard it as one of the most highly structured, biblical books. Due to its unity and literary complexity, there are divergent views on its interpretation. Both holistic (synchronic) and diachronic (reconstructing its redactional history) interpretations are noteworthy.[13] The influence of priestly

12 Majority of Ezekiel's scholars agree that the authentic words of the prophet are the core of the prophecy and the final composition being in the hand of the later redactor. This resulted in a remodeling, elaborating and supplementing of the original work. Among them we may name G. Holscher, Kessler, R. Kittel, C. C. Torrey, J. Smith, G. R. Berry, Walter Eichrodt, G. Fohrer, G. A. Cooke, J. W. Wevers, Walther Zimmerli, R. M. Hals, Leslie C. Allen, Daniel I. Block, John F. Kutsko, Andrew Mein, Christopher J. H. Wright, Margaret S. Odell, and Paul M. Joyce. See further discussion in Walther Zimmerli, *Ezekiel 1: A Commentary on the Book of Ezekiel, Chapters 1-24,* trans. Ronald E. Clements, (Philadelphia: Fortress Press, 1979), 2-8; Henry McKeating, *Ezekiel,* Old Testament Guides (Sheffield: Sheffield Academic Press, 1993), 30-61; Paul M. Joyce, *Ezekiel: A Commentary* LHB/OTE 482 (New York: T&T Clark, 2007), 7-16. Brian Neil Peterson, *Ezekiel In Context: Ezekiel's Message in Its Historical Setting of Covenant Curses and Ancient Near Eastern Mythological Motifs*, PTMS 182 (Eugene, Oregon: Pickwick Publications, 2012), 7-11. See also Tyler D. Mayfield, *Literary Structure and Setting in Ezekiel,* (Tubingen: Mohr Siebeck, 2010).

13 Moshe Greenberg, Lawrence Boadt, Julie Galambush, Thomas Renz, and others focus on its final form and they prefer to analyze the text in its present form. J. Garscha, F. L. Hossfeldt, Walther Zimmerli, Karl-Friedrich Pohlmann, and others discern multiple layers in its composition and reconstruct its redactional history in its interpretation. See Discussion in Joyce, *Ezekiel: A Commentary*, 13-16. Some interpreters use both the approaches. For example, Leslie C. Allen claims that he is representing both the approaches. He defines himself "like a householder who brings out of his store things new and old." See Leslie C. Allen, *Ezekiel 20-48,* WBC, vol. 29 (Waco: Word Books, 1990), xx. Cf. Matt 13:52.

thinking and ideology on its composition could not be overestimated.[14] At the same time, the visions of Ezekiel are expressed as prophetic passion in the form of a vision.[15] It is likely that the core of the oracles came from prophet Ezekiel, and the final form came to us through a priestly author (Ezekiel's school) sometime in the late sixth century BCE. A majority consensus exists on Babylonia as the location where Ezekiel's ministry took place.[16] Hence, the book must have been written and compiled in Babylonia. Throughout the book, both the authentic words of Ezekiel and the literary development of the literature through the hands of the redactors are considered. This book adds more knowledge in the understanding of purity in the book of Ezekiel and its interpretation in connection with communities of the Israelites who were in different locations during the exilic period.

14 Marvin A. Sweeney argues that a great many features of the book of Ezekiel are dependent upon the worldview and practices of the Zadokite priesthood. See Sweeney, *Form and Intertextuality in Prophetic and Apocalyptic Literature* (Tubingen, Germany: Mohr Siebeck, 2005), 126-172. See also discussion in Margaret S. Odell, "You are What You Eat: Ezekiel and the Scroll," *JBL* 117 (1998): 229-248.

15 Cf. Baruch J. Schwartz, "A priest out of Place: Reconsidering Ezekiel's Role in the History of the Israelite Priesthood," in *Ezekiel's Hierarchical World Wrestling with a Tired Reality*, eds. Stephen L. Cook and Corrine L. Patton (Atlanta: Society of Biblical Literature, 2004), 61-71 (especially 63). The book portrays Ezekiel as a prophet of judgment and hope. The book of Ezekiel addresses Judean community in Judah and the exiles, condemning their cultic and moral sin while also promising restoration.

16 For further discussion see Peterson, *Ezekiel In Context*, 6-17.

Chapter 1

Group Identity Models
Social Identity, Boundary Mechanisms and Purity in Intergroup Relationships

1. Introduction

Identity formation can be defined as an ongoing process of human action that defines group membership. "Identity" is an ambiguous term, rarely defined in a precise way. However, it can be understood as a product of social or political action wherein a group defines itself as having a distinctive history, experiences, and social locations that endow its members with unique perspectives on social issues.[1] An identity, whether personal or collective, depends on social processes whereby group values and norms define an individual and a group. Therefore, group relationships give a sense of identity defining who we are in a larger social world.

Social scientific research can be of immense help in exploring how group (social) identity is constructed using purity as an identity marker in the book of Ezekiel. I propose that Social Identity Theory (SIT) and its related concepts

1 Brubaker and Cooper argue that social sciences and humanities have surrendered the word "identity" and that it tends to mean too much, too little or nothing at all. Their idea is that the conceptual and theoretical work of identity might be better accomplished by other terms that offer less ambiguity. In their attempt to find alternative terms for "identity," they propose terms such as identification, categorization, self-understanding, social location, commonality, connectedness, and groupness. See Rogers Brubaker and Frederick Cooper, Beyond "Identity," *Theory and Society* 29, no. 1 (Feb 2000): 1-47.

are helpful tools for explaining group behavior and relationships. Therefore, this chapter reviews sociological, anthropological, and psychological paradigms as a tool to investigate how identity is constructed within social interaction and group relationships.[2] First, I will explain major approaches of social identity theory. I will discuss major questions such as the meaning and process of social identity formation. This is followed by a brief investigation of the relationship between identity and group conflicts, ideology and social identity, and boundary mechanisms in intergroup relationships. In the latter part of my discussion, I will deal with theories of purity developed by social anthropologists and biblical scholars. In my review of purity theories, I give emphasis to the meaning and function of purity systems, and to their functions as boundary markers in intergroup relationships.

2. Social Identity Theory

Social Identity Theory is a branch of social psychology that seeks to understand the effects of group membership on human identity. It was originally articulated by Henri Tajfel and John C. Turner in the 1970s, and has been extended in various ways by many sociologists.[3] According to Henry Tajfel, "Social Identity is understood as that part of the individual's self-concept which derives from the knowledge of their membership in a social group, together with the value and emotional significance attached to that membership."[4] According to Tajfel, group belonging has three dimensions: the cognitive dimension— simple recognition of belonging to a group, the evaluative dimension—negative or positive connotations of belonging, and the emotional dimension—attitudes that members hold towards insiders and outsiders.[5]

Turner further explains social identity as "that aspect of a person's self-concept that is based on their group memberships."[6] In his approach to self-

2 I agree with Jutta Jorikanta in the view that identity construction is a social-psychological phenomenon that relates to historical changes and the development of theological concepts. Cf. Jutta Jokiranta, *Social Identity and Sectarianism in the Qumran Movement*, Studies on the Texts of the Desert of Judah (Leiden: Brill, 2013), 87.

3 Apart from the articulation of the theory by Tajfel and Turner in the 1970s, many works on social identity and group relationships have been developed. Different works that contributed to the growth of social identity theory and its application in social sciences exist in compilations and edited volumes. For the lists of major works following Tajfel and Turner see footnote 7 of Introduction, p. 6.

4 Henri Tajfel, "Introduction," in *Social Identity and Intergroup Relations*, ed. Henri Tajfel (Cambridge: Cambridge University Press, 1982), 2.

5 Henri Tajfel, *Differentiation between Social Groups: Studies in Social Psychology of Intergroup Relations* (London: Academic Press, 1978), 87.

6 See John C. Turner, "Some Current Issues in research on Social Identity and Self-Categorization Theories," in *Social Identity Context, Commitment, Content*, eds. Naomi Ellemers, Russel Spears and Bertijan Doosje (Malden, Massachusetts: Blackwell Publishers, 1999), 8.

categorization theory, Turner postulates that "people stereotype themselves and others in terms of salient social categorizations, leading to an enhanced perceptual identity between self and ingroup members and an enhanced perceptual contrast between ingroup and outgroup members.[7] The ingroup is compared with the outgroup and evaluated positively as it is perceived as superior.[8] In short, the Social Identity Theory maintains that people categorize themselves into groups to establish a positive sense of value by distinguishing their group from other groups.

An important component of social identity theory is the establishment of boundaries (group norms). Tajfel and Turner argue that "pressures to evaluate one's own group positively through ingroup or outgroup comparisons lead social groups to differentiate themselves from each other."[9] Hence, a boundary is drawn between competing groups. In group conflict, the tendency of the dominant group is to maintain and justify the status quo and create new categories of differentiation.[10] To achieve positive social identity, individuals within a group would adopt varying approaches to drawing boundaries.[11] In boundary construction, norms or rules including ritual and purity systems play significant roles.[12] They play a central role in determining collective reactions by insecure group members in the social system. In short, a boundary is a norm or a distinguishing aspect in social identification. It is an identity marker in group relationships.

2.1. The Process of Social Identity Formation

In the process of social identity formation, there are different stages or characteristic modes of group interaction. They play important roles in defining one's identity in relation to others. I will explain them briefly as follows:

a. Categorization

Social identification presupposes that individuals tend to evaluate themselves and others in terms of a common category of membership. According to Michael A. Hogg, categorization is "an underlying process of social identity, which clarifies intergroup boundaries by producing a group's stereotypical and

7 Turner, "Some Current Issues," 11.

8 Cf. Rupert Brown and Dora Capozza, "Motivational, Emotional, and Cultural Influences in Social Identity Processes," in *Social Identities: Motivational, Emotional and Cultural Influences*, 3-30.

9 Tajfel and Turner, "The Social Identity Theory of Intergroup Behavior,"16.

10 Henri Tajfel and John Turner, "An Integrative Theory of Intergroup Conflict," in *Intergroup Relations*, eds. Michael Hogg and Dominic Abrams (Philadelphia, PA: Psychology Press, 2001), 98. Cf. Dominic Abrams and Michael Hogg, "An Introduction to the Social Identity Approach," in *Social Identity Theory: Constructive and Critical Advances*, eds. Dominic Abrams and Michael Hogg (New York: Springer-Verlag, 1990), 4.

11 See Turner, "Some Current Issues," 9.

12 See Anthony P. Cohen, *The Symbolic Construction of Community* (London/New York: Tavistock Publications, 1985), 12.

normative perceptions and actions."[13] Ingroup bias is a remarkable feature of intergroup relations.[14] Turner who offers the self-categorization theory argues that "an individual structures his or her perception of the self and others by means of abstract social categories and that these categories, as aspects of the self-concept that produce group behavior, are internalized by the individual."[15] Thus, categorization involves evaluation of both the self and the other with prejudice. In short, categorization is an evaluation of ingroup members positively, and categorizing others with bias to decide whether they are members of the ingroup or outgroup.

An extreme form of negative categorization in intergroup relationships is known as delegitimization. Daniel Bar-Tal, who popularized this theory, defines delegitimization as "categorization of groups into extreme negative social categories which are excluded from human groups that are considered as acting within the limits of acceptable norms and/or values."[16] It is an extreme negative attitude towards opposing groups to achieve a group's own goal. A group may delegitimize another group and devalue the delegitimized (outgroup) while elevating their own group. Groups may have based their delegitimization on ideology or delegitimizing belief. Delegitimization is thus a process of social identification whereby ingroup members exclude and devalue outgroup members in an extreme form.

b. Comparison

According to John R. Jost and Kimberley D. Elsbach, "the only way to assess value and regard in the social world is through processes of comparison, so that the value and worth of one group is always relative to the value and worth of the

13 Michael A. Hogg, "Intragroup Processes, Group Structure and Social Identity," in *Social Groups and Identities: Developing the Legacy of Henri Tajfel,* 67.

14 Cf. Henri Tajfel and John Turner, "An Integrative Theory of Intergroup Conflict," in *The Social Psychology of Intergroup Relations*, eds. William G. Austin and Stephen Worchel (Monterey: Brooks/Cole Publishing Company, 1979), 38.

15 John C. Turner, "Towards a Cognitive Redefinition of the Social group," in *Social Identity and Intergroup Relations, ed. Henri Tajfel* (Cambridge: Cambridge University Press, 1982), 16.

16 Daniel Bar-Tal, "Delegitimization: The Extreme Case of Stereotyping and Prejudice," in *Stereotyping and Prejudice: Changing Conceptions*, SSSP, eds. Daniel Bar-Tal, Carl F. Graumann, Arie W. Kruglanski and Wolfgang Stroebe (New York: Springer-Verlag, 1989), 170, 178-179. (169-182). Bar-Tal proposes six basic characteristics of delegitimization as: (1) extremely negative and salient basis of categorization; (2) permanent exclusion of the delegitimized group form the society; (3) extremely negative affective component; (4) institutionalized norms supporting delegitimization; (5) implication of a threat from the delegitimized group; and (6) prescription for extremely negative behaviors towards the delegitimized group. See above 178-179. See also Daniel Bar-Tal, "Causes and Consequences of Delegitimization: Models of Conflict and Ethnocentrism," *Journal of Social Issues* 46, no. 1 (1990): 65-81.

reference group."[17] Social identity theory holds the view that our sense of who we are is maintained through evaluative comparisons between ingroups and relevant outgroups.[18] In intergroup relationships, there is a social competition whereby the group members may seek positive distinctiveness through direct comparison with the outgroup.[19] Also similarity inside the group is emphasized when people categorize themselves as members of a group. Positive comparisons provide ingroup members high subjective status or prestige, whereas negative comparisons assign to outgroup members low prestige and negative social identity.[20] Competitions between religious groups for resources or value promotion likely foster prejudice against religious outgroup members.[21] Comparison is a means by which the value and worth of a group is described. It is motivated by the need for high self-esteem in the grouping process.

c. Stereotypes

Stereotyping is a phenomenon that frequently accompanies ingroup/outgroup differentiation. Tajfel defines stereotypes as "certain generalizations reached by individuals."[22] He states that "the main function of stereotyping is to simplify or systematize, for purposes of cognitive and behavioral adaptation, the abundance and complexity of the information received from its environment by the human organism."[23] Many times, our perceptions of others are determined by group identification instead of reacting to people as individuals. When we stereotype people, we attribute to them certain characteristics that are seen to be shared by all or most of their fellow group members.[24] Stereotypes are not simply expressions of ingroup preference, but they are assigning character profiles to others. Stereotypes serve primarily to justify and explain hostilities that derive from conflicts of

---

17 John R. Jost and Kimberly D. Elsbach, "How Status and Power Differences Erode Personal and Social Identities at Work: A System Justification Critique of Organizational Applications of Social Identity Theory," in *Social Identity Processes in Organizational Contexts*, eds. Michael A. Hogg and Deborah J. Terry (Philadelphia, PA: Psychology Press, 2001), 183.

18 Cf. Steve Hinkle and Rupert Brown, "Intergroup Comparisons and Social Identity: Some Links and Lacunae," in *Social Identity Theory: Constructive and Critical Advances*, eds. Dominic Abrams and Michael Hogg (New York: Springer-Verlag, 1990), 48.

19 Cf. Tajfel and Turner, "An Integrative Theory of Intergroup Conflict," 44.

20 Cf. Turner, "Towards a Cognitive Redefinition of the Social Group," 34.

21 Cf. Lynne M. Jackson and Bruce Hunsberger in "An Intergroup Perspective on Religion and Prejudice," in *Journal for the Scientific Study of Religion* 38, no. 1 (March 1999): 509-523.

22 Henri Tajfel, "Social Stereotypes and Social Groups," in *Intergroup Behaviour*, eds. J. C. Turner and Howard Giles (Oxford: Blackwell, 1981), 146.

23 Tajfel, "Social Stereotypes and Social Groups," 146-147.

24 Cf. Philip E. Esler, *Conflict and Identity in Romans: The Social Setting of Paul's Letter* (Minneapolis: Fortress Press, 2003), 21.

interest.[25] Therefore stereotyping is the evaluation of others and ourselves with generalized beliefs that can be both positive and negative.

2.2. Intergroup Conflict and Identity Construction

Social Identity as proposed by Tajfel and others suggests that the need to view oneself positively may heighten differences between groups and lead to conflict.[26] Group conflict may also heighten social identification. Social psychologists generally agree that socially constructed identities contribute to intergroup conflicts.[27] It is suggested that social identities create and exacerbate intergroup conflicts and intergroup conflicts influence social identity.[28] Conflicts often seem to involve groups' interests, whether ethnic, religious or cultural identities. In an intergroup conflict, cultural stereotypes and prejudices can lead groups to categorize another group to identify them as the outgroup, and then to stigmatize them. In his book *In Common Predicament: Social Psychology of Intergroup Conflict and Cooperation*, Muzafer Sherif maintains that "in intergroup conflict, a person belonging to one group locates other peoples as similar-dissimilar to himself and evaluates these similarities-differences as acceptable or unacceptable."[29] Ingroup bias is the outcome of group conflicts. Sherif upholds that in conflicts, the superior group that is in control exercised their power to maintain their status quo.[30] In short, conflicts enhance identity construction by exerting extreme negative analyses of outgroups. Hostile attitudes concerning the outgroup are the consequence of intergroup conflicts.

One of the aspects of intergroup conflict is ingroup attachment and outgroup antagonism known as 'ethnocentrism.' According to William G. Sumner, "Ethnocentrism is a universal characteristic of human groups that involves differentiation between the we-group or the in-group and the other-groups or

25 See discussion in Roger Brown, *Social Psychology* (New York: The Free Press, 1986), 533.

26 Cf. Robert W. White, "Social and Role Identities and Political Violence: Identity as a Window on Violence in Northern Ireland," in *Social Identity, Intergroup Conflict, and Conflict Reduction*, eds. Richard D. Ashmore, Lee Jussim and David Wilder (Oxford: Oxford University Press, 2001), 138-140.

27 Lewis Coser defines conflict as "a struggle over values and claims to scarce status, power, and resources in which the aims of the opponents are to neutralize, injure, or eliminate their rivals." See Lewis Coser, *The Functions of Social Conflict* (New York: The Free Press, 1956), 8.

28 Cf. Richard D. Ashmore, Lee Jussim and David Wilder, "Introduction," in *Social Identity, Intergroup Conflict, and Conflict Reduction*, 4.

29 Muzfer Sherif, *In Common Predicament: Social Psychology of Intergroup Conflict and Cooperation* (Boston: Houghton Mifflin Company, 1966), 13. Cf. Muzafer Sherif, *Group Conflict and Co-operation: Their Social Psychology* (London: Routledge & Kegan Paul Ltd., 1966), 37.

30 See Muzafer Sherif, *In Common Predicament: Social Psychology*, 13.

the out-groups."[31] Ethnocentrism creates differentiation within social groups with the production of dogmas. Antagonism and aggression against the outgroup may originate in the service of protection or enhancement of the ingroup.[32] Ethnocentrism thus provides mechanisms to promote positive attraction to ingroup norms and behavior as good and legitimate. On the other hand, it also encourages outgroup hostility.

2.3. Ideology and Identity Construction in Group Relationships

Social Identity Theory states that identity is shaped by self-concept and the tendency to favorably evaluate one's group. In a situation where identity consciousness is highly salient, people evaluate their identity through personal identification with some group. Ideologies are developed in such situations as sources of social identification. Ervin Staub defines ideologies as "visions of social arrangements that tell people how to live in difficult times."[33] Ann Swidler, in her book *Talk of Love: How Culture Matters,* argues that "an ideology usually defines a community."[34] In other words, in social engagements, actors or agents delineate group norms or ideologies. Ideologies are not merely visions of actors, they are systems or ideas sets for a community in social relationships.

Pierre Bourdieu seeks to explain how people conduct their ways of life in relation to one another and social institutions. He emphasizes the importance of domination and symbolic systems in the social structures of a society. His emphasis is on the importance of agents in social structures where a dominant class plays a decisive role.[35] For him, "the struggle between the dominant fractions and the dominated fractions in its ideological retranslation tends to be organized by oppositions, which produce strategies."[36] In other words, ideologies are created

31 Sumner who coins the term describes ethnocentrism as "a technical name for the view of things in which one's own group is the center of everything, and all others are scaled and rated with reference to it... Each group nourishes its own pride and vanity, boasts itself superior, exalts its own divinities, and looks with contempt on outsiders." William Graham Sumner, *Folkways: A Study of the Sociological Importance of Usages, Manners, Customs, Mores, and Morals* (Boston: Ginn & Company, 1906), 13.

32 See more discussion in Marilynn B. Brewer, "Group Identification and Intergroup Conflict: When Does Ingroup Love Become Outgroup Hate?" in *Social Identity, Intergroup Conflict, and Conflict Reduction, Conflict Reduction*, eds. Richard D. Ashmore, Lee Jussim and David Wilder (Oxford: Oxford University Press, 2001), 30.

33 Ervin Staub, "Individual and Group Identities in Genocide and Mass Killing," in *Social Identity, Intergroup Conflict, and Conflict Reduction*, 165.

34 Ann Swidler, *Talk of Love: How Culture Matters* (Chicago: University of Chicago Press, 2003), 97.

35 Pierre Bourdieu, *Distinction: A Social Critique of the Judgment of Taste,* translated by Richard Nice (Cambridge, Massachusetts: Harvard University Press, 1984, Original pub. in French 1979), 254.

36 Bourdieu, *Distinction*, 254.

by social structures where the dominant group and the dominated group engage in group relationships. In social identity terms, there is ingroup identification by focusing on distinct group norms on the part of the superior group. This is the case in the struggle between priestly groups of the exilic and the early postexilic period where the dominant group (Zadokite priests) cultivated their group's interest in their explication of group norms.

Bar-Tal also theorized how group beliefs (ideologies) function as defining factors in group relationships. He writes, "The contents of group beliefs provide the raison d'etre for a group's existence and delineate its uniqueness vis-a-vis other groups."[37] Group beliefs are tools or guidelines constructed for a coherent system of orientation in their social environment.[38] They are formally presented as defining repertoires of the group members. In other words, members of a group develop a group's norms out of conscious acts.

Michael Walzer discusses how rigorous ideologies are developed by groups of people who face uncertain situations, especially the situation of exile. He posits that the Puritan exiles, who constructed Puritan ideology rooted in Calvinism, shaped radical politics that subsequently played a decisive role in the English revolution.[39] Walzer argues that the Calvinist idea of radical politics was developed through a difficult process of invention and experimentation of the Calvinist saints in the historical situations in which they appeared.[40] He argues that the Puritans (exiled from England during the rule of the Catholic monarch, Mary) who were intellectuals exiled from their former land, deeply felt the urge to remake the world in the image of their own rigorous, demanding religion.[41] The returning Marian exiles responded to the experience of their exile with their own demanding theology. This includes their-self imposed authority and critique of existing social structures.

37 Daniel Bar-Tal, *Group Beliefs: A Conception for Analyzing Group Structure, Processes, and Behavior* SSSP (New York: Springer-Verlag, 1990), 46.

38 See Henri Tajfel, *Human Groups and Social Categories* (Cambridge: Cambridge University Press, 1981), 46. Bar-Tal proposes that group beliefs are part of individual's cognitive repertoires. They are inferred from leaders' speeches, documents of books. They are eventually formalized into group products such as in documents of books. See "Chapter 3: The Conception of Group Beliefs," in Daniel Bar-Tal, *Group Beliefs: A Conception for Analyzing Group Structure, Processes, and Behavior*, 35-46.

39 See detail in Michael Walzer, *The Revolution of the Saints: A Study in the Origins of Radical Politics* (Cambridge: Massachusetts, Harvard University Press, 1965).

40 Walzer examines the French Huguenots and English Puritans as examples to demonstrate how Calvinism has a new form in Western society. According to him, French Protestantism (the Huguenots) took up Calvinist concept of resistance with a new language of conscience in their justified resistance against kings. On the other hand, the Puritans (Marian exiles) took up Calvinist alternative political community of the Christian commonwealth, and therefore deprived of all official functions shaping another radical political figures. See Walzer, *The Revolution of the Saints*, 66-113.

41 Walzer, *The Revolution of the Saints*, 97.

In his other article entitled "Puritanism as a Revolutionary Ideology," Walzer argues that Puritanism was a "response to disorder and fear, a way of organizing men to overcome the acute sense of chaos."[42] The returning Marian exiles responded to particular experiences of confusion, change, alienation and exile by creating their own ideology. He considers that the responses were in the form of discipline and political activity. One trait of their response was a response to their own fear, "fear in themselves of the 'unsettledness.'"[43] Another aspect of their response was political activity "whose immediate purpose was to regain control of a changing world; hence the great concern with method, discipline, and order, and the frequent uneasiness with novelty."[44] The Puritan response to their social world not only aimed at coping with personal and social problems, but it was an intense response to transforming society, "to create a holy commonwealth."[45] Walzer's theory offers insight into the study of the radical politics/ideology of the priestly group of the exilic age. The priestly ideology of Ezekiel's author might be best understood in the light of Walzer's theory.

Religion is sometimes viewed as a defining characteristic of identity. In many instances, it plays a role of cultural characterization in group conflicts rather than being a purely spiritual alignment.[46] Nancy T. Ammermann argues that "religious organizations establish determinative narratives through elaborate sets of roles, myths, rituals, and behavioral prescriptions."[47] To put in another way, religious groups construct rules or norms as ideological innovations through social processes. Recently, Vyacheslav Karpov, Elena Lisovkaya, and David Barry

42 Michael Walzer, "Puritanism as a Revolutionary Ideology," in *Puritan New England: Essays on Religion, Society, and Culture*, eds. Alden T. Vaughan and Francis J. Bremer (New York: St. Martin's Press, 1977), 29. 19-41.

43 Walzer, "Puritanism as a Revolutionary Ideology," 32.

44 Walzer, "Puritanism as a Revolutionary Ideology," 35.

45 Walzer, "Puritanism as Revolutionary Ideology," 37. Cf. Walzer, *Revolution of the Saints*, 198. Kai T. Erikson, who wrote about the Puritan of the Massachusetts Bay maintains that Puritanism of seventeenth-century Massachusetts and the fifteenth-century France shared the same fatalism. He writes: "In their confessions they insist they are worthless and contemptible, but in their professions they declare that it is their special privilege and obligation to challenge all the established tradition in Christendom." See Kai T. Erikson, *Wayward Puritans: A Study in the Sociology of Deviance* (Boston: Pearson Education, Inc. 2005), 50-51.

46 Morgan Oddie claims that religion plays a crucial role in the in ethnic conflicts such as Bosnia-Hergovina, Catholic Croatians, and Muslim Bosniaks. See detail in Morgan Oddie, "The Relationship of Religion and Ethnic Nationalism in Boznia-Hergovina," *Religion in Eastern Europe* XXXII, no. 1 (February, 2012): 34-42.

47 See Nancy T. Ammerman, "Religious Identities and Religious Institutions," in *Handbook of the Sociology of Religion*, ed. Michele Dillon (Cambridge: Cambridge University Press, 2003), 213. Sociologists have addressed how the practices and activities of religious institutions create the culture of the community/identity. See Mark Chaves, Congregations in America (Cambridge, MA: Harvard University Press, 2004); also Penny Edgell Becker, Congregations in Conflict: Cultural Models of Local Religious Life (Cambridge: Cambridge University Press, 1999).

have proposed a theory known as 'ethnodoxy,' in which an ideology rigidly links a group's (ethnic) identity to its dominant faith. This theory claims that "cultures' normative lines are embodied in specific belief systems, discourse patterns, and ideologies."[48] Thus, individuals categorize and identify themselves with social groups in which religious doctrines (ideologies) and experiences play integral roles. Religion creates a sacred community and defines boundaries and identities.

3. Social Identity and Boundary Mechanisms in Intergroup Relationships

Social Identity Theory holds the view that "pressures to evaluate one's own group positively through ingroup/outgroup comparison lead social groups to differentiate themselves from each other."[49] In other words, boundary construction is one of the components of social identification. Sociologists, anthropologists, and social psychologists have devoted great efforts in explaining how and why people construct boundaries. By examining boundaries, they try to understand the rules or norms that determine the characteristics of religious and cultural institutions. They acknowledge that boundaries can be physically or conceptually expressed in ideas, rituals, and belief systems.[50] Boundaries may also be classified as symbolic and social.[51] Individuals and groups formulate either or both of these in order to maintain their group's cohesiveness. Emile Durkheim classically formulated the thought that groups have distinctive cultural boundaries. Along his line, Mary Douglas and others theorized how boundary maintenance played a vital role in social systems. In the following section I will discuss the approaches of some well-known social anthropologists whose theories are relevant for the discussion of boundary mechanisms in intergroup relationships.

---

48 See Vyacheslav Karpov, Elena Lisovkaya, and David Barry, "Ethnodoxy: How Popular Ideologies Fuse Religious and Ethnic Identities," *Journal for the Scientific Study of Religion* 51, no. 4 (2012): 638-655.

49 Tajfel and Turner, "The Social Identity Theory of Intergroup Behavior," 16-17.

50 See the discussion of various methods proposed by social anthropologists on boundary maintenance in the chapter entitled, "Maintaining and Transforming Boundaries: the Politics of Religious Identity," in Fiona Bowie, *The Anthropology of Religion: An Introduction* (Oxford: Blackwell Publishers, 2000), 70-90. See also Michele Lamont and Virag Molnar, "The Study of Boundaries in Social Sciences," *Annual Review of Sociology* 28 (2002): 167-195; John R. Hall, "The Capital(s) of Cultures: A Nonholistic Approach to Status, Situations, Gender, and Ethnicity," in *Cultivating Symbolic Boundaries: Differences and the Making of Inequality*, eds. Michele Lamont and Marcel Fournier (Chicago: University of Chicago Press, 1992).

51 Michele Lamont maintains that "symbolic boundaries are conceptual distinctions made by social actors to categorize objects, people, practices, and even time and space. They are tools by which individuals and groups struggle over to make agreement upon definitions of reality… Social boundaries on the other hand are objectified forms of social differences manifested in unequal distribution of resources and social opportunities." See Michele Lamont, *The Dignity of Working Men: Morality and Boundaries of Race, Class, and Immigration* (Cambridge, MA: Harvard Univ. Press, 2000), 168-169.

3.1. Emile Durkheim

Emile Durkheim analyzes the sacred-profane dichotomy to explain the central characteristic of religion. For him, the opposition between sacred and profane reflects a classification of the real or ideal things that man conceives of.[52] He writes:

> Sacred things are things protected and isolated by prohibitions; profane things are those things to which the prohibitions are applied and that must keep at a distance from what is sacred. Religious beliefs are those representations that express the nature of sacred things and the relations they have with other sacred things or with profane things.[53]

Thus for Durkheim, the beginning and maintenance of religion and preservation of the social system go together with the affirmation of the sacred and the profane.[54] They could not coexist in the same time and the same place. For him, a whole complex of rituals seeks to bring about the separation of sacred and profane.[55] Men observe both the negative cult and positive cult to demarcate and emphasize the separation between sacred and profane realms. These rites take the form of prohibitions (taboo) and sacrifice.[56] This approach insists that ideological communities preserve their unity by punishing deviance from normative behavior and mobilizing negative sanctions against such behavior. The function of cults (rites) is to prevent a mixture of the two domains or encroachment of one on the other. In short, religion provides a boundary to maintain group norms or behavior. Durkheim's binary conception of religious life has influenced many thoughts on the study of ritual systems and boundary studies. [57]

---

52 Durkheim, *Elementary Forms of Religious Life*, translated and with an Introduction by Karen E. Fields (New York: The Free Press, 1995; first published in French at Paris by F. Alcan in 1912), 34.

53 Durkheim, *Elementary Forms of Religious Life*, 38.

54 Cf. Jacob Pandian, *Culture, Religion, and the Sacred Self: A Critical Introduction to the Anthropological Study of Religion* (Englewood Cliffs, New Jersey: Prentice Hall, 1991), 37.

55 Durkheim, *Elementary Forms of Religious Life*, 303.

56 Durkheim, *Elementary Forms of Religious Life*, 303-319; 340-344.

57 The approach is applied in several works such as Mary Douglas, *Purity and Danger: An Analysis of Concepts of Pollution and Taboo* (New York: Oxford University Press Inc., 1966); Victor W. Turner, *The Forest of Symbols: Aspects of Ndembu Rituals* (Ithaca, New York: Cornell University Press, 1967); Roy Rappaport, *Ritual and the Making of Religion* (Cambridge: Cambridge University Press, 1999) and others among many. See a study on the influence of Durkheim's Elementary forms of Religion to a general theory of ideology in Kenneth Thompson, "Durkheim and Sacred Identity," in *On Durkheim's Elementary Forms of Religious Life*, eds. N. J. Allen, W. S. F. Pickering and W. Watts Miller, Routledge Studies in Social and Political Thought (London: Routledge, 1998), 94-104.

3.2. Mary Douglas

Mary Douglas, who follows Durkheim's analytic approach, also discusses boundary formation as a process that reflects divisions within society. According to Douglas, every culture has particular classifications for the world, which are necessary for social well-being and conceptual coherence.[58] Religious concepts such as ritual purity prevent confusion of categories and maintain the power inherent in orderly systems. In her book *Purity and Danger* she states, "Our pollution behavior is the reaction which condemns any object or ideal likely to confuse or contradict cherished classifications."[59] In other words, the creation of sacred boundaries can be seen in how order is maintained by excluding those items that would violate order. We draw lines of distinction to sustain norms of community life.

In her book *Natural Symbols* (1970), Douglas argues that society's structure is reflected in the understanding of cosmos and the human body. She maintains that a human body generates a symbolic meaning of social relationships.[60] She examines how a society cultivates behavior in human relationship. She asserts that "each social form and its accompanying style of thinking restricts individual thought and action."[61] In other words, the power of social structures generates symbols to control human behavior and identity. In order to control a body and identity, human groups "reject the bad outside and affirm symbolic means of purity of the group and of their inner selves."[62] Hence, a group's attitude is a factor of boundary construction in group relationships. Douglas' idea of pollution as boundary marker will be discussed under "purity and identity" in more detail.

3.3. Works Following Emile Durkheim and Mary Douglas

Following Durkheim and Douglas, other social anthropologists have described the role of boundaries in defining identity. Pierre Bourdieu maintains that symbolic classification is key to the reproduction of class privilege. He argues that the dominant groups generally succeed in legitimizing their own culture as superior to those of lower classes by demonstrating their distinction.[63] Michele Lamont illustrates how boundaries are constructed in social groups. She argues: "Boundaries are the lines that define some people, groups, and things while excluding others. These distinctions can be expressed through normative interdictions (taboos), cultural identities, attitudes and practices, and more

58 Douglas, *Purity and Danger*, 36.

59 Douglas, *Purity and Danger*, 35-36.

60 Mary Douglas, *Natural Symbols: Explorations in Cosmology* (New York: Pantheon Books, 1970). See especially pp. 65-82 and 140-155.

61 Douglas, *Natural Symbols*, 140.

62 Douglas, *Natural Symbols*, 146.

63 See Bourdieu, *Distinction: A Social Critique of the Judgment of Taste*, 254.

generally through patterns of likes and dislikes."[64] Boundary markers are vital when a group maintains its distinction in relation to other groups.[65]

Boundary construction is considered more salient when conflicting groups are too close. The level of otherness is more intense where the group that is too close to 'us' poses a threat to the group's own identity. Jonathan Z. Smith in his essay, "What a Difference a Difference Makes," argues that the most problematic challenge to an individual or group is always posed by what is called the "proximate other," that is when the "other (he/she) is too-much-like-us or when he claims to be us." [66] In other words, similarity of identity can become a severe threat to group identity. Nathaniel Deutsch applies this theory in his view of the relationship between Islam and Judaism. He argues that Islam's complex view of Jews and Judaism is contributed by similarity of identity.[67] In the same way, Maijastina Kahlos writes: "The most vehement attacks and demarcations of boundaries arise in situations in which the other group came alarmingly close to one's own group and had too many similarities."[68] This issue was found among interacting groups of the Greco-Roman period between Jews and Gentiles. This was also the case in the exilic period when different groups of the Israelites faced a crisis in defining their identities.

From these theories, we can infer that boundaries are shaped by identity threats. Cultural repertoires, traditions, and narratives are employed as boundary markers. Social interaction affects the permeability of boundaries in order to maintain the group's cohesiveness among interacting groups. When the identity of a group is in question, its history and cultural symbols are manipulated to favor at least one of the interacting groups.[69] The intensity of boundary maintenance is determined by ingroup perceptions of 'them' and 'others.' Thus, boundary mechanisms play a role in strengthening collective identity and group solidarity.

---

64 See Michele Lamont, "Culture and Identity," in *Handbook of Sociological Theory*, ed. Jonathan Turner (New York: Kluer Academic/Plenum Publishers, 2001), 172.

65 See Stephen Worchel, "A Developmental View of the Search for Group Identity," in *Social Identity: International Perspective*, eds. Stephen Worchel, J. Francois Morales, Dario Paez and Jean-Claude Deschamps (London: Sage Publications, 1998), 58-59.

66 Jonathan Z. Smith, "What a Difference a Difference Makes," in *To See Ourselves as Others See Us, Christians, Jews, "Others" in Late Antiquity*, eds. Jacob Neusner and Ernest Frerichs (Chico, California: Scholars Press, 1985), 46- 47.

67 Cf. Nathaniel Deutsch, "The Proximate Other: The Nation of Islam and Judaism," in *Black Zion: African American Religious Encounters with Judaism*, eds. Yvonne Chireau and Nathaniel Deutsch (New York: Oxford University Press, 2000), 91, 91-117.

68 Maijastina Kahlos, "Introduction," in *The Faces of the Other: Religious Rivalry and Ethnic Encounters in the Later Roman World*, ed. Maijastina Kahlos (Turnhout, Belgium: Brepols Publishers, 2011), 11.

69 Cf. Herbert J. Ganz, "Preface," in *Cultivating Symbolic Boundaries Differences and the Making of Inequality*, eds. Michele Lamont and Marcel Courier (Chicago: The University of Chicago Press, 1992), xiii.

4. Group Identity and Purity: Purity as a Boundary Marker in Intergroup Relationships

Sociologists, anthropologists, and biblical scholars study the idea of purity as an aspect of ancient religion. Scholars focus on the origin and development of purity concepts along with the study of the ritual systems of ancient societies. Major approaches to the study of purity and holiness are related to the concepts of taboo, totemism, and mana.[70] W. Robertson Smith, James G. Frazer and other theorists believe that originally the idea of purity was connected with taboo. These studies help in theorizing the origin and development of purity in primitive society. Smith brought to a wider knowledge the idea that ancient ritual systems in general and purity rules in particular are part and parcel of social systems. Mary Douglas enlisted Smith's method in her study of Levitical Laws of Purity. Biblical scholars such as Jacob Neusner, Jerome H. Neyrey, Jacob Milgrom, among many have done significant research on this topic that I find worth reviewing. There are many scholars who study purity/impurity of ancient Israel as they try to define the rationale for purity/impurity legislations in the Hebrew

70 The idea of taboo explains that in primitive society certain animals, objects, and conditions (eg. child birth, menstruation, etc.) are considered bearing sacredness or uncleanness. Society therefore observed rules of ceremonial purity. Totemism is the concept that certain animals or objects are forbidden to eat or touch, as they were totem (sacred) of a tribe. They become dethatched both from the human clan; in course of time they came to be sacred. W. Robertson Smith and James G. Frazer are well known anthropologists who studied taboo and totemism. Many social anthropologists and biblical scholars have developed their ideas. See W. Robertson Smith, *Lectures on the Religion of the Semites*, 3rd ed. (London: Adam and Charles Black, 1901; fist published in 1889); James G. Frazer, *The Golden Bough A Study in Magic and Religion* (Old Saybrook, CT: Konecky & Konecky, First published in 1890), 189-251. See other works such as Frank B. Jevons, *An Introduction to the Hebrew Religion* (London: Metuen & Co., 1896); The concept of mana states that certain things have power to bless or to curse. Something is filled with power. It is somehow related with the concept of taboo. It may be differentiated from taboo as the concept has a positive power which is different from the concept of danger or prohibition in taboo. For this discussion see R. H. Codrington, *The Melanesians- Studies in their Anthropology and Folklore* (New Haven: Hraf Press, 1957, first edition 1891); Mircea Eliade, *Man and the Sacred* (New York: Harper & Row, 1974). See also discussion on the general idea of taboo, totem, mana and ritual systems in ancient societies in Emile Durkheim, *The Elementary forms of Religious Life*; Clifford Geertz, *The Interpretation of Cultures: Selected Essays* (New York: Basic Books, 1974); Victor Turner, *The Forest of Symbols: Aspects of Ndembu Ritual* (Ithaca, New York: Cornell University Press, 1967); Fiona Bowie, *The Anthropology of Religion: An Introduction* (Oxford: Blackwell Publishers, 2000). Also see Nilton Dutra Amorim, "Desecration and Defilement in the Old Testament" (PhD Dissertation: Andrews University, 1986), 13-56.

Bible.[71] In this discussion, I will review methods of socio-anthropologists and biblical scholars in their attempt to define purity and impurity in relation to socio-cultural systems. I will explain how these theorists elucidate the role of purity as a boundary marker in group relationships.

4.1. W. Robertson Smith

W. Roberson Smith, in his book *Religion of the Semites*, argues, "It is impossible to separate the Semitic doctrine of holiness and uncleanness from the system of Taboo."[72] He states that ancient peoples maintained rules of holiness to protect themselves from the infection of supernatural powers. Hence, rules of holiness and purity are central to religious and cultural/social systems. Smith proposes that the Semitic law of uncleanness must be looked on as having survived from an earlier form of faith and society, which was developed into a higher spiritual religion.[73] For Smith, "By "ritual" is meant properly what is social-religious and not solely religious."[74] His main contribution lies in the recognition that ritual has a social function. He holds a view that sacrifice was not only meant for appeasement of the gods, but also for the joyous fellowship of the worshippers.[75] Armin Siedlecki, who has studied Smith's idea of purity systems, writes that for Robertson Smith, "beliefs and practices regarding the avoidance of defilement and the maintenance of purity ought to be seen in the same manner, as part of a social system that works toward its own preservation."[76] Smith understands that religious symbols are representations of a group's identity and values.[77] He considers ritual systems

71 Among them see G. W. Buchanan, *The Consequences of the Covenant* (Leiden: Brill, 1970); Jonathan Klawans, *Impurity and Sin in Ancient Judaism* (Oxford: Oxford University Press, 2000); cf. Jonathan Klawans, *Purity, Sacrifice, and the Temple: Symbolism and Supersessionism in the Study of Ancient Judaism* (Oxford: Oxford University Press, 2006); Philip Peter Jenson, *Graded Holiness: A Key to the Priestly Conception of the World*, JSOTSup 106 (Sheffield: Sheffield Academic Press, 1992); David P. Wright, "The Spectrum of Priestly Impurity," in *Priesthood and Cult in Ancient Israel*, eds. Gary A. Anderson and Saul M. Olyan (Sheffield: JSOT Press, 1991), 150-181; Also David P. Wright, "Unclean and Clean (Old Testament)," in *The Anchor Bible Dictionary* Vol. 6, 729-741; Saul Olyan, *Rites and Rank: Hierarchy in Biblical Representation of Cult* (Princeton: Princeton University Press, 2000); Christine E. Hayes, *Gentile Impurities and Jewish Identities: Intermarriage and Conversion from the Bible to the Talmud* (Oxford: Oxford University Press, 2002). I will not incorporate their approaches in this review as they are not relevant for my research.

72 William Robertson Smith, *Lectures on the Religions of the Semites: The Fundamental Institutions* (With an introduction and additional notes by Stanley A. Cook), (United States: KTAV Publishing House, Inc., 1969 third edition, first published 1927), 452.

73 Smith, *Lectures on the Religion of the Semites*, 449.

74 Smith, *Lectures on the Religions of the Semites*, 502.

75 See further discussion in Lecture 2 (sacrifice) in *Lectures on the Religion of the Semites*, 213-243.

76 See Armin Siedlecki, "Purity and Power: A Rhetorical Study of the Ideology of Purity and Defilement in the Book of Ezekiel" (MA Thesis: Wilfrid Laurier University, 1991), 11.

77 Smith, *Lectures on the Religion of the Semites*, 422, 447.

as symbolic expressions in human society. His understanding of taboo and ritual systems as having social function deserves commendation.

4.2. Mary Douglas

In her seminal work *Purity and Danger*, Mary Douglas wrote, "Where there is dirt there is a system."[78] That is, when we construct purity and impurity, we have a symbolic system of classification. Following Smith and Durkheim's functionalist line, she argues that religious beliefs, including the purity system, comprise a symbol system that reflects a set of criteria and values. Douglas argues that the idea of pollution displays the boundaries of cultural categories. She writes:

> (Dirt) implies two conditions: a set of ordered relations and a contravention of that order. Dirt then, is never a unique, isolated event. Where there is dirt there is system. Dirt is the by-product of a systematic ordering and classification of matter, in so far as ordering involves rejecting inappropriate elements. The idea of dirt takes us straight into the files of symbolism and promises a link-up with more obviously symbolic systems of purity.[79]

Douglas maintains that our idea of pollution is a response to anomalies, which are considered dangerous because they represent disorder.[80] In other words, the concept of pollution represents an attempt to prevent confusion or contradiction in human behavior. In her study of Israelite purity systems in the book of Leviticus, she argues that some animals are excluded from food as they do not fit the classification of ancient Israelite's classificatory paradigm.[81] Hence, she rejects views that interpret biblical dietary rules as aspect of primitive medicine and hygiene. Douglas' idea concerning purity and pollution entails not only ritual systems, but it also explains the structure, organization and operation of a larger social body.[82] In social identity terms, her idea of pollution illustrates a system of classification which defines who belongs and who is not in the group. [83]

Mary Douglas also argues that the physical body can act as a symbol of social identity. For her, the boundaries of the human body are a metaphor for the

78 Douglas, *Purity and Danger*, 36.

79 Douglas, *Purity and Danger*, 35.

80 Douglas, *Purity and Danger*, 36.

81 See Douglas, "Abomination of Leviticus" in *Purity and Danger*, 41-58.

82 Cf. Frank H. Gorman Jr., *The Ideology of Ritual: Space, Time and Status in the Priestly Torah*. JSOTSup 91 (Sheffield: Sheffield Academic Press, 1990), 10.

83 See Coleman A. Baker, "Social Identity Theory and Biblical Interpretation," *Biblical Theology Bulletin* 42, no. 3 (August 2012): 130.

boundaries of the group.[84] In her analysis of purity systems of Leviticus, she argues that Israelites in their belief systems maintained that all bodily issues such as blood, pus, excrement, semen, etc., were polluting. In their care for the integrity, unity, and purity of the physical body, they mirrored threatened boundary politics.[85] In other words, the law of purity of the body reflects group or society's aspiration for systematic maintenance of order. Douglas writes: "The analysis of ritual symbolism cannot begin until we recognize ritual as an attempt to create and maintain a particular culture, a particular set of assumptions by which experience is controlled."[86] We could formulate that the classic work of Mary Douglas (Purity and Danger), and her analysis of the purity systems of ancient Judaism, demonstrates that purity systems are the systematic structures, classifications, and evaluations of social groups. The methodology of Mary Douglas is not free from criticism.[87] However, the validity of her work is admired and applied in biblical studies in general and in studies of Israelite ritual (purity) systems.[88] Hence, Mary Douglas' theory of purity systems and her concept of pollution /impurity as a boundary marker in intergroup relationships are very useful.

4.3. Jacob Neusner

In his study of purity in Judaism, Jacob Neusner asserts, "Purity is an essential element in the interpretation of Israel's total religious system."[89] He argues that the Pentateuchal priestly code was developed in the post exilic setting (ca 450 BCE)

---

84 Douglas, *Purity and Danger*, 115. Cf. Jerome H. Neyrey, "The Idea of Purity in Mark's Gospel," *Semeia* 35 (1986): 102.

85 Douglas, *Purity and Danger*, 121.

86 Douglas, *Purity and Danger*, 128.

87 Many authors pointed out minor inaccuracies in her treatment of Leviticus 11 (Dietary Laws). See discussion in Jenson, *Graded Holiness*, 76-79. Even she admits her error in the earlier work, as she acknowledges in the later part of her writings. She expresses that the weakness of her theory is that local definitions of pollution are the negative aspect of specific normative schemas of the world, which should not be compared without also comparing the positive side. See detail in Mary Douglas, *Jacob's Tears, The Priestly Work of Reconciliation* (Oxford: Oxford University Press, 2004), 124-125. Jacob Milgrom rightly points out Douglas' defects in her failure to take into account the two pairs of antonyms laid down by the Priestly legislators: holy-common and impure-pure. For him, Douglas overlooks that there is a condition that a blemished animal or priest is not impure but common. See discussion in Jacob Milgrom, *Leviticus 1-16: A New Translation with Commentary* AB (Doubleday: New York, 1991), 1001.

88 Ronald Hendel expresses how the work of Mary Douglas has influenced the intellectual standards in the study of biblical ritual and culture. He notes that Mary Douglas' influence is seen in several works including Jacob Milgrom, Alfred Marx, Saul Olyan, Rudiger Schmidt, David Wright, Jenson, Gorman, Klawans, and others. See discussion in Ronald Hendel, "Remembering Mary Douglas: Kashrut, Culture, and Thought-Styles," *Jewish Studies* 45 (2008): 3-15.

89 Jacob Neusner, *The Idea of Purity in Ancient Judaism* (Leiden: Brill, 1973), 28.

to keep Israel holy, that is to separate it for God alone.[90] He contends that Israel's purity system has two main parts: (1) purity/impurity as a metaphor of morality (rejection of God, idolatry, sexual crime, and pollution of the land), and (2) purity/impurity in connection with the cult (unclean animals, menstruation, spots on the skin, mildew on the walls of the house, bodily discharge, sexual misdeeds, and the corpse).[91] Neusner believes that the idea of impurity, originally connected with loathing (i.e. of reptiles, dead bodies, menses, etc.), was transformed into a metaphor or simile for the good, right or even holy.[92] In other words, the purity system is divided into ethical categories of right and wrong, and into the cultic category of pure and defiled objects. His concept of purity shows how the day-to-day issues of community and common life were understood in terms of the cult. Hence, for Neusner, purity served a boundary in ancient Judaism in which society's structure was defined by the purity system embedded in the cult, which contributed to the ethics of the society. Neusner's category of ethical and cultic categories is not clearly seen in a strict sense in the Hebrew purity system. For example, in the book of Ezekiel, impurity of the people of Israel such as idolatry, bloodshed and others could be categorized as both ethical and cultic. However, his view of purity as a defining factor of society's structure in ancient Israel goes in line with that of Mary Douglas.

4.4. Jerome H. Neyrey

Following Mary Douglas, Jerome H. Neyrey claims that "purity in general is an abstract system of ordering and classifying, and a system whereby persons, objects, places, etc. are labeled pure or polluted in a given social group."[93] In other words, Neyrey understands purity as a cultural system and as the organizing principle of a group. Turning to the Jewish people of the first century CE, he defines purity as a systematic order categorized by differences between places (Holy of Holies, sanctuary, courtyards), by differences between people (priests, Levites, and Israelites), by differences between times (Sabbath, Passover, etc.), and by levels of uncleanness (lepers, menstruants, etc).[94] He uses the clause "purity means boundaries" to argue that external boundaries such as (a) Kosher diet, (b) circumcision, and (c) observance of the Sabbath serve as lines that distinguish

90 Jacob Neusner, *Purity in Rabbinic Judaism: A Systemic Account* (Atlanta, Georgia: Scholars Press, 1994), 33.

91 Neusner, *The Idea of Purity in Ancient Judaism*, 11-22.

92 Neusner, *The Idea of Purity in Ancient Judaism*, 12.

93 Jerome H. Neyrey, "The Idea of Purity in Mark's Gospel," *Semeia* 35 (1986): 92.

94 See his studies of the Jewish purity system in Jerome H. Neyrey, "The Symbolic Universe of Luke-Acts: They Turn the World Upside Down," in *The Social World of Luke-Acts*, ed. Jerome H. Neyrey (Peabody, MA: Hendrickson Publishers, 1991), 271-304. Neyrey also used the term "map" to refer to purity system. Hence he uses "map of places," "map of persons," "map of people," to describe the lines between pure and impure in the social system of Judaism of Jesus' times. See Neyrey, "The Idea of Purity in Mark's Gospel," 94-99.

Jews from other people.[95] He also uses "purity" as a sociological category to describe the boundary lines within first-century Judaism between categories like the "sick" and "sinners."[96] In short, Neyrey agrees with Mary Douglas that purity is a cultural system and a sociological category that defines a group. His phrase "purity means boundaries," reflects his idea of purity as a boundary marker in intergroup relationships.

4.5. Jacob Milgrom

Jacob Milgrom has carried out immense research in the study of the Priestly legislations of ancient Judaism. He agrees with Mary Douglas concerning purity as a system that serves to maintain the ideal pattern of a given society. He argues that "the entire system of purity has a single symbolic focus, which is death."[97] For him death is the common denominator of the purity system. In other words, for Milgrom, the Israelite purity system symbolically associates life with holiness and purity and vice versa. He holds the view that Israel's total system of life is connected with purity and that Israel's collective impurity (guilt) affects the sanctity of the temple.[98] He describes how impurity affects the entire cult as he says: "(the power of impurity) culminates in wanton, unrepented sin, which not only pollutes the outer altar and penetrates to the shrine but… pierces the veil to the Holy Ark and the very throne of God."[99] For Milgrom, the Israelite purity system is understood in relation to cultic acts in which defilement is systematically connected with the Temple. He differs from Mary Douglas in that, for him, not every form of impurity is equally defiling.[100] Although Milgrom does not emphasize purity as a cultural system, his concept of purity defines what is detrimental and what is beneficial before God. His binary approach helps in defining Israel's cultural

95 Neyrey, "The Idea of Purity in Mark's Gospel," 99-101.

96 Cited by Bart J. Koet, in *Dreams and Scripture in Luke-Acts Collected Essays* (Leuven: Peeters 2006), 83.

97 Jacob Milgrom, *Leviticus 1-16 A New Translation with Commentary* AB (New York: Doubleday, 1991), 46.

98 See Milgrom, *Leviticus 1-16*, 49-50. See also Chapter 6 entitled "Israel's Sanctuary: The Priestly Picture of Dorian Gray," in *Jacob Milgrom, Studies in Cultic Theology and Terminology* (Leiden: E.J. Brill, 1983), 74-84.

99 His thesis on purity/impurity and its effects may be summarized as: (1) To remain in a state of impurity is itself a sin, (2) states of human impurity affect the Temple from a distance, and (3) the purpose of the purification is to cleanse the Temple, not to atone for the offerer. See essay on "Milgrom on purity in the Bible," in *Hyam Maccoby, Ritual and Morality: The Ritual Purity System and its Place in Judaism* (Cambridge: Cambridge University Press, 1999), 165-181. Also see Andrew Mein, *Ezekiel and the Ethics of Exile* (Oxford: Oxford University Press, 2001), 153.

100 Milgrom, *Leviticus 1-16*, 1001.

system where purity plays a significant role. Therefore, for Milgrom, a purity system defines who is in the category of the godly (life) and who is not (dead).[101]

5. Summary and Conclusion

The preceding discussion of social identity theory and its related concepts and boundary maintenance in intergroup relationships demonstrates that group formation is a dynamic process in human social relationships. The Social Identity Theory of Tajfel and Turner suggests that social identification maintains the social identity of the ingroup (us) through the evaluation of the outgroup (others) through various processes such as categorization, comparison, and stereotyping. Evaluating the self positively, and evaluating the other negatively enhance group processes. This leads to the establishment of boundaries between groups. As part of social identification, group conflicts have resulted in delegitimization and ethnocentrism in which ideologies are evolved as group beliefs and religious values. As shown by the studies of Walzer, ideological innovations are the hallmark of a society in a transitional stage such as in migration or context change. The experiences of confusion, change, alienation and exile could heighten radical ideologies. The role of religion and belief systems in the formation of ethnic and social identity has long been acknowledged. Identity consciousness is sensitive and salient when similarity of identity becomes a severe threat to group identity. As proposed by social anthropologists, boundary construction is a relevant feature in social identification. The role of boundaries in social differentiation is explicitly highlighted here. Boundaries define who belongs in the group and who does not.

Social anthropologists such as Robertson Smith, Mary Douglas, and others explain how a purity system plays a role in the systematic classification of a social group. Researchers who study ancient purity systems posit diverse methods for explicating the meaning and function of purity and impurity in ancient society. Though differing in their approach, the majority consensus is that purity regulations are a symbolic system of a society where purity rules function to establish social order in intergroup relationships. They are not simply taboo or superstitions. Hence, "purity is boundary," as in the language of Neyrey, and it defines who is and who is not in the community.

As proposed by Mary Douglas and others, purity should be considered as a social force, which preserves the social system. The purity system maintains the integrity of the cognitive system, and the system of classification in a society. The

101 One disadvantage of his approach is the definition death as detrimental and impure as opposed to life. There is evidence in the Hebrew Bible to suggest that death, as the opposite of life, is not necessarily the opposite of purity. For example: in the priestly tradition and in Ezekiel, death is said to defiling only when a living person comes in contact with it. See Ezek 6:1-7; 39:11-20; 43:7-9. Death is not necessarily detrimental or defiling in the Hebrew Bible; it is rather portrayed as the destiny of a human being. For example: the death of the patriarch – Abraham, Isaac, and Jacob are described as "gathered to his people" (Gen 25:8; 35:29; 49:33); the death of Job as "death with full of life" (Job 42:17).

study of social identity theory and its related concepts prepares us to understand how groups interact in social relationships. It helps to us investigate how and why social identity is constructed in a particular context. Hence, it is a relevant theory for examining group relationship between different groups of the Israelites in the exilic age. It is a useful tool to investigate how interrelating groups of the Israelites were engaged in social relationships and how the literatures of the time developed ideologies to support their ingroup and outgroup bias.

The dynamics of boundary construction in intergroup relations help us to understand the book of Ezekiel, which gives extreme importance to purity. My argument is that it is in this process of maintaining a boundary of purity as a component in group identification, the book of Ezekiel, one of the exilic literatures intensifies the question, "Who is the true Israel." The question of social dynamics and group relationships during the exilic age needs to be investigated in order to determine the meaning and function of purity in the book of Ezekiel. This I will discuss in next chapter.

Chapter 2

Socio-Historical Situations of the Israelites in the Exilic Age
Intergroup Relationships, Group Identification, and Boundary Construction in the Exilic Literature

1. Introduction

The sixth century BCE has often been described as a "creative age," as it was a period in which political and cultural changes took place on a global scale. This period was significant for the Israelites, who experienced the end of monarchy and the exile over its duration. This century is also labeled the "Exilic Age," due to the exile of groups of people to Babylonia and Egypt during the Neo-Babylonian and the early Persian period. According to available biblical and extra biblical sources, tremendous political and sociocultural changes led to intergroup conflicts in this period. Literature of the period reflects those changes with ideological discussions on group identification.

By investigating the socio-historical situations of the exilic age and intergroup relationship in the literature of the exilic period, it is my hope to assess the dynamics of group relationship and identity formation. Hence, this chapter traces the socio-historical contexts of the exilic age[1] in order to explain

1 The exilic age of the Israelites may be said to have begun with the deportations after the conquest of Samaria in 722 BCE. However, in this paper, I will focus on the sixth century BCE, particularly between 597 to 520 BCE. This period covered the years between the first deportation of the Israelites under the Babylonian king in 597 BCE and the building of the Second Temple in 520 BCE.

the role of group dynamics in the formation of different Israelite group identities during this period. I evaluate available primary sources (biblical and extra-biblical texts, as well as archaeological findings) and the relevant secondary literature. I will also explore the connection between social identification and ideological discussions in exilic literature. By doing this I follow the methods of critics such as Charles E. Carter, Daniel L. Smith, and Dalit Rom-Shiloni among others, who contend that social identification was the force behind ideological and theological discussions of biblical literature, particularly in exilic literature.[2] I maintain that social relationships in the exilic age were the force behind the emergence of ideologies. Hence, I look into various examples of exilic literature in relation to group identification in the exilic age. This chapter serves as a backdrop to examine how the book of Ezekiel, one of the exilic texts that domesticates the concept of purity as an identity marker.

2. Israel in Exile

The rise of the Neo-Babylonian Empire was an important factor in the changing historical scene that affected the fall of Jerusalem, the end of Israel's (Judah's) independence, and consequent exiles in the sixth century BCE. [3] The Babylonian

2 Carter argues that a new ideology arose during the exilic age to explain the failure of the Judean kingdom and to endure the catastrophe of the exile in order to maintain the social identity of the Judean community. See Charles E. Carter, "Ideology and Archaeology in the Neo-Babylonian Period," in *Judah in the Judeans in the Neo-Babylonian Period*, eds. Obed Lipschits and Joseph Blenkinsopp (Winona Lake, Ind: Eisenbrauns, 2003), 318. Smith views the exile as a creative event in Judean history in which the *golah* community sought to find meaning (through literature) in their survival strategy that characterizes community in the crisis of exile. See Daniel L. Smith, *Religion of the Landless: The Social Context of The Babylonian Exile* (Bloomington, Ind: Meyer-Stone Books, 1989), 64-65. Rom-Shiloni ascribes many literary works during the 6th-5th century BCE as Babylonian exilic (group) ideologies. She argues that the conflicts between the Exiles and the people who remained in Judah "constructed and reconstructed group beliefs in the process of self-definition, and developed counter-definitions to delegitimize the others." See Dalit Rom-Shiloni, *Exclusive Inclusivity: Identity Conflicts Between the Exiles and the People who Remained* (6th-5th Centuries BCE) (New York: Bloomsbury, 2013). 23. See also Rom-Shiloni, "From Ezekiel to Ezra-Nehemiah: Shifts of Group Identities within Babylonian Exilic Ideology," in *Judah and the Judeans in the Achaemenid Period: Negotiating Identity in an International Context*, eds. Oded Lipschits, Gary Knoppers, and Manfred Oeming (Winona Lake, Ind: Eisenbrauns, 2011), 127-128.

3 The Neo-Babylonian Empire was established by Nebopolassar, the Chaldean, who captured the Assyrian capital Nineveh through an alliance of Mede, Cyarex and Scythian kings in 612 BCE. Nabopolassar then rebuilt his stronghold in Babylon as his capital. He moved towards the west to conquer Egypt. This led to the fall of Jerusalem and the exile. See Ancient Near Eastern Texts Relating to the Old Testament, ed. James S. Pritchard, translated by A. Leo Openheim (Princeton: Princeton Univ. Press, 1955), 303. Economic interests likely caused the campaign of the Neo-Babylonian power to the Southern Levant. Production of oil and wine are two important economic strength of Israel in ancient times. Remains of industrial installations found in Tell-en-Nasbeh, Tell Beit-Mirsim, Tel Beth-shemesh, Tel Geze, Tel Batash, and Tel Miane confirmed olive oil industry in the late Iron Age. Wine production which flourished

exile has been a subject of much discussion, with some OT scholars questioning its historicity. To be sure, the Old Testament accounts concerning the exile are scattered and must be taken from a variety of literary works. The book of Chronicles does not speak of the exile at all. Deuteronomistic history ends with the fall of Jerusalem in 587 BCE, and only touches lightly on further developments in Judah and Babylonia (2 Kings 25:22-30). Many biblical texts portray Judah after the deportations as "empty" or in "complete desolation" (Jer 52:27; Ezek 33:34; 2 Chro 36:20-21; Lev 26:32-34; 2 Kings 25:21).

On the other hand, traces of life in Judah can be found in other texts (2 Kings 25:22-26; Jer 40-41). Biblical scholars address many issues regarding the exile. First, the period of the exilic age is a matter of discussion. Traditionally, scholars have defined it lasting from 597-539 BCE (First deportation to Edict of Cyrus). For others, 587 BCE (the final destruction of Jerusalem) is the real beginning of the exilic age.[4] The end of the exilic age for others is 515 BCE.[5] In my discussion, I assume that the exilic age began in 597 BCE, the year Jerusalem was captured and the first group of deportees left Jerusalem for Babylon. It ended in 520 BCE when the rebuilding of the Jerusalem temple was undertaken at the decree of the Persian king Darius I.[6]

The historical reality of the exile is also at issue. C. C. Torrey questions whether there ever was an exile, claiming that the story was invented to justify the existence of Jews in Babylonia at a later period.[7] Following Torrey, Robert Carroll,

---

in Gibeon during this time, could have attracted the Babylonians to extend their imperial expansion. See discussion in Hans M. Barstad, "After the Myth of the Empty Land:" Major Challenges in the Study of the Neo-Babylonian Judah," in Judah and the Judeans in the Neo-Babylonian Period, 3-20.

4 Cf. Rainer Albertz, *Israel in Exile: The History and Literature of the Sixth Century BCE*, trans. David Green, SBL 3 (Atlanta: Society of Biblical Literature, 2003), 2.

5 Thus Middlemas defines the exilic age as the "Templeless Age" (587-515) based on the books of Haggai, Zechariah 1-8, and the Holiness Code. See Jill Middlemas, *The Templeless Age: An Introduction to the History, Literature, and Theology of the Exile* (Louisville: Westminster John Knox Press, 2007).

6 I assume 520 BCE as the end of the exile because it was the year when the construction of the Jerusalem temple was actually taken up. Following the decree of Darius I (522 BCE), the repatriates under the leadership of Zerubbabel and Joshua took active part in rebuilding the temple. Ezra 6, Haggai 1 and Zechariah 1:16; 4:8-10 indicate this. This is also hinted in Jeremiah 15:11-12; 29:10, Zechariah 1:12; 7:15, and 2 Chronicles 36:21, which allude to a "70 years-long exile." Recent studies suggest that a large number of exiles did not return to Judah until shortly before the rebuilding of the temple around 520 BCE. Rainer Albertz, Vanderhooft, and John J. Ahn, among others hold this position. See Rainer *Albertz, Israel* in Exile, 2; Vanderhooft, *The Neo-Babylonian Empire*, 104 -114. John J. Ahn, *Exile as Forged Migrations: A Sociological, Literary, and Theological Appropriation on the Displacement and Resettlement of the Southern Kingdom of Judah*, BZAW 147 (Berlin: De Gruyter, 2011), 38, 40.

7 Charles. C. Torrey, *The Composition and Historical Value of Ezra-Nehemiah*, BZAW 2 (Giessen: J. Ricker, 1896), 62-65.

H. M. Barstad, and Thomas L. Thompson (among others) suggest that exile was an ideological construct that had little historical reality.[8] On the other hand, scholars such as Ralph E. Klein, P. R. Ackroyd, Rainer Albertz, Oded Lipschitz, Avraham Faust, and many others advocate the reality and importance of the Babylonian exile as a major influence for formulating biblical literature.[9] Extra-biblical and archaeological artifacts from different sites confirm the historical reality of the fall of Jerusalem and the consequent deportations and settlements in Babylonia and Egypt. The total figure of exiles in the book of Kings is 18,000 (10,000+8,000) (2 Kings 24:14, 16). The book of Jeremiah records three deportations which add up to 4,600 (the first deportation – 3,032 (Jer 52:28), the second deportation – 832 (Jer 39:9-10; 52:29), and the third deportation 745 (Jer 43:5-6; 52:30).[10] Josephus has two deportations: the first deportation with Jehoiachim, 3000 in number; and the second deportation with Jehoiachin, 10,832 in number.[11] Demographic studies of the century, with the help of archaeological data, support opposing views.[12] Even though we cannot determine the exact number of people displaced

8 See Robert P. Carroll, "Exile! What Exile? Deportations and the Discourse of Diaspora," in *Leading Captivity Captive: "The Exile" as History and Ideology*, ed. L. L. Grabbe, JSOTSup 278 (Sheffield: Sheffield Academic Press, 1998), 62-79; Hans M. Barstad, *The Myth of Empty Land A Study in the History and Archaeology of Judah During the "Exilic" Period* (Oslo: Scandinavian University Press, 1996); Thomas L. Thompson, *The Mythic Past: Biblical Archaeology and the Myth of Israel* (New York: Basic Books, 1999).

9 See Ralph W. Klein, *Israel in Exile: A Theological Interpretation* (Philadelphia: Fortress Press, 1979); Peter R. Ackroyd, *Exile and Restoration: A Study of Hebrew Thought of the Sixth Century* (London: SCM Press Ltd., 1968); Rainer Albertz, "More or Less than a Myth: Reality and Significance of Exile for the Political, Social, and Religious History of Judah," in *By the Irrigation Canals of Babylon: Approaches to the Study of the Exile*, LHE/OTS 526, eds. John J. Ahn and Jill Middlemas (New York: T&T Clark, 2012), 20-33. Oded Lipschits, *The Fall and Rise of Jerusalem: Judah Under Babylonian Rule* (Winona Lake, Ind: Eisenbrauns, 2005), Avraham Faust, *Judah in the Neo-Babylonian Period: Archaeology of Desolation*, SBL ABSS 18 (Atlanta, Georgia: SBL, 2012).

10 Mowinckel believes that Jeremiah records only the number of deportees from Judah outside Jerusalem, and that about 10, 000 people from Jerusalem and it surrounding areas are to be added. Cited in Joel Weinberg, *The Citizen-temple Community* JSOTSup 151; trans. Daniel L. Smith-Christopher (Shefield: Sheffield Academic Press, 1992), 36.

11 Flavius Josephus Judean Antiquities, 238, 240. The second number is the total number of exiles for Josephus. He apparently adds up the round number of 2 Kings 24:14 -10,000 and the number of second deportation in Jeremiah 52:29 - 832, which is 10, 832.

12 Studies by Barstad and Zorn argue for smaller numbers. On the other hand, recent studies of excavations and surveys done by Oded Lipschits and Avraham Faust favor a major decline in the settlement of Judah during the Neo-Babylonian and early Persian period. The population of the southern kingdom by the end of the eighth-seventh century BCE was calculated to be approximately 300,000 (Albright) or 250,000 (Weinberg). Cf. William F. Albright, "A Brief History of Judah from the Days of Josiah to Alexander the Great," BA 9 (1946): 4; Joel Weinberg, *The Citizen-Temple Community*, 35. Lipschits calculates the decline of population to be about 70 percent and Avraham Faust estimates up to 80-90 percent decline. See Oded Lipschits, "Demographic Changes in Judah between the Seventh and the Fifth Centuries

in the successive deportations, we may roughly estimate the number to be around 20,000.[13] If the population of Judah in the seventh century was approximately 200,000 the number of the exiles may have added up to approximately ten percent of the total population.

3. Socio-Historical Situations of the Israelites in the Exilic Period

3.1. Community of the Exiles in Babylonia

The exilic age began in 597 BCE with the first deportation under Nebuchadnezzar. He was a strong king who assembled further campaigns in the west after the destruction of Jerusalem.[14] It is plausible that Nebuchadnezzar had an enlightened policy in his treatment of the exiles. Jorn Kiefer argues that Judean deportees received equal treatment with those of other ethnic groups. He writes: "Die judischen Deportierten teilten das Schicksal zahlreicher anderer Minderheiten im multiethnischen und multikulturellen Babylon."[15] After the death of Nebuchadnezzar, in 562 BCE, Babylonian power rapidly declined.[16] A record of the Babylonian Court list reveals that Jehaoiachin was released from prison and was given a royal status in Babylonia during the reign of Awil Merodach.[17] The Weidner Tablets allude to the rations the exiled Judean king Jehoiachin and his sons received.[18] A document from the Eanna archive contains information about a shipment of kurummat sarri (provisions of the king) for dinner at the

---

B.C.E." in *Judah and the Judeans in the Neo-Babylonian Period, 356; Faust, Judah in the Neo-Babylonian Period*, 246.

13 This calculation is made on the basis of biblical records, Josephus, and other scholars. The number in 2 Kings (10000+8000) are the first and the second deportations, and Jeremiah's record total of 4600 includes the three deportations from the northern regions. Mowinckel's thesis that Jeremiah records only people from the Northern sites is convincing as Jeremiah lived in Mizpah. Hence, the total could be 10,000+8,000 from Jerusalem and its surrounding areas, and about 4,600 from Benjamin area. This calculation comes close to Josephus and many other scholars.

14 *ANET*, 305. Cf. *Flavius Josephus Judean Antiquities* 8-10, 264; Ezek 26, 28 & Jer 52:30.

15 Jorn Kiefer, *Exil und Diaspora: Begrifflichkeit und Deutungen im Antiken Judentum und in der Hebraischen Bibel* (Leipzig: Evangeische Verlagsanstalt, 2005), 74-75.

16 See *ANET*, 311.

17 *ANET*, 308. Cf. 2 Kings 25: 27-30. Goulder compares this record with other Old Testament figures such as Joseph, David, and Second Isaiah, and concludes it is an ideological construction. See M. Goulder, "Behold my Servant Jehoiachin," *Vetus Testamentum* 52, no. 2 (2002): 176.

18 The Weidner Chronicles are fragments of cuneiform tablets discovered at Sippar, a supposed Neo-Babylonian temple library. It is named after the excavations of E. F. Weidner in 1926. The texts list the rations Jehoiachin and his sons received in the Babylonian province. This is parallel with Amel-Marduk's treatment of Jehoiachin in 2 Kings 25:30 and Jer 52:31-34. See *ANET*, 308. See also Laurie E. Pierce, "Judean" A Special Status in Neo-Babylonian and Achaemenid Babylonia?" in *Judah and the Judeans in the Achaemenid Period*, 269; See the translation of The Weidner Chronicle in A. K. Grayson, *Assyrian and Babylonian Chronicles* (Locust Valley, NY: J. J. Augustin, 1975), 145-156.

palace, which resonates with "Jehoiachin dined regularly in the king's presence" in 2 Kings 25:29.[19] The special status of Jehoaichin may be limited among the Judean exiles and he could have died early.[20] Evidence of the settlements of the Babylonian exiles can be found in the Murashu Tablets.[21] The tablets represent the archives of an agricultural banking firm of the Murashu family at Nippur, in the town of Yahudu (al Yahudu) in which nearly hundred Judean names are identified. Many of those names are Yahwistic, and several of them are similar to the names found in Ezra-Nehemiah. The persistence of Yahwistic names could be interpreted as an attachment to the traditional onomastic repertory. Only Judeans of the Neo-Babylonian and Persian period in Babylonia used Yahwistic names.[22] They demonstrate self-identification of the Judeans amidst other groups. The tablets demonstrate that the Judeans in Babylonia had been fully integrated legally and could make their livelihood through normal economic means.[23] From these documents we can reconstruct the context of the Babylonian exiles and determine that they were well established and had adjusted well in their settlements, which continued into the Persian period as is evidenced from the Murashu archive.

---

19 This document is dated the spring of 579 BCE. It is found within the records of the conveyance of foodstuffs from the Eanna temple to the court of Nebuchadnezzar. The account is contradicted with the book of Kings, which dates the event at the time of Evil-Merodack, the son of Nebuchadnezzar. See detail in David B. Weisberg, "A "Dinner at the Palace" During Nebuchadnezzar's Reign," in *Homeland and Exile: Biblical and Ancient Near Eastern Studies in Honour of Bustenay Oded*, eds. Gershon Galil, Mark Geller and Alan Millard (Leiden: Brill, 2009), 263.

20 The book of Ezekiel suggests this where priests and elders took leadership role in the aftermath of the fall of Jerusalem in Babylonia. The kingship or leadership role of Jehoiachin is not mentioned.

21 The 730 tablets belonging to the archives of the house of Murasu were discovered in May 1893 in a room at Nippur during the excavations sponsored by the University of Pennsylvania. The tablets contain collections of names that include a large number of individual with Babylonian names, Persians, Medes, Egyptians and West Semites (including biblical personal names). See detailed study of the onomasticon of the Murasu tablets in Michael David Coogan, *West Semitic Personal Names in the Murasu Documents* (Missoula, Montana: Scholars Press, 1976).

22 Ran Zadok claims that Jews can be distinguished comparatively easily from the other West Semitic ethnic groups since the theophoric element YHW is practically confined to Jewish names in the Neo Babylonian and Late Babylonian period. For him, those names are plausible proof that Jews lived in Babylonia in the Neo Babylonian and Achaemenian period around the Nippur region. See Ran Zadok, *The Jews in Babylonia During the Chaldean and Achaemenian Periods According to the Babylonian Sources* (Haifa: University of Haifa, 1978), 5, 13.

23 Cf. Albertz, Israel in Exile, 102. In her detailed study of the Murashu tablets, Laurie E Pearce concludes that Judeans were not given any special status, although they were involved in business transactions. See Laurie E. Pierce, "Judean:" A Special Status in Neo-Babylonian and Achaemenid Babylonia," in *Judah and the Judeans in the Achaemenid Period*, 274. See also Pierce, "New Evidence for Judeans in Babylon, in Judah and Judeans in the Persian Period," eds. Oded Lipschichts and Manfred Oeming (Winona Lake, Ind: Eisenbrauns, 2006), 399-411.

From biblical texts, we know that the exiles transitioned smoothly into their new settlements. They maintained correspondences with those who remained in Judah (Ezek 33:21-22; Jer. 29). They built houses, planted gardens, enjoyed their products, and lived normal lives (Jer. 29:5-7). The books of Ezra, Haggai and Zechariah confirm that the repatriates were economically sound and able to contribute to the rebuilding of the Jerusalem temple (Ezra 2:69; Haggai 1:2; Zech 6:10-11). They assembled under the leadership of elders and priests (Ezek. 8:1; 14:1; 20:1; Jer. 29:1). The book of Daniel and Esther imply that they were able to rise to higher positions while in exile. There is a possibility that the deportees built their own temple at Casiphia, from whence Ezra was able to recruit cultic personnel (Cf. Ezra 8:15-20). Frequent usage of "assembly of the elders," in Ezekiel may have liturgical connections (Ezek 8:1, 11; 14:1; 20:1). Certain religious practices like circumcision, observance of the Sabbath, and dietary laws received emphasis, during this period, perhaps as markers of Judean identity. It is believed that the exile was a time of religious activity, a time of concentrated focus on Israel's religious heritage, the formation of profound literary works, and gathering together and editing of earlier texts.[24] Yet life in exile was not all positive. The exiles longed for their homeland (Ps 137), and looked forward to the coming of Cyrus to liberate the group (Isa 45:1-7; 51:12-16). In spite of favorable conditions for a rise in socioeconomic status, the exile was a major uprooting as the groups lost their homeland and original social status.

The book of Ezekiel claims that the exiles settled down in different parts of Babylonia, perhaps somewhere near the river (canal) Chebar, such as Tel-abib (Ezek 1:1-3; 3:15). The Murashu documents show that many Judeans settled around Nippur, which lay between the Tigris and Euphrates about 150 km southeast of Babylon. The Chebar canal also flows near the city of Nippur and hence this appears to be one of the main settlements of the Babylonian exiles.[25] Other settlements, according to biblical sources are Tel-melah and Tel-harsa (Neh 7:61), Ahava (Ezra 8:15, 21, 31), and Casiphia where a leader, Iddo, lived with other temple personnel (Ezra 8:17). Even though we cannot locate the exact locations of these sites where the exiles lived, it is certain that they lived in communities, located somewhere along the riverbanks of the Tigris and Euphrates.

---

24 Some critics such as Klein, Brueggemann, Ackroyd, Albertz, and others advocate this idea. For example, Klein emphasizes seven literary works as the outcome of the exile, such as Lamentations, selected Psalms, Deuteronomistic History, Priestly writings of the Pentateuch, prophets of Jeremiah, Ezekiel and Deutero-Isaiah. See Klein, *Israel in Exile*, 7. See also Walter Brueggemann, *Hopeful Imagination: Prophetic Voices in Exile* (Philadelphia: Fortress Press, 1986); Peter R. Ackroyd, *Exile and Restoration*, Rainer Albertz, *Israel in Exile*.

25 Cf. Charles Francis Whiteley, *The Exilic Age* (Philadelphia: Westminster Press, 1957), 70.

3.2. Community of Those Who Remained in Judah

Questions of continuity and discontinuity of life in Judah after the deportations have been a contentious issue. Robert Carroll, who coined the term "myth of the empty land," argues that there was no such empty land in Judah after the collapse of Judah.[26] Others argue for partial disruption and less decline in settlements.[27] On the other hand, many studies demonstrate that Judah was in ruin and that there is no evidence of proper settlement in the Neo-Babylonian period. Archaeological discoveries of the Neo-Babylonian and early Persian Period (sixth century) are published in many surveys and publications, however the results of archaeological studies reflect polarizing views.

Since the work of Albright in the 1920s, archaeological exploration in Palestine gained new impetus with excavations of different sites in the ancient biblical world.[28] A number of studies and surveys have reconstructed the history of Judah in the sixth century BCE through the study of archaeological artifacts; such as, architecture, pottery, ceramics, and tombs in different regions. The results of excavations of Jerusalem by Kathleen Kenyon were interpreted as supporting a continual habitation of Jerusalem in the sixth century BCE.[29] One archaeological result is interpreted by Bastard who writes: "Life went on after 586 pretty much in the same way as it did before the arrival of Nebuchadnezzar's armies, possibly, but not necessarily, on a reduced scale."[30] Jeffrey R. Zorn's extensive research on the material remains of Tell en-Nasbeh (Mizpah), including architecture (room-building patterns), pottery, and stamped jars, suggests a flourishing provincial

---

26 See Robert P. Carroll, "The Myth of the Empty Land," *Semeia* 59 (1992): 79-93.

27 For example Hans M. Barstad, *History and the Hebrew Bible: Studies in Ancient Israelite and Ancient Near Eastern Historiography* (Tubingen: Mohr Siebeck, 2008), Jeffrey R. Zorn. "Tell-en-Nasbeh and the Problem of the Material Culture of the Sixth Century," *Judah and the Judeans in the Neo-Babylonian Period*, 413-447.

28 Following the landmark work of Albright (1920-1930), biblical archeology wrote new chapters with excavations in various places including but not limited to the Benjamin region (William F. Bade 1926, 1935, Finkelstein 1993); Transjordan (Nelson Glueck 1932-1947); Jericho and Jerusalem (Kathleen Kenyon 1952-1958); Sechem (G. E. Wright 1957-1968); Gibeon (James B. Pritchard 1956-1962); Ai (Joseph A. Callaway 1964-1969); Tell-el-full (Paul W. Lapp - 1964-1967); Judean Hills (Avi Ofer 1993); She`phelah; Jerusalem and its environs (Gabriel Barkay 1994, Amos Kloner, 2000, 2001, Ephraim Stern 2001). Dever outlines different stages of the archaeology of the "Holy Land" as: (1) The exploratory era (19th century), (2) The classificatory period (1920-1950), (3) The heyday and decline (1950-1970), (4) The new archaeology (1970-present). See William G. Dever, *What Did the Biblical Writers Know and When Did They Know it? What Archaeology Can Tell Us about the Reality of Ancient Israel* (Grand Rapids, Michigan: Eerdmans Pub. Co., 2002), 54-60.

29 Cited in Efrain Velazquez II, "The Persian Period and the Origins of Israel: Beyond the "Myths," in *Critical Issues in early Israelite History*, eds. Richard S. Hess, Gerald A. Klingbeil, and Paul J. Ray Jr., (Winona Lake, Ind: Eisenbrauns, 2008), 67.

30 Hans M. Barstad, *History and the Hebrew Bible*, 159.

center of Mizpah in the sixth century.[31] Continued settlement in Judah, particularly in the Benjamin region, is likely.

In opposition to the proposal of continued settlement, many investigations argue for a major decline in the population of Judah in the Neo-Babylonian and early Persian period.[32] One of the most important contributions is found in the publications of Oded Lipschits. Through his survey of the excavations of various sites of Judah, he claims that the data and surveys reveal that "between the end of the Iron Age and the Persian period there was a decline of approximately seventy percent in the size of settled area."[33] In line with Lipschichts, Avraham Faust recently lays out a strong case for the desolation and depopulation of the land in the sixth century.[34] His study implies that not only Jerusalem and its environs, but also the whole land of Judah including Benjamin were heavily damaged.

If we review various archeological data and surveys, we can conclude that life in Judah in the sixth century BCE was marked by decline, which was caused not only by deportations, but also by famine, economic downturn, and attacks by neighboring nations emboldened by a weak political establishment. It is evident that Jerusalem and its surrounding areas were severely desolated and depopulated, whereas there were relatively stable settlements in the Benjamin region. I argue this for the following reasons: (1) archaeological data provides mixed results and are

---

31 Zorn, "Tell-en-Nasbeh and the Problem of the Material Culture of the Sixth Century," 413-447. See also Ephraim Stern, *Archaeology of the Land of the Bible* Vol. II: *The Assyrian, Babylonian, and Persian Periods (734-332 BCE)*, (New York: Doubleday, 2001), 312-327.

32 See for example, William F. Albright, *The Archaeology of Palestine* (Harmondsworth, Middlesex: Penguin Books 1949); Ephraim Stein, *Archaeology of the Land of the Bible* Vol. II; Charles E. Carter, *The Emergence of Yehud in the Persian Period: A Social and Demographic Study*, JSOT Sup294 (Sheffield: Sheffield Academic Press, 1999); Charles E. Carter, "Ideology and Archaeology in the Neo-Babylonian Period," in Judah and the Judeans in the Neo-Babylonian Period, 301-322; B. Oded, "Where Is the "Myth of the Empty Land" To be Found? History versus Myth," in *Judah and the Judeans in the Neo-Babylonian Period*, 55-74.

33 According to Lipschits, the decline of settled areas (settled dunams) at the end of the Iron Age (7th century BCE) to the Persian period (5th century BCE) is as follows: Benjamin - 56.5%, Jerusalem environs 89.0%, Northern Judean Hills - 2.0%, Southern Judean Hills - 71.7%, The Shephelah - 66.7%, Beer-Sheba-Arad Valleys - 75.0%, Eastern Strip - 88.9%. Total decline - 72.3% See Oded Lipschits, "Demographic Changes in Judah between the Seventh and the Fifth Centuries B.C.E.," in *Judah and the Judeans in the Neo-Babylonian Period*, 356. See also Oded Lipschits, The Fall and Rise of Judah under Babylonian Rule (Winona Lake, Ind: Eisenbrauns, 2005).

34 He claims that the land was not empty; but there were probably thousands of people in Judah in the Neo-Babylonian period. See Faust, The Archaeology of Desolation, 233. See also Faust, "Settlement Dynamics and Demographic Fluctuations in Judah from the Late Iron Age to the Hellenistic Period and the Archaeology of Persian-Period Yehud," in *A Time of Change: Judah and its Neighbours in the Persian and Early Hellenistic Periods*, LSTS 65, ed. Yigal Levin (London: T&T Clark, 2007), 23-64; and Faust, "The Shephelah in the Iron Age: A New look on the Settlement of Judah," *Palestine Exploration Quarterly* 143, no. 3 (2013): 203-219.

subject to interpretation;[35] (2) there is no explicit record the wholesale desolation of Judah in Babylonian or Persian texts; (3) biblical texts suggest continuity in the Benjamin region of Judah, around Mizpah and Bethel; and (4) when exiles returned, the land was already inhabited by a significant number of peoples.

How do biblical texts explain the social history of the Judahite community in the period? Biblical texts illustrate that life continued in Judah around Mizpah and Bethel after the destruction of Jerusalem. Gedaliah formed a center in Mizpah around which the Judeans who had not been taken into exile might gather (Jer. 40). Biblical texts indicate that a certain group of priests known as the Shaphanids took control of the political and religious institutions.[36] Biblical sources testify that the consequent attacks from foreign nations, along with occasional confrontations with the Babylonian power, would have worsened the socioeconomic life of the people of Judah (Jer. 49:1-6 Cf. Ezek 25:1-11; 35:1-15; Lam. 5:12-13; Amos 1:11f). The (possibly partial) removal of royalty, officials, priests, and landed citizens favored a social revolution in Judah. This could have been affected by the "poorest of the land" מדלת הארץ (2 Kings 25:12) rising to positions of greater influence. The presumably propertyless members of the community, who now happened to be landholders under the Babylonian authority, occupied royal lands and perhaps also took over lands from other property-owners (Ezek 11:15; 33:24).

Historical notes from the biblical texts suggest that the Temple was destroyed and that sacred vessels were stolen in the second Babylonian invasion (2 Kings 25:9; 2 Chro 36:18f). Whether worship occurred after the destruction of the Temple is uncertain. According to Jeremiah 41:5, after the destruction of Jerusalem, people came from Shechem, Shilloh, and Samaria, possibly for pilgrimage to Jerusalem. Mizpah and Bethel increased in importance, possibly for administrative purposes and religious assembly.[37] Religious life was marked by the decline of worship at Jerusalem on the one hand, and the revival of the ritual importance of Bethel/Mizpah on the other.

---

35 Lipschits recognizes two big problems of archaeology: (1) the lack of uniformity in the survey resulted partially by differences in the type of area surveyed, and (2) different worldviews of the surveyors. See Lipschits, "Demographic Changes in Judah between the Seventh and the Fifth Centuries," 325.

36 2 Kings 25:22; Jer 40:7-12. Gedaliah, the ruler at Mizpah, was the grandson of Shaphan, secretary and priest of the royal court at the time of Josiah (2 Kgs 22:3; 1 Chro 8:17; Jer 39:14, 40:5-6). Blenkinsopp argues that the Shaphanids claimed leadership of the Judean community of Judah. This is also suggested by the continuation of their descendants as temple priests, found in 2 Kings 22:12; Jer 29:3; 36:10. See Joseph Blenkinsopp, "Judeans, Jews, Children of Abraham," in *Judah and the Judeans in the Achaemenid Period*, 465.

37 In many instances, biblical texts provide the cultic role of Bethel (Gen 12:18; 35:1; Judg 20:18; 1 Sam 10:3; 1 Kings 12:2-32; Amos 5:5). People gathering at Mizpah for political and religious assembly are recorded in several instances (Judg 20:1; 1 Sam 7:5; 10:17; 2 Kings 25:23; Jer 40). Interestingly, Bethel is very close to Mizpah about 6 km north of the site. Hence, the political and religious significance of Mizpah and Bethel in the exilic period is unquestionable.

3.3. Judean Community in Egypt

According to biblical literature, Egypt is the land where the people of Israel experienced settlement, captivity, and immigration. The traditions of the ancestors, the Exodus, the monarchy, and the exile have extensive ties with Egypt and its people. The cooperative relationship between Pharaoh Apries (biblical Hophra) and the Judean king Zedekiah is said to have encouraged the voluntary immigration of Israelites to Egypt.[38] Deuteronomistic history and the book of Jeremiah describe immigration to Egypt in 582 due to fears of reprisal from the Babylonian king (2 Kings 25:26; Jer 44:1). Settlements in Egypt possibly began during the reign of Manasseh or Josiah.[39] A plausible scenario is that some priests of Yahweh escaped Manasseh's polytheistic campaign and fled to Egypt.[40] The discovery of the Elephantine Papyri is helpful for reconstructing the social history of the exiles in Egypt.[41] According to the papyri, Judeans built an ethnic community in Elephantine sometime in the sixth-fifth century BCE. They also built a temple of Yahu in Elephantine before Cambyses conquered Egypt in 525 BCE.[42] It is plausible that the Judean community had already settled in the seventh century, to which additional exiles fled in the Neo-Babylonian period.

38 Cf. Charles F. Pfeiffer, *Exile and Return* (Grand Rapids, Michigan: Baker Book House, 1962), 27.

39 Letter of Aristeas 13 alludes to the help rendered by Judeans for Egyptian king Psammetichus who campaigned against the king of Ethiopians. The Psammetichus mentioned in this text appears to be Psammetichus I, who ruled Egypt during 671-617 BCE. Hence, the existence of the Judeans in Egypt by the end of the 7th century is plausible. See comments on the text in Herbert T. Andrews, "The Letter of Aristeas," in *The Apocrypha and Pseudepigrapha of the Old Testament in English with Introductions and Critical and Explanatory Notes to the several Books*, ed. R. H. Charles (Oxford: Clarendon Press, 1913), 96. In agreement with the seventh century origin, Bezalel Porten dates the establishment of the Jewish community at Elephantine about 650 BCE. See Bezalel Porten, "Settlement of the Jews at Elephantine and the Arameans at Syne," in *Judah and the Judeans in the Neo-Babylonian Period*, 466.

40 Leo Dupree Sandgren, *Vines Intertwined: A History of Jews and Christians from the Babylonian Exile to the Advent of Islam* (Peabody, Massachusetts: Hendrickson Publishers, 2010), 51. Cf. 2 Kings 21:5-16.

41 The Elephantine Papyri are a group of papyrus documents and fragments written in Demotic Egyptian, Aramaic, Greek, Coptic, and Latin dating from the 5th century BCE originating at Elephantine, a site in Upper Egypt. They are classified as: Letters, Contracts, Literary Texts, Historical Texts, Accounts, and Lists. Of the Papyri, some of them, including Letters have generated interest in biblical studies. See Gary A. Herion, "Elephantine Papyri," in *ABD* Vol. 2, 445-455. Though they are late, they help in reconstructing the history of the Judean community in Egypt that may have been established in the 7th/6th centuries BCE.

42 See "The Jedinah Archive," B19.TAD A4.7, in *Bezalel Porten, The Elephantine Papyri in English: Three Millennia of Cross-Cultural Continuity and Change* (Leiden: E. J. Brill, 1996), 141.

The Jewish names found in the papyri, most of which go back to the pre-exilic period, confirm a settlement in the seventh century.[43]

The papyri suggest that the exiles sought and made their living as soldiers in Egyptian service.[44] It appears that mixed marriage was accepted.[45] The community retained its own religio-cultural values of worshiping Yahu through a well-established cultic system.[46] Bob Becking contends that the Yehudites in Elephantine were "the descendants of a branch or various branches, of the poly-Yahwism that existed in Judah before the Yahweh-alone movement."[47] The names of deities associated with temples at Syne, such as Banit, the Queen of Heaven, Bethel and Nabu, support the probability of polytheistic worship.[48] We have limited evidence of the relationships between the Elephantine community and other groups of Israelites. What we know is that there were communications between the exiles in Egypt and the Judeans in the land in the sixth-fifth century BCE.[49] We may summarize that the Judeans in Egypt during the exilic age were the group of exiles from the Neo-Babylonian period, who mingled with the Judean community already settled.

4. Judah in the Early Persian Period

The traditional understanding of the early history of the Israelites in the Persian period is that, after the triumph of Cyrus over king Nabonidus in 539, a group of Babylonian exiles returned to their homeland.[50] The appendix of 2 Chronicles (36:22-23) tells of the decree of return. Ezra 1-2 reports the return following the

43 Names include Ananiah, Azariah, Gemariah, Hosea, Jedaniah, Menahem, Uriah, Zechariah, among many. See Porten, *The Elephantine Papyri in English*, 26.

44 This is shown by their involvement in military, economic activity, and their contribution for the temple of Yahu. See "Miscellanous Letters" B8-12 and "the Jedaniah Archive" B13-22.

45 In the Mibtahiah Archive, there is a marriage contract between Mahseiah, son of Jedaniah and Egyptian daughter called Eshor. See "The Mibtahiah Archive" B28 TAD B2.6, 177-183.

46 This is evident in the Jedaniah Archive, which calls for the observance of Passover and of some provisions of the Torah, such as abstention from work on Nissan 15 and 21, abstention from the consumption of leaven during the seven days of the feast, regulations concerning the obligations of purity during the week, and the prohibition of fermented drink. See "The Passover Letter," B13 TAD A4.1, 125-126.

47 Bob Becking, "Yehudite Identity in Elephantine," in *Judah and the Judeans in the Achaemenid Period*, 415.

48 The letters to Syne open with a greeting to the temples of Bethel, the Queen of Heaven, Banit, and Nabu. See "The Mikkibanit Letters" B1 TAD A2.1, B2 TAD A2.2, B3 TAD A2.3, and B4 TAD A2.4.

49 In a letter sent by Jedaniah, a leader of Jewish community, to the Persian-named Bagavahya, governor of Judah, he narrates the destruction of the temple of Yahweh by the Egyptians. See "The Jedaniah Archive" B20 TAD A4.8.

50 For recent discussions on the history of the fall of Babylonia and the rise of Persian Empire see Megan Bishop Moore and Brad E. Kelle, *Biblical History and Israel's Past: The Changing Study of the Bible and History* (Grand Rapids: Eerdmans, 2011), 396-464.

decree of Cyrus, however the reports are contradictory.[51] The decree of Cyrus, as found in the Cyrus Cylinder, records a return of the gods and their peoples to their respective lands.[52] Some scholars deny any mass return, claiming that such a decree is unlikely because the Judeans refused to return, remaining in exile along with their descendants for many generations.[53] While some deny mass return to Judah in the sixth century BCE, archaeological finds suggest a repopulation of Judah in the late sixth to the fifth centuries BCE.[54] A number of sites in Judah were occupied during the Neo-Babylonian period, to which new settlements were added during the Persian period.[55] Hence, the gradual return to Judah in the late sixth-fifth century is generally accepted.

Despite scholarly consensus on the return of the Judeans from Mesopotamia in the early Persian period, the high number detailed in Ezra-Nehemiah is not corroborated by a long-term return from Babylon. In other words, settlement took place gradually in the late sixth-fifth century BCE. The continued settlements of Judeans in Babylonia, recorded in the book of Esther and Daniel, also indicates this. The edict of Cyrus appears to be fully realized by the time of Darius I (522-486 BCE) (Ezra 6:1-12). After seizing the throne of Persian Empire from Cambyses, Darius I extended his imperial power to Syria-Palestine in the West. His brilliant administration is exhibited in his organization of the empire into provinces, each under the charge of a satrap or a provincial governor. It is probable that the new system of administration gave opportunities for the exiles to return

---

51 For example, the book of Ezra that tells the return of the first group under the leadership of Sheshbazzar in the first year of Cyrus (Ezra 1:7-11) is contradicted with Ezra 2 about the list of returnees in which Sheshbazzar is not mentioned at all among the returnees.

52 Cyrus Cylinder lines 32-34 reads: "I returned to (these) sacred cities on the other side of the Tigris, the sanctuaries of which have been ruins for a long time, the images which (used) to live therein and established them permanent sanctuaries. I (also) gathered all their (former) inhabitants and retuned (to them) their habitations." See the text in Irving Finkel, "The Cyrus Cylinder: the Babylonian Perspective," in *The Cyrus Cylinder: The King of Persia's Proclamation from Ancient Babylon*, ed. Irving Finkel (London: I. B. Tauris & Co. Ltd., 2013), 4-34.

53 Lester L. Grabbe argues that a small numbers of Jews returned to Yehud in the early Persian period, while the bulk of the Jews stayed in Mesopotamia. See discussion in Lester L. Grabbe, "They Shall Come Rejoicing to Zion' or Did They? The Settlement of Yehud in the Early Persian Period," in *Exile and Restoration Revisited: Essays on the Babylonian and Persian Periods in Memory of Peter R. Ackroyd*, LSTS 73, eds. Gary N. Knoppers and Lester L. Grabbe with Deirdre N. Fulton (New York: T&T Clark, 2009), 124.

54 See Faust, "Settlement Dynamics and Demographic Fluctuations in Judah," 48-49.

55 Edelman confirms the repopulation focusing on archaeological evidence. She illustrates that in the Benjamin region, fifty-two sites already occupied in the Neo-Babylonian period continued to be occupied in the Persian period. In addition, twenty-three sites were added during that time. Likewise, thirty-six sites in the Judean hill country increased from fourteen, seven sites in northern Shephelah increased with the addition of sixteen newly established Persian-Era sites. See more detail in Diana Edelman, "Settlement Patterns in Persian-Era Yehud," in *A Time of Change: Judah and Its Neighbours in the Persian and Early Hellenistic Periods*, 54-58.

and to build the temple under the governorship of Tettanai, the governor of the Beyond the River satrapy, and Jerubbabel, the governor of Judah (Ezra 6:13-15). While many Judeans remained in Babylonia and Egypt, it is plausible that the groups of Judeans who returned to Judah were responsible for the rebuilding of the Jerusalem temple in the early period of Darius I.[56] Biblical sources suggest that for more than two decades after Cyrus' decree, the construction of the temple of Jerusalem had not been completed (Cf. Hag 1:1-5; Zech 1:16; Ezra 5:1). Rebuilding and completing the temple is dated a few years after Darius I, who came into power in 522 BCE.[57] It is likely that the work of temple construction achieved its peak under the leadership of Zerubabbel in 521/520 BCE (in the first/second year of Darius) and was completed six years later in 516/5 BCE (Cf. Ezra 6:15; Hag 1:1), which is approximately the seventieth year of exile, according to the prophet Jeremiah (Jer 5:12; 29:10-15 cf. 2 Chro 36:21; Dan 9:2). We therefore, claim that the exilic age extends from the fall of Jerusalem in 597 BCE until the completion of the second Temple in 516/515 BCE.

Ezra-Nehemiah records a return under the leadership of Sheshbazzar (Ezra 1:11), Zerubabbel (Ezra 2:2; Neh 7:7), and Ezra (Ezra 8). The number of returnees is hard to fix with precision. By adding the individual entries in Ezra and Nehemiah, the number of repatriates comes to 31,089 (Neh 7) or 29,818 (Ezra 2) men.[58] This contradicts the total number given by Ezra and Nehemiah.[59] The purpose of the lists, and when they were written, is uncertain, as they may have been recorded from different censuses.[60] Assuming that the book of Ezra-Nehemiah is from a late date, the lists may represent the population of Judah in the sixth-fifth century BCE following consecutive returns from Babylonia and likely also from Egypt.

The repatriates from Babylonia, and possibly Egypt, formed a new community with those who remained in Judah. Side by side with the returning exiles were also groups of people who disapproved of rebuilding the Temple. The

56 The book of Haggai and Zechariah detail that it was "in the second year of King Darius, in the sixth month, on the first day of the month, the word of the Lord came by the prophet Haggai to Zerubbabel son of Shealtiel, governor of Judah, and to Joshua son of Jehozadak, the high priest to start rebuilding the temple." (Hag 1:1ff. Cf. Zech 4:9).

57 Cf. Ezra 6:1-12. Here it is reported that Darius found the decree of Cyrus at Ectabana, the capital of the province of Media. Accordingly he gave permission to rebuild the house of God with the expense borne by the king.

58 Cf. Joel Weinberg, *The Citizen-Temple Community*, 42.

59 The entries in Ezra and Nehemiah are contradicting the total number of people reported in Ezra 2:66 & Neh 7:66 which is 42, 360 men. If we add women and children in the lists, the number could become that large.

60 For example, some critics assume that the names recorded in Ezra-Nehemiah were repatriates in 539. Some argue that they were repatriates between 539 and 515 BCE. Some have argued for a census of the population of Judah at the time of Cyrus or Nehemiah, or the population around 519-517. See Weinberg, *The Citizen-Temple Community*, 41-42.

names found in the lists of repatriates suggest that the Judeans at the time of the return were already mixing with other ethnic groups.[61] Biblical texts attest to group conflicts in the land. Those who remained in Judah during the exilic age were described as "the people of the land" עם הערץ (Ezra 4:4; 9:1-2). Foreign wives and their children were separated and rejected (Ezra 10; Neh 13). Mixed marriage was condemned (Neh 13:23-29). The issue of who was the "true Israel" became more important. The exiles of Babylonia appear to have gained political control along with the appointed leaders who represented the monarchy of Persia.[62] A council of elders and priests replaced the monarchic type of administration, missing since 586 BCE, and it is possible that the priestly group of the Babylonian exiles dominated the new system of administration.

5. Intergroup Relationships in the Exilic Age

From the first deportation in 597 BCE until the construction of the Second Temple in 520 BCE, Israelites living in Babylonia, Judah and Egypt engaged in intergroup relationships. Interaction of the Israelite community in the exilic age was characterized by group conflict, competition, and (re)identification. As reflected by the history of Judah during the exilic period, those who remained in Judah established political and religious stronghold around Mizpah and Bethel. The exiles and those who remained in Judah had been in conflicts since separation. It is plausible that a *Golah* group dominated Judah in the early Persian period when they returned with wealth and power. With the backing of priestly theology they tackled the Judean group who was already in the land and was in constant danger from the surrounding nations. A general overview of intergroup relationships in the exilic age is discussed as follows:

5.1. Political Divide

Traces of life in the exilic age demonstrate a great divide in the political features of the communities of that period. During the Neo-Babylonian period, the exiles in Babylonia were without a strong political administration aside from Jehoaichin, who survived as the representative of the exiles in the Babylonian court. However,

61 These include names: Mordekai - which contains the name of the Babylonian deity Marduk (Ezra 2:2; Neh 7:7), Bilsan - which contains the name of Babylonian deity Bel (Ezra 2:2; Neh 7:7), Bigvai - a Semitic rendering of the Persian personal name (Ezra 2:2, 14; Neh 7:7, 19; 10:16), Elam - a name related to a territory in Iranian plateau (Ezra 2:7; Neh 7:12), and Azgad - a non–Semitic name (Ezra 2:12; Neh 7:17). See discussion in Bob Bekcing, "On the Identity of the 'Foreign Women in Ezra 9-10," in *Exile and Restoration Revisited: Essays on the Babylonian and Persian Periods in Memory of Peter R. Ackroyd Library of Second Temple Studies* 73, ed. Gary N. Knoppers and Lester L. Grabbe with Deirdre N. Fulton (New York: T&T Clark, 2009), 35-36.

62 According to Haggai and Ezra-Nehemiah, administrators of Judah in the early Persian period included repatriates such as Jeshua, Sheshbazzar, Zerubbabel, Nehemiah, and Ezra. See Hag 1:1; Ezra 3:1; 8; Neh 2:1.

they enjoyed social stability under the leadership of priests and elders. In the meantime, Judah enjoyed a semblance of political establishment at Mizpah with Gedaliah and the Shaphanids.[63] When Jerusalem fell at the hands of the Babylonians, the absence of a monarchy created a political vacuum that became a bone of contention between the groups. Political divide between the Shaphanid family and the Jerusalemite leadership could be observed during and after the fall of Jerusalem.[64] This is culminated in the exilic period when Gedaliah grandson of Shaphan took leadership and shifted the national capital from Jerusalem to Mizpah (2 Kings 25:22; Jer 40:7-12). In the early period of the Persian period, the political clash between the two groups, led by repatriates and the Shaphanids, worsened. As Joseph Blenkinsopp says, "The Shaphanids were… certainly in favor of maintaining the status quo."[65] However, other exilic groups did not accept the non-Davidic ruler and the non-Jerusalemite administration.

5.2. Conflict over Cultic Center and Priesthood

Biblical texts relate many instances of the gathering of the Israelites at Bethel and Mizpah for religious purposes.[66] One can assume that worship took place in the sanctuary of Yahweh at Bethel and at Mizpah, whereas sacrifice and religious gatherings were unlikely to have been held in Jerusalem during the exilic period due to the destruction of the Temple. The Deuteronomistic Historian condemned cultic activities and its priesthood at Bethel and Mizpah.[67] Bethel was a subject of hidden polemic because of its potential as an alternative to Jerusalem.[68] It is not surprising to find the exclusive claim for priesthood of the Zadokite family in the book of Ezekiel 40-48 because of the other forms of priesthood in the land of Benjamin at Bethel and Mizpah. The competition between the Babylonian sponsored sanctuary at Bethel/Mizpah and the repatriates' claim of the centrality

63 This is also shown by archaeological findings of significant occupation in the period. See more detail in Zorn, "Tell-el Nasbeh and the Problem of Material Culture of the Sixth Century," 413-447.

64 The Shaphanid family played a crucial role in political and religious affairs both before and after the fall of Jerusalem. Shaphan appears to be secretary to Josiah; his three sons and two grandsons took leadership during the crisis of Judah in the sixth century BCE (See 2 Kings 22:3-10; 1 Chro 8:17, 9:7-8; Neh 11:7; Jer 29:3; 36:10; 39:14, 40:5-6; 29:1-28).

65 Blenkinsopp, "Judaeans, Jews, Children of God," 465.

66 See for Bethel: Gen 12:18; 35:1; Judg 20:18; 1 Sam 10:3; 1 Kings 12:2-32; Amos 5:5; for Mizpah: Judg 20:1; 1 Sam 7:5; 10:17; 2 Kings 25:23; Jer 40.

67 Cf. 1 Kings 12:31; 13:1-10. Blenkinsopp finds the politics of cult in the Deuteronomistic history in which cultic activities at Bethel was downgraded and delegitimized in the literary framework of the Deuteronomic history. See more detailed discussion in Joseph Blenkinsopp, "Bethel in the Neo-Babylonian Period," in *Judah and the Judeans in the Neo-Babylonian Period*, 102-103.

68 Yarah Amit, "Epoch and Genre: The Sixth Century and the Growth of Hidden Polemic," in *Judah and Judeans in the Neo-Babylonian Period*, 142.

of Jerusalem and its temple could have created conflicts in the sixth century.[69] Conflict between cultic officials concomitant with conflict over cultic sites created greater division between the Shaphanids (perhaps the forerunners of the sons of Aaron) and the Zadokites.[70] Egyptian exiles were not treated well, perhaps due to conflict over cultic matters.[71]

5.3. Class Conflict

The Deuteronomistic history records that "the poor of the land" מדלת הארץ were left behind to cultivate and inhabit the land (2 Kings 24:14). For them, the exile was Yahweh's judgment on the exploitation of the upper class. The claims to land ownership by the common people were oppositionally received as – legitimate (Jer 32) and illegitimate (Ezekiel 11, 33). The books of Jeremiah and Ezekiel demonstrate class conflict between the exiles (elite) and the inhabitants of Jerusalem and Judah (poor of the land). When some of the exiles returned in the early Persian period, they came with economic, social, and political power and the blessing of the Persian king and overwhelmed the existing late exilic community. As reflected by the history of Judah during the exilic period, those who had remained in Judah established political and religious stronghold around Mizpah and Bethel. The *Golah* group, which dominated the early Persian period, renewed its connection with Jerusalem as its center of administration and worship. With their temple theology they tackled the Judean group who were already there and who were already in constant danger from the surrounding nations. The upper class did not even recognize the poor as worthy for counting as citizens. They were the outgroup whose claim of land and cultic center were unacceptable. Hence, class conflict began as early as deportation and continued through the late exilic period.

5.4. Theological Difference

With the decline of the priesthood and monarchy in Judah, Deuteronomism shaped a theology of covenant for those who remained in Judah. Sin-punishment-repentance-restoration had become the guiding principles reflected in some of the exilic literature. In Babylonia, the growing influence of priestly leadership supported strict rules of religiosity, including circumcision, Sabbath-keeping,

69 Cf. Blenkinsopp, "Bethel in the Neo-Babylonian Period," 104-105.

70 Blenkinsopp argues that both the sons of Aaron and the sons of Zadok are the products of the second temple period, who emerged out of the struggle for control of the cult between the first temple and the second temple. See Joseph Blenkinsopp, "Judean, Jews, Children of Abraham," in *Judah and the Judeans in the Achaemenid Period*, 465.

71 Jedaniah and the priests of Elephantine sent letters to Bagahaya, governor of Judah, and to the priests of Judah, reporting their struggles at Elephantine. There is a mention that no reply texts have been found. This suggests an unpleasant relationship between the two groups. See "The Jedaniah Archive" B19 TAD A4.7, 142.

food laws, and varieties of purity systems.[72] When these groups interacted during the early Persian period, theological differences created conflicting ideologies and theologies. The exilic group invented ritual symbols to define who was in the group in order to maintain their identity. Religion became more important in the (re)identification of community as Albertz observed, "In the exilic period, Israel acquired for the first time, characteristics of a religiously constituted community."[73]

5.5. Ethnic Conflict

The deportations and exiles resulted in an engagement with people of other cultures in Babylonia, Egypt and in the homeland. That different groups of the Israelites mingled with other people was acknowledged.[74] By supporting strong relationships during their exile in foreign lands, both the Egyptian and Babylonian exilic groups were able to maintain their identities. When they interacted with those who remained in Judah, identity issue was more salient. Debates over the identity of "true Israel" became an important issue in the exilic age. The claims of descendants of Abraham and the inheritance of the land had become interpretative theological issues that defined group identity in the time of exile. Those who are not deported from the land are represented as not qualified to be sons of Abraham (Ezekiel 11:14-16; 33:24; 36:1-5).[75] Ezra-Nehmiah shows that endogamous boundaries became determining factor of group membership right from the early Persian period. The Exiles, who claimed themselves to be "the true Israel," in their attempt to consolidate social structure of the pure community, erected purity as a defense mechanism to maintain social boundaries.

5.6. Dominance of Other Groups by the Babylonian Exilic Group

The dominance of the Babylonian exiles in Judah is shown by the varied literature of the exilic age. Biblical records attest that the exilic group consisted of the elites such as king Jehoiachin, royal family, priests, and prophets (2 Kings 25; Ezek 1). Dominance of other groups by the Babylonian exiles may have been caused by the stable socioeconomic conditions of the repatriates, who returned to Judah in the early Persian period. Studies confirm that the Babylonian exiles successfully integrated into the business affairs in Babylonia.[76] This, together with the gifts

72 For a detailed discussion see H. Wheeler Robinson, *The Religious Ideas of the Old Testament* (London: Gerald Duckworth & Co. Ltd., 1956), 207. Also Ralph W. Klein, *Israel in Exile: A Theological Interpretation* (Philadelphia: Fortress Press, 1979).

73 See Albertz, *Israel in Exile*, 137.

74 This is shown by lists of repatriates, mixed marriage issue, interaction with other groups such as the Samaritans, Moabites, Ammonites, etc., in Ezra-Nehemiah.

75 Cf Gen 12:2; 13:16; Exodus 6:8. Abraham was bestowed blessing of descendants and land (Gen 12:2; 13:16).

76 See Pierce, "Judean:" A Special Status," 267-277.

of Darius I (Ezra 6:8-9), could have helped them to achieve dominance when they returned to the homeland. This economic status, supported by priestly influence, encouraged them to focus on ideologies about group identification. They established a strong influence through various means, including literature. A substantial amount of the exilic literature emerged from the Babylonian exilic ideology.

6. Group Identification and Boundary Construction in the Exilic Literature

In response to the exilic experience and intergroup processes and conflicts, biblical literature developed as a strategy for social identification and negotiation among the divided communities. Scholars generally agree that much of the biblical literature was written, redacted, and compiled during this period. Steed Davidson rightly points out that "in a vacuum created by lack of institutions such as monarchy, prophets, and temple, biblical texts emerged to represent divine speech as survival mechanism."[77] In social identity terms, groups set up their own ideologies by differentiation to delegitimize the other group. During this time different groups tried to explain the catastrophe of the Babylonian destruction and exile and fostered an ideal vision for the new Israel or the true Israel. The Judeans in Babylonia, who were most threatened by the danger of loss of identity are probably most responsible for the innovation of religious and ritual elements. To legitimize their group identity, they constructed boundaries as markers of identity. Group dynamics within the communities is reflected in the ideologies of different exilic literature.[78] In this discussion, I will elucidate how different ideologies emerged as identity markers in exilic literature as a preview to my study of the book of Ezekiel. I will limit my scope to the literature from which we can assess group identification, specifically among the communities of Israel in the exilic age. I will also demonstrate how ideologies or group norms were cultivated to foster group interests.

---

77 Steed Vernyl Davidson, *Empire and Exile: Postcolonial Readings of the Book of Jeremiah* (New York: T&T Clark, 2011), 181-182.

78 Exilic literature here designates a large corpus of biblical literature authored or edited during the exilic age. The literature written in the exilic age but received their final forms in the period of the Persian period are also included in this list. Scholars do no share consensus around the attribution of "exilic literature." For example, Rainer Albertz includes the Book of the four prophets, Habakkuk, Exilic Patriarchal history, Deuteronomistic History, Jeremiah, Ezekiel, and Deutero-Isaiah as Exilic literary works. See Rainer Albertz, Israel in Exile. Dalit Rom-Shiloni assigns Ezekiel, Deutero-Isaiah, Ezra-Nehemiah, Haggai, and Zechariah 1-8 as exilic literature. See Dalit Rom-Shiloni, "From Ezekiel to Ezra-Nehemiah: Shifts of Group Identities within Babylonian Exilic Ideology," in *Judah and the Judeans in the Achaemenid Period*, 127-128.

6.1. The Empty Land and Desolation of Judah

The idea of empty land and desolation of Judah is one aspect of group identification. It marks the distinction between those of the exilic group and those who remained in Judah in the exilic age. This idea is found in several exilic texts including in the Deuteronomistic history, 2 Chronicles, Leviticus (the Holiness code), Jeremiah, Ezekiel and Ezra-Nehemiah. First, The Deuteronomistic history promotes a negative attitude towards those who remained in Judah narrating about the last days of Judah and the exile.[79] It depicts that "Nebuzaradan carried into exile the rest of the people who were left in the city, except "the poorest of the people" (2 Kings 25:11, 21). Those left behind in the land suffered whereas the deported group with king Jehoiachin received favor (2 Kings 25: 22-30). Condemnation of political power at Mizpah and emphasis on the desolation of Judah are ideological modes of alienation of those living in Judah during the exile. Secondly, in 2 Chronicles 36, the "empty land" ideology occurs in the narration of the last days of Judah in the same manner as in the Deuteronomistic history.[80] There is an emphasis that "the land was desolate for seventy years until it had compensated for the neglect of its Sabbaths." (2 Chro 36:21 cf. Lev 26: 43). The exile and the empty land idea are presented as compensation for the Sabbaths, as the land had been desolated for so long. This implies that only after the seventy year Sabbath rest will the repatriates reestablish a community of God.[81] The exile and desolation of the land for the Chronicler is a purifying process in which the newly purified community should be defined by the purity of the repatriates. There is also the same idea of "empty land" in the priestly literature, particularly in the Holiness code (Lev 36:43) and in the book of Ezekiel (Ezek 33:24; 36:3). The socio-historical situation of Judah, as indicated above, shows that the land was not empty and many people were left behind in Jerusalem and the Benjamin

---

79 Martin Noth popularized the theory that Deuteronomy-2 Kings is a composite work written in Palestine around the middle of the sixth century BCE, using numerous old traditions and sources. Through a revision of his idea, new approaches emerged. Some have even argued for post-exilic redaction. In spite of diverse ideas, it is commonly accepted that Deuteronomistic History (Deuteronomy-2 Kings) received its final form sometime in the exilic period. See Martin Noth, The Deuteronomistic History (Sheffield: JSOT, 1981), 4. See recent studies on the Deuteronomistic History in Stephen L. Mackenzie, "Deuteronomistic History" *ABD* Vol. 2, 160-168.

80 Scholars situate the book of Chronicles in the historical contexts of the late sixth century. The earliest strata may have come from the late sixth century BCE and was compiled in the late fourth century in its present form by an anonymous author(s). The chronicler's great interest in Davidic promises and Solomon's temple matches the era of Haggai, Zechariah, and Ezekiel 40-48. Hence, the early strata may have come in the late sixth century. See the detailed discussion on the debate over authorship and date of Chronicles in Gary N. Knoppers, *I Chronicles 1-9: A New Translation and Commentary, AB* Vol. 12 (New York: Doubleday, 2003), 101-117.

81 Cf. Albertz, *Israel in Exile*, 13-14.

region. Hence, this idea of the empty land and desolation of Judah may be viewed as an attempt to disenfranchise the people who remained in Judah.

6.2. The Idea of the Remnant (Remnant of Israel)

The term שרית (left over, remained - remnant) characterizes one form of Israel's response to severe crisis that threatened its national existence. It could initially refer to those who survived the destruction and those who remained in the land. Ideologically, it also refers to the exiles and refugees in Babylonia.[82] R. E. Clements writes: "The notion of a recognized status as "remnant of Israel" served as a basis of religious and social identity for the growing number of Jews who lived outside the territorial boundaries of the earlier kingdoms of Judah and Israel."[83] We find a significant usage of this term in the book of Jeremiah.[84] In the book, the idea of the remnant of Israel has a complex identity. First, the remnant of Israel in the land will be eliminated (6:9; 8:3; 11:23; 15:29). Second, those who were deported into exile will constitute the true remnant (24:4-7; 31:7; 39:9). Third, there was absolutely no hope for those who fled to Egypt (42:7, 12). We find two important issues here. (1) The book of Jeremiah exhibits a development in which the originally negative fate predicted for the remnant of Israel is altered by expressions of positive hope in the reestablishment of the nation with the Babylonian exilic group. (2) By contrast, absolutely no hope remains for those who fled to Egypt.[85] The book of Ezekiel conveys a similar perspective to Jeremiah. After the catastrophe of 587 BCE, we find a complete rejection of any claims on the part of surviving inhabitants of Jerusalem (33:23-29). The book refers exclusively to the Babylonian exiles as the basis for the believing remnant (11:16; 36:2-36). In social identity terms, "remnant" became a self-categorizing word for the exilic group to claim themselves as the people of God.

6.3. Exilic Experience as an Identity Marker

An explicit comparison of the exilic group (הגלה) and those who remained in Judah is found in the book of Ezekiel. This I will discuss in more detail later. Apart from Ezekiel, in the book of Ezra-Nehemiah we find explicit identification of the exilic group as the true Israel.[86] Ezra-Nehemiah argues that the exilic

82 See Dalit Rom-Shiloni, *Exclusive Inclusivity*, 81-98. See also Katherine Southwood, "The Holy Seed: Significance of Endogamous Boundaries and Their Transgressions in Ezra 9-11," in *Judah and the Judeans in the Achaemenid Period*, 206.

83 R. E. Clements, "שאר" *TDOT* Vol. XIV, 278.

84 The nominative/noun שרית is found 24 times in the book of Jeremiah out of 66 occurances in the Hebrew Bible. See Clements "שאר," *TDOT* Vol. XIV, 273.

85 Cf. Clements "שאר," *TDOT* Vol. XIV, 281.

86 The unity of Ezra-Nehemiah is attested by ancient texts and versions including LXX, Vulgate, and others. The most common proposal regarding authorship and date is successive redactions and expansions of earlier sources (the oldest sources perhaps are as early as the late sixth century)

community in Babylon represents the true Israel.[87] It narrates the exilic experience as a prerequisite for group membership. The exilic community is distinguished from those who remained in Judah with the designation of "the peoples of the lands" אמי הרזות (Ezra 4:4; 9:1-2). The repatriates' identity is articulated on the basis of their experience of exile as attested in the names used for them – the exiles הגלה (Ezra 1:11; 4:4; 10:6,8), son of the exiles בן הגלה (Ezra 4:1; 6:16, 19-20; 8:35, 10:7, 16) and other related identifications.[88] Those remaining in Judah (the peoples of the land) are identified as self-confessed foreigners, a threat to the community, rebels, and Samaritans (Ezra 4:1-25; Neh 6:6-9; 4:1-4; 13:23). The new community is shown to be dependent on the Babylonian-Persian exiles for community leadership.[89] The book of Haggai also delegitimizes those who remained in Judah by the use of the designations "this people/this nation" העם הזה/הגוי הזה in 2:10-19.[90] In these passages, descriptions of the people העם הזה/ הגוי הזה are used in the context of worship and temple construction. They refer to the religious community of those left in the land, whose sacrifice and worship were categorized as unclean. Since they did not experience the exile, those who remained in Judah are categorized as the outgroup.

6.4. Ethnicity, Genealogy, and Group Membership

In the book of Ezekiel and Ezra-Nehemiah we find identification of Israelite groups in which ethnicity is a determining factor. In Ezekiel, we find the denial

at the hands of golah editors in the fourth century BCE. The book(s) of Ezra-Nehemiah in its present form is dated late due to successive redactions See Jacob M. Meyers, *Ezra-Nehemiah: Introduction, Translation, and Notes*, AB (Garden City, New York: Doubleday, 1965), xxxviii-lii. Also Juha Pakkala, "The Exile and Exiles in the Ezra Tradition," in *The Concept of Exile in Ancient Israel and Its Historical Contexts*, BZAW 104, eds. Ehud Ben Zvi and Christoph Levin (Berlin/New York: De Gruyter, 2010), 91-101.

87 Esler claims that the narratives represent the segment of the people of Israel who create stories, a narrative that, by selecting, plotting and interpreting particular events in its history, captures key understandings of what it means to be a member of their group. See Philip F. Esler, "Ezra-Nehemiah as a Narrative of (Re-Invented) Israelite Identity," Biblical Interpretation 11 (2003): 418.

88 Other related designations of the Babylonian exiles are: "the rest of their people" (Ezr 3:8), "the people who came from exiles (Ezr 2:1; Neh 6:6), "all the assembly of those who had returned from the captivity" (Neh 8:17); "who had returned from exile," (Ezr 6:21), "remnant," (Ezr 9:13-15; Neh 1:3), "Israel," (Ezr 2:2, 70; 3:1, 11).

89 Such as Ezra, Nehemiah, Jerubbabel, Sheshbazar, Joshua/Jeshua. Ezra is a scribe, priest, and representative of the imperial ruler. The combination of the leadership roles of Ezra is a necessity to reify authentic leadership of the golah group. Cf. Mark Leuchter "Coming to Terms with Ezra's many Identities in Era-Nehemiah," in *Historiography and Identity (Re)formulation in Second Temple Historiographical Literature*, LHB/OTE 534, ed. Louis Jonker (New York: T&T Clark, 2010), 62.

90 The oracles in the book of Haggai are usually dated to 520 BCE, as implied by the contents of the book The book suggests that the house of the Lord is still in ruin and the will to build the house of the Lord is already achieved, as Haggai encouraged leaders of the land and the people.

of the claim of those remained in Judah as "sons of Abraham" and "heir of the land" (Ezek 33: 23-29 Cf.11: 14-21). Their purported impurity and disobedience to the covenant delegitimized them to become the sons of Abraham. Ezekiel uses genealogy as identity maker in a group membership in a specific way. Ezek 16:1-43 portrays Jerusalem originating from the land of Canaanites "Your father was an Amorite and your mother a Hittite (v. 3). With this genealogy, Ezekiel accuses Jerusalem as the non-people of God. Her sin and misconduct such as idolatry, bloodshed, adultery, and so on are connected with her parents – Amorite, Canaanites, and Hittite (16:2-8). In contrast, the exiles are depicted as the chosen race, the descendants of the stock of Jacob (Ezek 20:5). This analogy portraying the dichotomy of Jehoiachin exiles versus Jerusalem as Israel versus the foreign people is an ideological device in the internal conflict.[91] Genealogy is a very important source of identity marker in the P source of the Pentateuch and in Ezra-Nehamiah (Gen 28:3; 35:11; 48:3-5; Ezra 4:1-6). In Ezra-Nehemiah we find a more stringent rule of group identification based on marriage. The book reflects the maintenance of symbolic boundaries that separate Israelites from other groups. It imposes a separation of foreign wives (Ezra 9-10) and keeping a distance from foreigners (Neh 10, 13).[92] This might imply a rejection of those who remained in Judah and their cult.[93] In Ezra-Nehemiah, ethnic cleansing is enforced through reviewing the Golah list (Ezr 2; Neh 7); lists of the returned exiles function to establish that they belong to Israel, according to the line of their father's house (בת אב). Daniel L. Smith argues that what we see in the Golah list is "not necessarily the determination of 'relatives,' but the determination of the true Israelites, or true members of the purified "sons of the exile."[94] In other words, the Golah list determines who truly belongs to the community of Israel, and therefore also defined who was the outgroup.

6.5. The Whole House of Israel - An Inclusive Perspective

While some exilic literature promote exclusivity in regard to group membership, other exilic texts such as Deutero-Isaiah, Zechariah, Trito-Isaiah, and some parts

91 Dalit Rom-Shiloni, "Shifts of Group Identities," 141.

92 Cf. Deut 7:1-4; 23:4-6; Ezek 44:9. The prohibition was against the traditional custom of the Israelites. In many instances we find endogamous marriage and intermarriage among the Israelites. For example, Abraham married two Arab women (Gen 16:15-16; 25:1-6); Moses married two Midiante women (Exod 2:21-22; Num 21:1); Joseph married the daughter of an Egyptian priest (Gen 41:45). David and Solomon showed no signs of reluctance to marry foreign wives. The law demonstrates how the community needs to adopt strategies in order to avoid assimilation and to maintain group integrity.

93 Bob Becking argues that "foreign women" in Ezra-Nehemiah are not other ethnic women, but rather inner Yehudite group who assessed as strange and dangerous for their otherness, who might have been connected with sanctuaries across the border. See "On the Identity of the 'Foreign Women in Ezra 9-10," 42-43.

94 Daniel L. Smith, *Religion of the Landless*, 105.

of Jeremiah, present a more inclusive perspective. These books look for the restoration of the whole house of Israel. For example in the book of Deutero-Isaiah we find equal status for Israel and Jacob, a plausible metaphoric representation of the repatriates and those who remained in Judah (Isa 41:14; 43:1; 44:1; 45:4; 48:1).[95] There is also an explicit inclusion of the unknown group - "who called you by name" בשם הנקרעים (Isa 43:1; 48:1) or "who swear by the name of the Lord" (Isa 48:1) in the community of Israel.[96] The term "the nations" (הגוים) is used five times to refer to all displaced, survivors, and known nations who will be restored (Isa 40:17; 42:1; 43:9; 45:20; 52:10).

Secondly, the book of Zechariah 1-8 maintains an inclusive view on group identification.[97] The book looks for the future re-gathering of the house of Israel so that Yahweh's purpose of restoration will be achieved when the entire community dwells in Judah (8:7-8). This inclusive view is illustrated by an acceptance of the priests of Bethel into the new community (7:2-7). Members are seen as living in the East and West. The mention of מארץ מבוא השמש "from the land of the setting of the sun" (8:7) could be understood to mean an Egyptian diaspora, or exiles wherever they are.[98] Zechariah's "whole house of Israel" encompasses the exilic group (the southern), the non-deported population (the northern group), and those from the west (the Egyptian diaspora).

---

95 The book of Isaiah, chapters 40-55, has been considered the work of unknown prophet/prophets called Deutero-Isaiah or Second Isaiah, coming from the Babylonian exiles before the dawn of the Persian Empire. It was Bernhard Duhm who distinguished the three units of Isaiah1-39, 40-55, and 56-66 characterized by distinctive historical backgrounds and literary characters. The texts suggest a Babylonian exilic experience and it anticipates. The coming of Cyrus is anticipated in the passages and that a kind of polemic against Babylonian religion is suggested in many of the references. Therefore, scholars conclude that the prophecy comes from the late exilic age, possibly by about 550-540 BCE. See Bernhard Duhm, *Das Buch Jesaia, Handkommentar zum Alten Testamentum* (Gottingen: Vandenhoeck & Rupreckt, 1892); See also discussion in Joseph Blenkinsopp, *A History of Prophecy in Israel*, revised and enlarged (Louisville, Kentucky: Westminster John Knox Press, 1996), 181-193.

96 John J. Ahn believes that in Deutero-Isaiah, the nameless group is those who seek recognition in the second generation Judeo-Babylonian community. See Ahn, *Exile as Forged Migrations*, 196-197.

97 Zechariah 1-8 is characteristically distinctive and different in literary style from Chapters 9-14 and hence considered separate literary unit. The majority of commentators agree that Zechariah 1-8 is composed in the late sixth or early fifth century BCE, perhaps the time around 515 BCE. See John Kessler, "Diaspora and Homeland in Early Achaemenid Period: Community, Geography and Demography in Zechariah 1-8," in *Approaching Yehud: New Approaches to the Study of the Persian Period*, Semeia Studies 50, ed. Jon L. Berquist (Atlanta: Society of Biblical Literature, 2007), 138. The opening verse accounts that Zechariah received a vision in the "eighth month of Darius's second year," i.e. 520 BCE.

98 Cf. Sara Japhet, "The Concept of the "Remnant" in the Restoration Period: On the Vocabulary of Self-Definition," in *From the Rivers of Babylon to the Highlands of Judah: Collected Studies on the Restoration Period*, ed. Sara Japhet (Winona Lake, Ind.: Eisenbrauns, 2006), 436-437.

There are also hints of inclusive view of group identity in Jeremiah, particularly in the Book of Consolation (Jer 30-33). This collection clearly recalls Deutero-Isaiah's salvation oracle.[99] Judeans who remained in the land would be saved from the Babylonians (30:10); the people who survived the sword would find grace in the wilderness (31:2). Ingathering will take place from the land of the north (31:8 cf. 16:15). Jeremiah's symbolic purchase of a field at Anathoth in the Benjaminite region demonstrates that the remnants have the right to own lands (32:6-25).[100] This ideology contradicts Ezekiel 11, which rejects ownership of the land by the non-exilic group.

Trito-Isaiah promotes an inclusive view of group membership based on ethics and religion.[101] Access to the Temple comes from moral and faithful worship of the Lord, not ethnicity (56:1-6). The definition of the community was expanded on the basis of Sabbath worship, covenant keeping, and behavior pleasing to Yahweh. (56:2, 4, 6; 58:13; 63:8). Foreigners are included to minister and participate in Israel's worship (56:6). Divine salvation is for all, not for a specific community.[102] The community of Yahweh is not determined by ethnicity, lineage, nationality, or geography, but rather by the obedience to the law of God.

7. Pure and Impure Communities in the Book of Ezekiel

The book of Ezekiel has been accepted as written by the prophet Ezekiel, who also experienced the exilic catastrophe. It is generally agreed that the book received its final and fullest redaction sometime in the late exilic/ early post-exilic period by a priestly school or schools, who ascribed the formation of Judean

---

99 This unit may be from the A material, demonstrating the perspective of the prophet. Though some of the oracles may come from the period after 598/587, the perspective remains focused on the land of Judah. See discussion in Robert R. Wilson, "Forced Migration and the Formation of the Prophetic Literature," in *By the Irrigation Canals of Babylon: Approaches to the Study of the Exile*, LHB/OTS 526, eds. John J. Ahn and Jill Middlemas (New York: T&T Clark, 2012), 137.

100 The right to land ownership in this text suggests the middle of the exilic period, or it may be the genuine sayings of Jeremiah edited to address the issues of a later exilic generation. See William R. Domeris, "The Land Claim of Jeremiah-Was Max Weber Right?" in *Jeremiah (Dis)placed: New Directions in Writing/Reading Jeremiah*, eds. A. R. Pete Diamond and Louis Stulman (New York: T&T Clark, 2011), 139.

101 The collection of materials in Isaiah 50-66 comes from the early period of the Persian Empire is generally accepted. Joseph Blenkinsopp summarizes the majority opinion that the bulk of Isaiah 56-66 reflects the situation in the province of Judah (Yehud) during the first century of Persian rule, corresponding more or less to the reigns of Darius I (522-486), Xerxex (486-465), and Artexerxex I (465-424). See Joseph Blenkinsopp, *Isaiah 56-66: A New Translation with Introduction and Commentary*, AB Vol. 19B (New York: Doubleday, 2003), 43.

102 The oracle of salvation in 56:1-8 predict a positive future for foreigners (*goel*), and son of foreigners (56:3), eunuchs (56:4-5), the outcasts of Israel (56:8). Also included are: those in Jacob (59:20), Jerusalem (65:18; 66:12), descendants from Jacob (59:20), inheritors of my mountain from Judah (65:9), and kindred from all nations (66:2).

community after the exile to Ezekiel.[103] It is plausible that the book of Ezekiel went through revisions, and that the present form demonstrates the heavy hand of the Babylonian exilic group, possibly Zadokite priests. The book's distinctiveness comes from its emphasis on purity/impurity. There are several references to group identification in the book of Ezekiel. Interestingly purity and group identification are well connected in the book.

First, we find an explicit reference to the choice of Babylonian Exiles in Ezekiel 11:14-21.This oracle is a disputation speech directed against the Judahite community who remained in their homeland, as well as a thesis that affirms the choice of the exiles who were in Babylonia. The text appears to address the immediate situation after 597 BCE.[104] The non-exiled Judahites console themselves by a theological claim to the land (11:15), in which Ezekiel denies that Yahweh will give the land to the exiles (11:18), and argues that those remain in the land will be punished because of their impurity (11:21). Ezekiel affirms Yahweh's choice of the exiles as his people, with whom his presence is to be felt as a sanctuary to them even though they are removed from their land (11:16). They will be gathered and restored (11:17) and he will give them the land of Israel (11:17). Here purity/impurity is a defining factor of divine choice and rejection. Hence it is a pro-Babylonian view of group identification.

Secondly, Ezekiel uses land rights to disenfranchise those remaining in Judah. The claims of descendants of Abraham and inheritance of the land had become an interpretative theological term that defines group identity in the time of exile. This is found in Ezekiel 33:21- 24 (Cf. 11:14-21; 36:1-5). This oracle echoes Ezek 11:14-21 in its emphasis on the idea of "empty land." The setting is post-587 BCE, as the picture of desolation "laid waste" points to a drastic destruction of Jerusalem.[105] In this oracle, we find the claim of the inhabitants of the 'waste places,' who claim possession of the land" (33:24 Cf. 11:15). Emphasizing the genealogical bond between Abraham and the present community in Jerusalem, those who remained in the land claim their rightful possession of the land (cf. Gen 15:7; 17:8; Exo 6:4). This is refuted by

103 See the discussion of scholarship on the authorship of Ezekiel in Brian Neil Peterson, Ezekiel in Context: Ezekiel's Message Understood in Its Historical Setting of Covenant Curses and Ancient Near Eastern Mythological Motifs (Eugene, Oregon: Pickwick Publications, 2012). Also see Meindert Dijkstra, "The Valley of Dry Bones: Coping with the Reality of the Exile in the Book of Ezekiel," in *The Crisis of Israelite Religion: Transformation of Religious Tradition in Exilic and Post-Exilic Times*, ed. Bob Becking and Marjo C. A. Korpel (Leiden: Brill, 1999), 114-133.

104 Zimmerli argues that the oracle undoubtedly goes back to the period when the Jerusalem sanctuary was still standing, before the year 587 BCE. See Walther Zimmerli, *Ezekiel 1* trans. Ronald E. Clements, eds. Frank Moore Cross, Klaus Blatzer and Leonard Jay Greenspoon (Philadelphia: Fortress Press, 1979), 263.

105 Cf. Walther Zimmerli, *Ezekiel 2*, trans. James D. Martin, eds. Paul D. Hanson and Leonard Jay Greenspoon. (Philadelphia: Fortress Press, 1983), 198.

Ezekiel who accuses them of disobeying the purity rules of the priestly laws and Deuteronomic teaching against eating bloody meat, idol worship, murder, and adultery. This disobedience invalidated their claim. The case is clear for Ezekiel that those who are not deported could not claim to be authentic descendants of Abraham and then could not claim the land. This response endorses an understanding of landownership based on purity/impurity.

Another identity marker for group membership is cultic and moral purity/impurity. Many oracles denigrate Jerusalem (Judah) for her sinful conducts.[106] Among them, Ezekiel 22:1-31 contains a series of diatribes against Jerusalem and its inhabitants. The majority of critics agree that the oracle pertains to the Babylonian exiles and historical situation of 597 and 587.[107] The oracle may originally have come from the prophet Ezekiel or the Ezekiel's school may have logically arranged it in the late exilic or postexilic period.[108] The systematic presentation of the case against Jerusalem, and particularly her political leaders, suggests rulers such as Jehoaichim and Zedekiah, or perhaps Gedaliah and the Shaphanids.[109] Jerusalem, her rulers, and her inhabitants are charged for their cultic and moral sins. Rom-Shiloni rightly points out that Ezekiel's intensive references to Jerusalem (those who remained in Judah) and its fate are a response to both his immediate audience in exile and to the need to redefine the religio-national identity of the Exiles.[110] In short, for Ezekiel, the impurity of those who remained in Judah disenfranchised them from the community of Yahweh.

Finally, the clearest example of boundary construction between the varied communities of Israel is found in 44:1-31. This passage represents an exclusive Zadokite view on other priestly families and foreigners. The text assumes its present form in the Persian period, probably during the reign of Darius I.[111] The second generation of Ezekiel's disciples (Zadokite lineage) downgraded other priestly families by claiming that the latter led Israel into sin during the pre-exilic period (Ezek 44:10, 12). This section protects the purity of worship by forbidding foreigners to worship in the temple (44:9), because mingling with

106 Clear examples of these types of oracles are found in Ezekiel 6:1-14; 7:1-27; 11:1-13; 16:1-43; 21:1-32; 22:1-31; 24:1-14.

107 See Leslie C. Allen, *Ezekiel 20-48*: WBC Vol. 29 (Dallas: Word Books, 1990), 34; Peter Craigie, Ezekiel (Philadelphia: Westminster Press, 1983), 165.

108 Block argues that the logical arrangement may be occasioned by the need to address the postexilic community to explain the rationale for judgment on Jerusalem. See D. I. Block, *The Book of Ezekiel Chapters 1-24* NICOT (Grand Rapids, Michigan: Eerdmans, 1998), 700.

109 Allen, *Ezekiel 20-48*, 36. G. A. Cook, *A Critical and Exegetical Commentary on The Book of Ezekiel* Vol. 1, ICC (Edinburgh: T&T Clark, 1937), 241.

110 Dalit Rom-Shiloni, "Ezekiel as the Voice of the Exiles and Constructor of Exilic Ideology," in *HUCA* LXXVI (Cincinnati: Hebrew Union College-Jewish Institute of Religion, 2006), 41-43.

111 Cf. Steven Shawn Tuell, *The Law of the Temple in Ezekiel 40-48*, HSM 49 (Atlanta, Georgia: Scholars Press, 1992), 14.

foreign counterparts defiles the temple. (44:6-9). It is therefore also an exclusive view of the Babylonian exilic group. From the perspective of Michael Walzer's "Revolution of the Saints," this view reflects a radical ideology of Zadokite priests, who out of their exilic experience and struggles fabricated their vision of a pure society.[112]

8. Summary and Conclusion

In the exilic era, from the fall of Jerusalem until the rebuilding of second temple, Israel underwent great social changes as the result of several factors. Undoubtedly, deportations created intergroup relations in the exilic era. The Babylonian exilic group maintained a normal life through their involvement in the social systems of the Babylonian and Persian empires. They also developed a more stringent form of Yahwism. In the same way, the Egyptian exiles maintained their Judean identity with the temple at Elephantine. The Judahite community remaining in Judah established political and religious strongholds around Mizpah and Bethel. With the rise of Cyrus and Darius I, the Persian exiles returned to Judah in a series of events. A new (restored) community was formed with new social structures. Intergroup relationship between the three groups from the first deportation (597) until the building of the second temple (520) was not peaceful. Conflict and competition marked the social structure of the exilic period, in which the Babylonian exilic group dominated the community.

As exemplified in the above, exilic literature developed in the midst of identity crises of the sixth century BCE Israel. Traditions of the past were revised to offer new meaning for the suffering communities. Differing perspectives on the identity of Israelite groups reflect group conflicts in the exilic period, with the main contenders being the Babylonian exilic group and those remaining in Judah. The ideas of "the empty land"/ "desolation of Judah," and "the remnant of Israel," were revised and appropriated in the Deuteronomistic history, Jeremiah, 2 Chronicles, the Holiness Code, and Ezekiel. Explicit group comparison and identification - the ingroup (the exiles) and the outgroup (people of this/the land) were promulgated by Haggai, Ezra-Nehemiah, and Ezekiel. In contrast, some writings such as Deutero-Isaiah, Trito-Isaiah, Zechariah, and the Book of Consolation (Jeremiah 30-33) include "all Israel" in the community, transcending group boundaries. From these literatures, we can infer that the socio-historical situations of authors and redactors played vital roles in the ideological discussions and group identifications. As shown in the above, we find that Babylonian *golah* group led by priestly groups greatly influenced ideological discussions with a strong boundary construction. The exiles in Babylonia, who were most threatened by the loss of identity, were the ones most responsible for the innovation of religious and

112 For more detail on Michael Walzer's method see Michael Walzer, *Revolution of the Saints: a Study on the Origins of Radical Politics* (Cambridge, Massachusetts: Harvard University Press), 1965.

ritual elements. To maintain group identity in such a situation, a process called "boundary mechanism" was necessary. New ritual innovations, with new ethnic and religious boundaries, were established as sociological tools in which purity laws became vital criteria for group membership.

As Mary Douglas conceives, the idea of purity became a great concern, expressed symbolically to preserve the integrity of the social group. As discussed in the above, there are indications of group identification in which purity/impurity sets a boundary in the book of Ezekiel. Ezekiel disenfranchises those who remained in Judah because they were impure. They were not fit to be descendants of Abraham and heir of the land of Israel. Thus, purity concept had a new meaning and function in socio-historical contexts of the book of Ezekiel. It is evident that purity is a vehicle for Ezekiel to identify group membership in the exilic period. This demands serious inquiry. In order to evaluate the role of purity in group identification in the book of Ezekiel, I will first investigate the meaning and usage of purity in the book of Ezekiel in my next chapter.

Chapter 3

Purity in the Book of Ezekiel

1. Introduction

The idea of purity occupies an important place in the book of Ezekiel. Ezekiel employs the vocabulary of holiness and purity more than any other canonical prophet. Ezekiel shares the priestly conception that impurity defiles the land, the temple, and the name of God. Therefore, purity is foundational in the theology of the book of Ezekiel. The basic Hebrew root for pure is טהר which usually stands in opposition to טמא (impure/unclean). The term טמא is frequently used to describe Israel's sin, which signifies concepts connected to impurity, uncleanness, defilement, and pollution.

In this chapter, I will discuss the basic idea of purity in the book of Ezekiel. I will first briefly define terminologies used to define purity and holiness in Ezekiel followed by an investigation of the relationship between holiness and purity, and the connection between impurity and sin. Then I will delve into a study on different types of purity/impurity, and purification in the book of Ezekiel. This study will form a basis for the next chapter in which I discus purity and identity in the book of Ezekiel with exegetical studies of selected texts.

The relationship between the priestly writings (P) and the book of Ezekiel is obvious.[1] I assume that Ezekiel and P are in the same priestly milieu but

1 Some scholars argue that P predates Ezekiel and there is literary dependence of Ezekiel on the writings of P or at least Ezekiel makes use of the Holiness Code. For this approach see See Avi Hurvitz, *A Linguistic Study of the Relationship Between the Priestly Source and the Book of Ezekiel: A New Approach to an Old Problem* (Paris: J. Gabalda, 1982); Risa Levit Kohn, *A New Heart and a New Soul; Ezekiel, the Exile and the Torah*, JSOTSup 358 (Sheffield: Sheffield Academic

their relationship is not a matter of direct literary dependence.[2] As Menahem Haran argues, Ezekiel and P are relatively homogenous entities, both of which originated in similar, but distinct, priestly circles.[3] I believe that the distinctive nature of Ezekiel in relation to purity ideas is determined by the background and circumstances of the author(s). In my study, I will incorporate the priestly texts (and H) when and where necessary.[4] Since the idea of purity cannot be considered in isolation from the idea of holiness. I will also discuss the idea of purity in its relation to holiness. A detailed study on the concept of holiness however, is beyond the scope of this work.

2. Purity in the Book of Ezekiel

The programmatic statement of Ezekiel concerning purity is that "the priest's duty is to distinguish between the holy and the common, and between the unclean and the clean" (Ezek 22:26; 44:23). The holiness of God and the purity of his people are fundamental in the book. Yahweh visits Israel because its idolatry and other abominable actions have defiled (חלל/טמא) his temple (5:11; 8:5-18; 23:38-39), his land (36:16-18), his people (20:7, 31, 43), his Sabbaths (20:13, 21, 24), and his name (20:39). Ezekiel stresses the sin of Israel as impurity (defilement) and pollution (desecration). The verbal form of the root טמא (to defile) is the most common term used in Ezekiel to express the impurity of Israel. Defilement is enacted through what is portrayed as cultic offences and other moral impurities. In Ezekiel, Israel's history is depicted as disloyalty to Yahweh through the practice of cultic/ritual and moral impurities. According to Ezekiel, if Israel is to be God's people, it must tolerate no defilement or

Press, 2000); Michael A. Lyons, *From Law to Prophecy: Ezekiel's Use of the Holiness Code* (New York/London: T&T Clark, 2009).

2 I hold this view because there are literary synonymy as well as divergent perspectives in the texts. For example, while ritual and cultic purity are the main concerns of the priestly writings, Ezekiel emphasizes more on ethical (moral) purities. While the priestly writings emphasize complicate sacrificial rites, this is not the concern of Ezekiel, except in chapters 40-48. See this view in William H. C. Propp, "The Priestly Source Recovered Intact?" *Vetus Testamentum* XLVI (1996), 478; Jacob Milgrom, *Leviticus 1-16: A New Translation with Introduction*, AB (New York: Doubleday, 1991), 39.

3 See Menahem Haran, "The Law Code of Ezekiel 40-48 and Its Relation to the Priestly School," in *Hebrew Union College Annual*, Vol. 50 (Cincinnati: Hebrew Union College, 1980), 61-66.

4 The Holiness Code (H) (Lev 17-26) is considered a separate unit on the ground that there is distinctive holiness legislation given to the whole Israel in this chapters, whereas in the remainder of the Priestly work the idea that the entire Israelite people is holy is never mentioned (except once in Num 16:3). So, H's contention that all Israel is holy marks a development in priestly thought or possibly a distinct work from P. See discussions in Baruch Levine, "Late Language in the Priestly Source: Some Literary and Historical Observations" in *Proceedings of the Eighth World Congress of Jewish Studies* (Jerusalem: World Union of Jewish Studies, 1983), 69-82.

infidelity in its midst.[5] But on the contrary, Israel is represented as failing to maintain the required state and engaged in various forms of impurity.

2.1. Purity/Holiness Word Group טהר, טמא, קדש, חלל

Before we move into discussion of various types of impurities in Ezekiel, let me define four purity and holiness terminologies commonly known as the purity/holiness word group. First, טהר is the principal root for pure/clean. It usually stands in opposition to טמא. It is translated variously: (qal) be clean, pure, cleansed, purified; (piel) cleanse, purify; (adj) clean, pure; and (noun) purifying, cleansing.[6] The root טהר is found 16 times in Ezekiel.[7] The root referring to a physical state denotes the absence of physical dirt, as very similar to the English term "pure." It can denote the absence of impurities like זהב טהר (pure gold). It is understood as a rather neutral condition, in the sense that it is not contagious.[8] In Ezekiel, the verb forms of חטר are used in varying meanings: to cleanse from filthiness/lewdness (24:13; 37:23), cleansing from iniquities (36:33), cleansing the land (39:14). It also conveys the idea of cultic purity as found in the pair "the altar should be atoned for (כפר) and purify it (טהרו)" (Ezek 43:26).

Second, the root טמא is primarily translated as impure, unclean, defile, and pollute. Of 283 occurrences in the Hebrew Bible, we find 44 instances of it in Ezekiel.[9] In the book of Ezekiel, the meanings of the verb form are: (1) (qal) to become unclean, ceremonially unclean (22:4; 23:17), (2) (niphal/hithpael/pual) to defile oneself /themselves/myself (20:43; 14:11), and (3) (piel) defile/make unclean sanctuary, etc., (5:1; 43:8). The adjectival form amj means 'impure' or 'ceremonially unclean such as unclean/defiled food (4:13; 22:10). The (noun) טמאה is a state of uncleanness (22:15; 36:17), usually translated as defilement.[10] Impurity/defilement (טמאה) refers to those items, which threaten the pure status of Israel and its sanctuary. Certain physical processes, such as death, leprosy and sexual discharges, brought about impurity (Ezek 44:26-27). Many impurities are not due to transgression or rebellion but simply the result from the human condition. Impurity is also a moral condition of violation of God's law through rebellion and immoral acts, such as sexual misconduct, idolatry, etc.

5 Cf. Lawrence Boadt, "Book of Ezekiel," *ABD* Vol. 2, 720.

6 See "טהר," *BDB*, 372-373. See also Hannah K. Harrington, "Clean and Unclean," *NIDB*, Vol. 1 (A-C), 681.

7 Of 212 occurrences we find in Leviticus & Numbers = 93, Exodus = 33, Ezekiel = 16, Chronicles = 15, Others = 55. See Jacob Neusner, *The Idea of Purity in Ancient Judaism*, SJLA 1 (Leiden: Brill, 1973), 26.

8 Nilton Dutra Amorim, "Desecration and Defilement in the Old Testament" (PhD Dissertation: Andrews University, 1986), 248.

9 Jacob Neusner, *The Idea of Purity in Ancient Judaism*, 26.

10 See "טמא," *BDB*, 379-380. See also Ludwig Koehler and Walter Baumgartner, "טמא" *HALOT*, Vol. 2, 375-376.

Third, sacred/holy is the translation of the root קדש. Biblical scholars in their study show that the exact etymology of the root קדש and its derivatives is still unresolved.[11] The term with all its derivatives is a religious one, having the implication of "holy" "pure" "consecrated one."[12] Although קדש is not synonymous with טהר, it is related to pure/purity (טהר) since being consecrated or sanctified presupposes a condition of cultic or moral acceptability. We find the pair and the opposites of "holy and common" (קדש/קל) in a comparison with the pure and the impure (טהר/טמא) (Ezek 22:26; 44:23).[13] The Hebrew root קדש occurs 105 times in the book of Ezekiel.[14] Ezekiel places great importance on the holiness of both the temple and cultic acts.[15]

Fourth, the Hebrew root חלל is translated as profane, defile, pollute, desecrate (piel), be profaned (niphal), let be profaned, and begin to make invalid (hiphil). The nominative and adjective meanings are – profane, common, ordinary, forbid.[16] It is the opposite of holy (קדש). קדש and חלל are frequently used in parallel with טהר and טמא (Ezek 22:26; 44:23 cf. Lev 10:10). In the Hebrew Bible, the verb חלל is used 134 times; in 75 cases it conveys the meaning of "profane." Most of these cases are found in the book of Ezekiel (31 times) and in the Holiness Code (16 times).[17] Profanation for Ezekiel refers to any cultic and moral offences

---

11 Two popular suggestions are (1) קדש might have come from a combination of יקד (burn) and אש (fire); and (2) the root קד and קדש as having the basic meaning of "separate/asunder." See discussion in Kornfeld, "קדש," *TDOT* Vol. XII, 521-527.

12 Cf. In the Akkadian, Ugaritic, and West Semitic inscriptions the root קדש and its derivatives imply religious sense as "consecrated" or "dedicated things" such as the deity, priestly class, and objects related to the deity. See Kornfeld, "קדש," 523.

13 Jenson describes חלל the opposite of קדש which may well imply a lack of holiness. See Philip Peter Jenson, *Graded Holiness: A Key to the Priestly Conception of the World*, JSOTSup 106 (Sheffield: Sheffield Academic Press, 1992), 45.

14 The root occurs about 842 times in the Hebrew Bible. Significant concentrations are found in the book of Leviticus (152), Ezekiel (105), Exodus (102), Numbers (80), and Isaiah (73). See Kornfeld, "קדש," OT Word Field," *TDOT* Vol. XII, 527.

15 See Yahweh's holy name (20:39; 36:20; 39:7), the holy sanctuary (5:11; 8:6; 23:38-39; 45:3) and in general as a referring to the new temple (43:21; 44:1; 45:3-4; 47:12; 48:8); holy chambers (42:13; 44:19; 46:19); holy territory/portion (45:6,7; 48:10), holy mountain (20:40; 28:14); holy things/offerings (22:26; 42:13; 44:8). The verb form of the root is used to "sanctify/consecrate" the Sabbath (20:12); "sanctify" Israel (37:28).

16 While the root חלל is the only term in Hebrew that means, "to desecrate" there are several different חלל roots. These are – "to pierce" "to begin," "to play the flute." See discussion in Hilary Lipka, "Profaning the Body" חלל and the Conception of Loss of Personal Holiness in H," in *Bodies, Embodiment, and Theology of the Hebrew Bible*, eds. S. Tamar Kamionkowski and Wonil Kim, LHB/OTE 465 (New York: T&T Clark, 2010), 90-113. In my discussion here, חלל will always refer to "to profane/desecrate" unless otherwise indicated.

17 See more detail in Robert H. O'Connor, "חלל," *NIDOTTE* Vol. 2, 146.

that defame the name and prestige of Yahweh.[18] The term is used interchangeably with טמא in some instances (Lev 10:10; Ezek 44:23). Their distinction however, is that the expression חלל knows no source of uncleanness, as is the case of טמא. חלל signifies action that deprives something or someone of holiness, while טמא adds to such a defiling dimension. While חלל may have Yahweh as subject or object, טמא acts have no effect on him, nor does he perform amj activity.[19]

2.2. Purity and Holiness

As suggested by their usages in the book of Ezekiel, purity and holiness are very close in meaning and usage. Sometimes they are used synonymously or at least having the same connotation. Some scholars consider the terms "pure" and "holy" to be essentially synonymous.[20] Jacob Milgrom illustrates the relationship between holiness and purity with the four possible states as follows:[21]

Sacred/holy	Common
Pure	Impure

This illustration suggests that sacred (holy) is the opposite of impure. Either sacred or common and either pure or impure can exist simultaneously. Whereas the common may be either pure or impure, the sacred may not be impure. Jenson draws the holiness spectrum in a scheme of "very holy (קדש קדשים) – holy (קדש) – pure (טהור) – unclean (טמא) – very unclean (טמא)."[22] In their attempt to explain the relationship and connection of holiness and purity, Milgrom and Jenson emphasize the continuum according to some criteria of graded holiness, which is not valid in certain cases.[23] Hence holiness and purity could not be explained in terms of a gradation, but rather through their with interacting with each other.[24]

18 Ezekiel speaks about profanation of Yahweh's name (20:9, 14, 39, 36:21-22; 39:7; 43:7-8), profanation of Yahweh (13:19); profanation of the sanctuary (7:22, 24:21; 23:39; 44:7), of the Sabbath (Ezek 20:13, 16, 21, 24).

19 Cf. Amorim, "Desecration and Defilement in the Old Testament," 216-218.

20 See Neusner, *The Idea of Purity in Ancient Judaism*, p. 18ff. Also cited in E. Jan Wilson, *"Holiness" and "Purity" in Mesopotamia* (Neukirchen, Vluyn: Neukirchener Verlag-des Erziehungsvereins GambH, 1994), 3. Walter Eichrodt, *Ezekiel: A Commentary*, trans. Cosslett Quin; OTL (Philadelphia: Westminster Press, 1970), 333.

21 Jacob Milgrom, *Leviticus 1-16*, AB (New York: Doubleday, 1991), 616.

22 Jenson, *Graded Holiness: A Key to the Priestly Conception of the World*, 44. The use of the same word טמא to represent both "unclean" and "very unclean" is confusing.

23 For example, the distinction between pure and common could not be ascertained. The criteria to distinguish between very holy and holy, impure and very impure is not obvious. One Hebrew root – חלל is not included in both of the scheme, which is very prominent in the book of Ezekiel. The meaning of the pair holy-profane found in the priestly writings and the book of Ezekiel is not explained by this scheme.

24 Ka Leung Wong, *The Idea of Retribution in the Book of Ezekiel* VTSup 87 (Leiden: Brill, 2001), 124.

In many instances holiness usually generally belongs to the realm of the divine, and purity to the human realm, and has both cultic and ethical aspects. Holiness is the essence of God and Israel could have holiness only with divine action (Ezek 20:12; 37:28 cf. Lev 17-26). Purity is necessary for the activation of holiness (Ezek 43:26 cf. Exo 22:30). Impurity of any kind, ritual, or moral, can impinge on God's realm and bring destruction on the community.[25] Because of the holiness of God, the house of God, the priests, as well as gifts brought to him must be pure in order for the system to be effective. Purity and impurity then may have no intrinsic meaning, but may derive their significance from their relation to the holiness of the God and the Temple.[26]

The interconnectedness of holiness and purity is found in the expression in Ezekiel 44:23 that "the duty of the sons of Aaron is to teach my people the difference between the holy and the common, and show them how to distinguish between clean (pure) and the unclean (impure)" (Ezek 22:26; Lev 10:10). Ezekiel views the states of holiness, profaneness, purity, and impurity in terms of two pairs of opposites: pure vs. impure and holy vs. profane." [27] In a few cases the roots חלל (profane) and טמא (defile) connote the same meaning.[28] Though used interchangeably in certain texts, we also have a clear distinction between the two concepts and Ezekiel indeed chose his words with precision.[29] Thus, for Ezekiel, the sanctuary and the name of God are both defiled and profaned; the land is defiled through sexual misconduct, idolatry, and contact with corpse, not profaned. The Sabbath is not defiled but profaned. In short, in Ezekiel, holiness and purity interact with each other which indicates the state of aptness, but they remain specifically distinct. They are neither totally overlapping nor totally separated.

2.3. Impurity and Sin

It is a general consensus that sin and impurity are not the same thing but closely related. Very often in the Hebrew Bible, impurity is equated with sin.[30] In "Impurity and Sin in Ancient Judaism," Jonathan Klawans maintains that certain

25 Jacob Milgrom, *Leviticus 1-16*, 47.

26 Cf. Marcel Poorthuis & Joshua Schwartz, "Purity and Holiness: an Introductory Survey," in *Purity and Holiness: The Legacy of Leviticus*, eds. M.J.H.M. Poorthuis & J. Schwartz (Leiden: Brill, 2000), 12.

27 See Ezek 22:26; 42:20; 44:23 Cf. Lev 10:10; 11:471 Sam 21:5.

28 Israel defiled (טמאו) the holy name of God (43:7, 8); they also profaned (ויחללו) it (36:20; 39:7).

29 In Ezekiel, defilement (טמאה) is used extensively in relation to sexual misconduct. We see examples in 18:6, 11, 15; 22:11; 23:13, 17; 33:26. We find examples of defilement through idol worship in 20:7, 26, 30, 31; 22:3, 4; 23:7; 36:18; 37:23; 43:8. The land is defiled not profaned (36:17; 22:24). Profanation (חלל) is the only term used to describe Sabbath profanation (20:13, 16, 21, 24; 22:8; 23:38). Cf. Tova Ganzel, "The Defilement and Desecration of the Temple in Ezekiel," *Biblica* 89, no. 3 (2008): 369-370.

30 See Lev 5:2-3; 16:16; Eccl 9:2; Isa 6:5; 64:6.

grave sins have their own distinct defiling force.[31] And certain impurities are so severe that they have defiling force. These include sexual sins (Ezek 22:10-11 cf. Lev 18:24-30), idolatry (Ezek 16, 23 cf. Lev 20:1-3), and bloodshed (Ezek 23:45 cf. Num 35:33-34). They defile a person (sinner), the land (Ezek 36:17 cf. Lev 18:25), and the sanctuary (Ezek 5:11 cf. Lev 20:3). Sin is described in the language of defilement in Ezekiel and in the priestly writings (Ezek 5:11; 23; Lev 18:5, 9).

Jay Sklar demonstrates that sin and impurity are closely related as they both pollute and endanger the sinner and the sanctuary.[32] In many cases, impurity refers to uncleanness in general, such as unclean animals, unclean food, leprosy and menstruation (Lev 11-15 & Num 19; Ezek 7:19-20). These are not mentioned as sinful. Impurities such as corpse contamination and idolatry are not only impure but also sinful as they defile the sanctuary (Ezek 43:7-9 cf. Num 19:11-13). Sin is a kind of uncleanness, a moral deflection from the will of God, like breaking a divine prohibition (Ezek 20:43; Lev 4), or neglecting cultic and judicial order (Ezek 23:17; Lev 5:1-4). Purification of the sanctuary is necessary in certain cases of impurity. Thus a חטאת offering is offered as part of the ritual of the Day of Atonement (Ezek 45:18, 20 Cf. Lev 16:16, 19, 33). While only washing and absolution are enough for cleansing, חטאת is required to atone for sin (Ezek 43: 21, 22; 45:15 Cf. Lev 12:6; 14:10). From the above, it is clear that natural impurity is generally not sinful whereas severe impurities that defile the sanctuary, the land, and the name of God are sinful.

2.4. Types of Purity/Impurity

Biblical scholars have diverse approaches to categorizing purity/impurity. One commonly accepted type is called permanent impurity. This includes animals that cannot change from clean to unclean or vice versa (Lev 11-12; Deut 14). They are not contagious unless they are dead.[33] David P. Wright delineates the discussion of purity/impurity in two broad types: (1) permitted impurity (2) prohibited

31 Jonathan Klawans, *Impurity and Sin in Ancient Judaism* (Oxford: Oxford University Press, 2000), 21.

32 Jay Sklar explores the close relationship between sin and impurity in relation to כפר in the priestly writings. He demonstrates that since both sin and impurity pollute and endangers the sinner and the sanctuary. כפר (ransom/atonement/purgation) is necessary for atonement/purification. See detail in Jay Sklar, "Sin and Impurity: Atoned or Purified? Yes!," in *Perspectives on Purity and Purification in the Bible*, eds. Baruch J. Schwartz, David P. Wright, Jeffrey Stackert, and Naphtali S. Meshel LBH/OTS 474 (New York: T&T Clark, 2008), 23-31.

33 Cf. Jacob Milgrom, *Leviticus 1-16*, 669. Also Gordon J. Wenham, *The Book of Leviticus*, NICOT (Grand Rapids, Michigan: Eerdmans, 1979), 50.

impurity.[34] Some have a scheme of severe (major) impurity and lesser (minor) impurity,[35] or "real and "abstract" impurity.[36]

The most popular categorization is ritual and moral purity/impurity. Jonathan Klawans, who follows this scheme, concedes that ritual impurity includes natural processes such as menstruation, blood, and skin diseases, which are the result of contact with natural processes, more or less unavoidable, generally not sinful, and typically permanent.[37] On the other hand, moral impurity is violation of God's laws such as idolatry, sexual crimes, bloodshed, and others which were considered heinous and defile humans, the land of Israel, and the sanctuary of God.[38] There are some problems with Klawans' scheme of ritual and moral impurity. First, animal species are not fit to categorize as ritually or morally pure or impure. Second, the type of gentile impurities mentioned in the book of Ezra-Nehemiah is accounted for neither by ritual nor moral impurity."[39] There is also a problem of ascribing "ritual" as opposed to "moral" in ancient Israel because such a distinction is not explicit in ancient (biblical) Israel.[40] The distinction is less clear in the book of Ezekiel because both defile the Temple, land and the name of God.[41] We could also argue that food purity rules could come under both ritual

34 Permitted impurity includes – (1) death related – human corpse and animal carcasses, (2) sexual impurities – discharge, (3) diseases – leprosy, (4) cultic – the blood of purification (חטאת), the scapegoat, the red cow and its ashes, שׂרעת bird and bird blood. Prohibited impurity includes – (1) corpse contamination, (2) delaying purification, (3) sexual transgressions, (4) idolatry, (5) homicide, and (6) polluting the Sacred. See David P. Wright, "Unclean and Clean (OT)," *ABD* Vol. VI, 729-741.

35 Severe impurities include – corpse, leprosy, discharge, flow of blood with childbirth, corpse impure-priest and corpse-impure Nazirite. Lesser impurities include – corpse-impure-lay person, menstruant, emission of semen, and carcass-contaminated person. See Harrington, *The Purity Texts,* 11. In other explanation, major impurities require various other rites for cleansing such as sacrifice. Minor impurities are those which are typically cleansed through bathing and or laundering, which are not contagious. See Sklar, "Sin and Impurity," 26 and Philip Peter Jenson, *Graded Holiness*, 225-226.

36 Tarja S. Philip, *Menstruation and Childbirth in the Bible: Fertility and Impurity, Studies in Biblical Literature* 88 (New York: Peter Lang, 2006).

37 Jonathan Klawans, *Impurity and Sin in Ancient Judaism* (Oxford: Oxford University Press, 2000), 41. Cf. Jonathan Klawans, *Purity, Sacrifice, and the Temple: Symbolism and Supersessionism in the Study of Ancient Judaism* (Oxford: Oxford University Press, 2006), 145-174. In his article in the Jewish Study Bible, Klawans lists the distinctions of ritual and moral purity in more detail. See Jonathan Klawans, "Concepts of Purity in the Bible," in *The Jewish Study Bible*, eds. Adele Berlin and Marc Zvi Brettler (Oxford: Oxford University Press 2004), 2045-2046.

38 Jonathan Klawans, *Impurity and Sin in Ancient Judaism,* 41.

39 Eve Levavi Feinstein, "Sexual Pollution in the Hebrew Bible: A New Perspective," in *Bodies, Embodiment, and Theology of the Hebrew Bible*, 119-121.

40 Cf. Jacob Neusner, *The Idea of Purity in Ancient Judaism*, 1-2.

41 Tova Ganzel, "The Concept of Holiness in the book of Ezekiel," (English Abstract of PhD Dissertation: Senate of Bar-Ilan University, Ramat-Gan, 2005), 16.

and moral categories.[42] Therefore, I will not follow a strict rule of categorization in this study. In the following discussion I will briefly explain different types of purity/impurity found in Ezekiel.

a. Menstruation

The impurity of menstruation was generally accepted among all traditional societies. This is not an exception in Israel. Milgrom writes: "Menstruant is an untouchable state of separation from society; it is "a metaphor for extreme pollution, ultimate revulsion."[43] The Hebrew term for menstruation is נדה. The term comes from the root נדד or נדה which share the same meaning "chase away, drive away."[44] It means 'distancing', both in a physical sense and in an emotional sense.[45] The noun נדה occurs 29 times in the Hebrew Bible with three semantic domains: (1) Impurity in connection with menstruation; (2) Impurity in general, abomination; and (3) purification.[46]

The root נדה in Ezekiel has the general meaning of menstruation and an image/synonym of impurity.[47] The term occurs five times, which has a meaning of both "menstrual impurity," and "an embodiment of menstrual impurity." Ezekiel is the only biblical text that deploys the term נדה as a moral category.[48] In Ezekiel 7:19, 20 the word probably refers to impurity in general or a figurative meaning. The text refers to the ornaments of the inhabitants of the land of Israel (7:1) and the survivors (7: 16), which Yahweh is making an unclean thing (הנדה) to them (7:19, 20). Here "their gold shall be an impure thing," זהבים לנדה (v.19) could imply denigration of their fortune. Verse 20 accuses the beauty of ornaments (made with gold and silver) "made with abominations which Yahweh will make unclean" (לנדה). It could also refer to the ritual impurity of the inhabitants who

42 Cf. Harrington, "Clean and Unclean," *NIDB* Vol. 1, 483.

43 Jacob Milgrom, *Leviticus 1-16*, 952.

44 Milgrom-Wright, "נדה," *TDOT* Vol. IX, 232.

45 Moshe Greenberg, "The Etymology of נדה (Menstrual Impurity)," in *Solving Riddles and Untying Knots: Biblical, Epigraphic, and Semitic Studies in honor of Jonas C. Greenfield*, eds. Ziony Zevit, Seymour Gitin, and Michael Sokoloff (Winona Lake, Ind.: Eisenbrauns, 1995), 69.

46 Milgrom-Wright, "נדה," 233.

47 This use of נדה as a synonym of impurity is common in late books of the Bible. For example in Ezra 9:11 we see, "The land you are about to possess is a land unclean (נדה) through the uncleanness (נדה) of the peoples of the land." See also Zech 13:1, 2; 2 Chro 29:5. See more discussion in Tarja Philip, "Gender Matters: Priestly Writing on Impurity," in *Embroidered Garments: Priests and Gender in Biblical Israel,* HBM 25, ed. Deborah W. Rooke (Sheffield: Sheffield Phoenix Press, 2009), 40-60.

48 See Charlotte Elisheva Fonrobert, *Menstrual Purity: Rabbinic and Christian Reconstructions of Biblical Gender* (Stanford, California: Stanford University Press, 2000), 223.

make idols with their gold and silver; this is considered an abomination.[49] It has a figurative meaning of a ceremonially unclean thing.

Embodiment of menstrual impurity "a menstruant woman" טמאת הנדה is found in Ezekiel 18:6; 22:10 and 36:17. The usage has a parallel reference with defilement of one's neighbor. Impurity of the land of Israel is depicted as "defiling neighbor's wife (טמא את) and coming near to a menstruating woman" (18:6). In 22:10, one of the crimes committed by Jerusalem is sexual intercourse with a menstruant, which defiles her. This reflects the prohibition of sexual intercourse with a menstruant in Leviticus 15:18-24. Ezek 36:17 also describes the impurity of Israel (when they dwelt in the land) with the expression כטמאת הנדה היתה (like the uncleanness of a menstruant). In short, we identify two things from this type of impurity: (1) Menstruation, as a female impurity, is used figuratively to explain the impurity of the inhabitants of Jerusalem; (2) As the root meaning presupposes, the inhabitants of Judah are excluded from the society of Israel as they are ritually impure due to their illicit sexual impurity related to menstruation.

b. Corpse Impurity

According to the priestly writings, the corpse is the most contaminating of all the impurities. Bearers of this impurity who became impure by contact with the dead or simply by entering a house where the dead lay, had to undergo a week of purification before they returned to community life (Lev 7:21; 15:31; Num 19:11-13, 20). The corpse-contaminated person was forbidden to approach the sancta and could not offer anything at the Temple (Lev 7:19-20; Num 9:7-11; Deut 26:14). The concern to ban corpses from settlement is alluded to in certain extra-priestly texts.[50]

In the book of Ezekiel, corpses are frequently subjected to anti-ideal treatments. They are connected with impurity and rejection.[51] In Ezekiel 43:7-9 we find a tension that describes the ideal state of holiness and purity of the temple and its environs. The passage indicates that the corpses (פגרים) of the kings interred near the sanctuary defiled the holy name of Yahweh; He could not dwell with

---

49 Gold and silver are beautiful ornaments with which idols are made. This is a frequent emphasis in prophetic literature. See for example Isaiah 2:20; 30:20; 31:7; 40:19. See also discussion in Wong, *The Idea of Retribution*, 138.

50 See Josh 24:33; Judg 16:31; 2 Kings 13:20f. 23:6, 16; Isa 22:16. While it is prohibited, there are certain texts that show the accounts of burial of Judah's kings inside towns and even in houses. The books of Kings report that thirteen kings of Judah were buried in the city of David. See 1 Kings 2:10; 11:43; 14:31; 15:8; 15:24; 22:51; 2 Kings 8:24; 9:28; 12:22; 14:20; 15:7; 15:38; 16:20. Josh 24:33; Judg 16:31; 2 Kings 13:20f., 23:6, 16; Isa 22:16. See discussion in David Pearson Wright, "The Disposal of Impurity in the Priestly Writings of the Bible with Reference to Similar Phenomena in Hittite and Mesopotamian Cultures" (PhD Dissertation: University of California, Berkeley, 1984), 119.

51 Cf. Francesca Stavrakopoulou, "Gog's Grave and the Use and Abuse of Corpses in Ezekiel 39:11-20," *JBL* 129, no. 1 (2010): 67-84.

them.[52] Rejection of פגר in Ezekiel could be a warning against the performance of an idolatrous sacrificial practice.[53] The exact meaning of פגרים in this text is debatable. If the use of the term in the Hebrew Bible is examined, we find that it is usually used to refer to dead bodies of animals or human.[54] For the book of Ezekiel, the custom of burying the dead bodies (corpse) of kings inside the city of Jerusalem compromises the purity and holiness of the sanctuary. The concern of removal of corpses from the Temple area (corpses of kings) in the book of Ezekiel reveals the desire to maintain the purity of the sanctuary from defilement.

Ezekiel 6:1-7 also seems to reflect ritual impurity in relation to corpse contamination. The text talks about the punishment of Israel that Yahweh is about to destroy cultic places of the inhabitants of Judah. In this speech, the terrible punishment includes "putting down the dead bodies/corpses of the sons of Israel before their idols and scattering their bones around their altars" (6:5). Idolatry and the presence of dead bodies in the precinct of the sanctuary indicate defilement. In the language of Milgrom, corpses and bones defiled the sanctuary because they are associated with death. Thus, Ezekiel shows that corpses or bones contaminate the purity of the sanctuary. Thus, this prohibition denounces the cultic impurity of the Jerusalem rulers.

In 39:11-20, we find the burial of Gog[55] by the house of Israel to cleanse the land. It will take seven months to cleanse the land, and only after that do they observe a sacrificial feast in the land (11.17). The elimination of the corpses of Gog and his warriors represents .the return of the exiles and Israel's claim to its land and legitimize the exiles' return.[56]In this corpse desecration motif of Ezek 38-39, we can infer the rhetorical function of divine judgment, in that only the remnant (exiles) avoids the punishment.[57] Other examples are also found in 35:8

52 In Ugaritic texts, the term has a meaning of "stele" or "offering." See D. Neiman, "פגר: A Canaanite Cult-Object in the Old Testament," *JBL* 67 (1948): 55-60.

53 J. Ebach, M. Dietrich, O. Loretz, and H. Sanmartin among many supported this interpretation. See more detail in David Pearson Wright, *The Disposal of Impurity in the Priestly Writings,* 121.

54 See Lev 26:30; Num 14:29, 32, 33; 1 Sam 17:46; 2 Kings 19:35; Isa 14:19; 34:3; 37:36; 66:24; Jer 33:5; 41:9; Ezek 6:5; Amos 8:3; Nah 3:3; 2 Chro 20:24.

55 There have been various attempts to explain the identity of Gog in this chapter. Some have argued that Gog is to be identified as one of the nations in the Ancient Near East as referred in the table of the nations in Gen. 10:2. Some others identify it with Gyges, the Lydian king (ca. 660BCE), or to the apocalyptic synonym for the Babylonians, Scythians, Old Testament antichrist, Alexander the Great, Gagu-a city prince, and so on. See more detail in Walther Zimmerli, *Ezekiel 2: A Commentary on the Book of Ezekiel 25-48,* trans. James D. Martin, ed. Paul D. Hanson, (Philadelphia: Fortress Press, 1983), 301f., Daniel I. Block, *The Book of Ezekiel 25-48,* NICOT, (Grand Rapids, Michigan: Eerdmans, 1998), 433f.

56 Stavrakopoulou, "Gog's Grave and the Use of Abuse of Corpses," 84.

57 Divine judgment fall upon all three groups–Gog, (the identity of whom is uncertain), the Judean remnant who have remained in Jerusalem, and the Judean exiles of Babylonian invasion who are slain and their corpses defiled. But finality of punishment seems to fall on Gog and the inhabitants of Jerusalem, while the remnant of the exile are revived and transported back

that tells about the desolation of Mount Seir with dead bodies. Ezekiel 37:1-14 records the unburied bones, which indicates the lifeless situation of the exiles. The experience of exile is a veritable graveyard; to live again is to return to the land.[58] One may also include 24:16-24, the command not to mourn his wife as the anti-treatment of corpses.[59] The above emphases on corpses show purity of the sancta, and rejection of foreign nations, and defilement of the people and the land. It also shows that the land of Judah is in a state of impurity and that it also needs a seven month long cleansing. Giving new life to the dead bodies signifies restoration of the exiles to their own land.

c. Food

Food purity/impurity is frequently found in the Levitical laws. According to Milgrom, the purpose of food prohibitions is to inculcate a root principle of ethics, such as the inviolability of life.[60] Food has a natural religious value. Religious and social groups define themselves by their dietary regulations.[61] Walter Houston argues that "food defines and protects equally Israel's vertical relationship to God and their horizontal difference form all other peoples."[62] In other words, Israel's dietary system may be viewed as preventive measure to maintain their identity.

One clear example of food purity is found in Ezekiel 4:9-15. This text – "eating a mixture of food" seems to express the dearth of food in the besieged city. In vv. 9-11 we see a command to prepare food with a mixture of different kinds of cereals and vegetables. The prophet is commanded to bake them into bread. Hence, the idea of uncleanness may be exhibited in this command as Ezekiel has to bake mixtures of cereals and vegetables.[63] But, nowhere in biblical texts and even in the Mishnah, do we find any anxiety of the sacred related to the mixing

---

to their homeland. See more in Nathanael James Warren, "A Cannibal Feast in Ezekiel," *JSOT* 38, no. 4 (2014): 501-512.

58 Leslie C. Allen, *Ezekiel 20-48*, WBC Vol. 29 (Dallas, Texas: Word Books, 1990), 186.

59 Stavrakopoulou, "Gog's Grave and the Use of Abuse of Corpses," 84.

60 According to him, the system teaches to have reverence to life by (1) reducing his choice of flesh to a few animals, (2) limiting the slaughter of these few permitted animals, and (3) prohibiting consumption of the blood. Reduction of Israel's diet to a few herbivores is based in a reverence for blood and life. See Jacob Milgrom, "Biblical Diet Laws," *Studies in Cultic Theology* (Leiden: EJ Brill, 1983), 110.

61 Cf. Eyal Regev, "Non-Priestly Purity and its Religious Aspect According to Historical Sources and Archaeological Findings," in *Purity and Holiness: The Heritage of Leviticus*, eds. M.J.H.M. Poorthuis & J. Schwartz (Leiden: Brill, 2000), 238.

62 Walter Houston, *Purity and Monotheism: Clean and Unclean Animals in Biblical Law*, JSOTSup 140 (Sheffield: Sheffield Academic Press, 1993), 260.

63 Sowing a field with two kinds of seed is prohibited in Lev 19:19 (cf. Deut 22:9).

of different kinds of cereal in food.[64] The command therefore intended to give opportunity that the prophet is to sustain himself with those foods.

Ezekiel, at the request of God, recoils at using human excrement as fuel for cooking food (vv. 12-15). The impurity is caused by the way the food is prepared. The use of human excrement is irregular and defiling (Cf. Deut 23:15).[65] The prophet protests that he has never defiled himself with forbidden food. Forbidden food in Ezekiel's reply contains "what died of itself (נבלה) or was torn by animals (חרפה), and carrion flesh (פגול)." These are unclean as they cause defilement to the priests (Lev 22:8; Ezek 44:31). God gives the dung of cattle instead. Permission to use cow dung for baking bread – is a linked to the harsh conditions of captivity. The food prescribed for the prophet illustrates "the unclean food among the nations, to which they are driven" (v.13). Hence, it is food prepared in a foreign land that is impure (Cf. Am 7:17; Hos 9:3; Ezek 36:18b). There is a practical solution for the exiled Judeans on how to survive in an unclean land. A symbolic example of this is that the prophet and his fellow countrymen were permitted to use cow dung, which was the common type of fuel in a country deficient in firewood.[66] This text shows that food purity is a concern of Ezekiel, but that the law was not to be enforced strictly in a foreign land, or could be modified for those in exile.

d. Idolatry

The most common mode of defilement in Ezekiel is idol worship. The most striking expression that Ezekiel uses to characterize idolatry is גלולים. The noun גלולים occurs 48 times in the Hebrew Bible, always in the plural. Ezekiel contains 39 out of 48 occurrences.[67] In most of the cases it is connected with impurity. The

---

64 Walther Zimmerli, *Ezekiel 1: A Commentary on the Book of the Prophet Ezekiel 1-24*, trans. Ronald E. Clements. Eds. Frank Moore Cross, Klaus Blatzer and Leonard Jay Greenspoon (Philadelphia: Fortress Press, 1979), 169.

65 Deut 23:13-15 says that human excrement should be covered up to make the camp holy so that the Lord shall not see something indecent and turn away from them. The passage is not related with food impurity. Milgrom and Harrington concede that this passage may have been an influence on the Dead Sea sectarians. See Hannah K. Harrington, *The Purity Texts*, Companion to the Qumran Scrolls, 5 (London/New York: T&T Clark, 2004), 107; Greenberg, *Ezekiel 1-20*, 107.

66 See discussion in Meindert Dijkstra, "The Valley of Dry Bones: Coping with the Reality of the Exile in the Book of Ezekiel." in *The Crisis of Israelite Religion: Transformation of Religious Tradition in Exilic and Post-Exilic Times*, eds. Bob Becking and Marjo C. A. Korpel (Leiden: Brill, 1999). 131.

67 It is significant to note that all of the texts that speak about גלולים are generally considered exilic and post exilic, either in its original or redactional form. Cf. Lev 26:30; Deut 29:16; 1 Kings 15:12; 21:26; 2 Kings 17:12; 21:11, 221; 23:24; Jer 50:2. See also in John F. Kutsko, *Between Heaven and Earth: Divine Presence and Absence in the Book of Ezekie*l (Winona Lake, Indiana: Eisenbrauns, 2000), 32.

etymological meaning of גלולים is not certain.[68] Due to its frequent association there with טמא, it is most likely that it is derived from גלל meaning "to be dirty."[69]

In Ezekiel, the term is used frequently to express the charge against the people in Judah. It usually denotes a sin of idolatry committed by Israel in the past and also in the present. It is most commonly found in announcement of judgment (Ezek 6:2-10, 11-14; 16: 36; 20; 23; 36). In 36:18 we find the summary of the fall of Jerusalem: "So I poured out my wrath upon them for the blood which they had shed in the land, for the idols with which they had defiled it." The prophet conceives of idolatry as the root cause of sin.[70] The frequent connection between גלולים and טמא are found in Ezekiel in many instances (20:7, 18, 31; 22:3f.; 23:7,30; 36:18, 25; 37:23 Cf. Hos 5:3; Jer 2:23). It is used as a metaphor for the sin of Judah. Since the term is frequently connected with טמאת, it is used in Ezekiel to express both cultic and moral impurity.

There are many instances where idolatry is in combination with abomination (תועבה).

Abomination in Ezekiel is a peculiar term used frequently to refer to the radical nature of sinful acts.[71] It refers fundamentally to any actions or objects that are found to be disgusting, revolting, or repulsive, on the basis of group norms.[72] But in Ezekiel (and in Deuteronomy) the term is almost entirely used for improper sacrifice or ritual acts. It also refers to something repugnant and despicable in either the religious-cultic or social-moral sphere. [73] It is shown that in Ezekiel, idolatry is something repugnant for the group's purity norms, and that those who practice it are doomed to punishment.

Detestable thing (שקץ) is another term used as an equivalent to גלולים. The root שקץ occurs 8 times in the book of Ezekiel. Ezekiel's use of the word pair (here in Ezek 5:11, et al) "detestable things and abominable practices" to "idolatrous

---

68 It may have come from the root גלל - to roll (sacred stones/images), גלל - dung (and dirty), or Sumerian *gullullu* - commit crime. See Preuss, "גלולים," *TDOT* Vol. III, 2.

69 See Kutsko, *Between Heaven and Earth*, 33.

70 The expression, "for their heart went after their idols" frequently explains the sins of Israel.

71 The term is found 117 times in the Bible, and 45 of these occurrences are found in Ezekiel. See Tova Ganzel, "The Defilement and Desecration of the Temple in Ezekiel," *Biblica* 89, no. 3 (2008): 371.

72 Gen 46:34 describes shepherds as תועבה to the Egyptians, 43:23 asserts that it was תועבה for the Egyptians to eat with Hebrews. In Psalm 88:9, the psalmist complains about having become תועבה to his acquaintances. It has a social meaning of something repugnant in human relationship. But in the book of Deuteronomy and Ezekiel, the use shift in relation to God. See also Daniel I. Block, *The Book of Ezekiel 1-24*, NICOT (Grand Rapids, Michigan: Eerdmans, 1997), 203.

73 Ezek 14:6; 16:36; 18:12 Cf. Deut 32:15-18. See discussion in Daniel L. Smith-Christopher, *A Biblical Theology of Exile* (Minneapolis: Fortress Press, 2002), 160.

objects and practices" reflects strong Deuteronomic influence.[74] The expression of the pair is found in Leviticus, but it is never used with reference to idolatry.[75] It denotes things ceremonially unclean (Ezek 5:11 cf. Lev 7:21), unclean animals (Ezek 8:10), and idolatry (Ezek 14:6; 16:36; 18:12). This practice defiles the sanctuary (5:11).

In Ezekiel, idolatry and alliance with foreign nations are seen as defilement. In these accusations, recognition of allies' gods (idolatry) is portrayed as sexual misconduct and unfaithfulness. Israel's political and economic alliances with foreign powers, which implied recognition of the allies' gods, amounted to a desertion of Yahweh in all respects like (1) a wife's abandoning her lawful husband and (2) prostitution. Chapter 16 takes up the theme of the harlotry of Israel following other gods who are the adopted and wedded maiden of Yahweh. Israel has become an unfaithful maiden pursuing other men just as she follows other gods. Ezekiel 23 describes Samaria and Jerusalem as two sisters, Oholah and Oholibah, who engage in prostitution with other nations.[76] The motif of harlotry is bound up with both cultic and political unfaithfulness. Therefore the harlotry of Samaria and Jerusalem is a national sin and pollution.[77] With these practices Israel has reneged on its oath by breaking the covenant (16:60), defiled herself (23:13), the sanctuary (with child sacrifice to idols) (23:38, 39), and desecrated the Sabbath (23:38).

e. Sacrifice of Children to Idols

Ezekiel 23:38-39 contains explicit reference to defiling the sanctuary by sacrificing children to idols. The defilement and desecration results not only from the introduction of foreigners, but also from the arrival of the Israelites themselves for the purpose of slaughtering children to fetishes.[78] The prophet combines the defilement of the temple with its desecration, thereby emphasizing the severity of the people's wrongdoing and thus justifying the impending destruction of the Temple. Ezekiel perceives the defilement and profanation of the Temple and profanation of the Sabbath as the result of their abominable acts (v. 36),

74 See the use in 7:20; 11:18, 21; 20:7, 8, 30; 37:23. Cf. Deut 7:26; 29:16; 1 King 11:5, 7; 2 Kings 23:13, 24; Isa 66:3; Jer 4:1; 7:30; 13:27; 16:18; 32:34.

75 Cf. Block, Daniel I. Block, *The Book of Ezekiel Chapters 1-24*, NICOT (Grand Rapids: Eerdmans, 1997), 208.

76 Oholah and Oholibah are identified as Israel and Samaria in 4c. Kutsko argues that the use of Samaria and Jerusalem for the Northern and Southern Kingdoms is clear here. See Kutsko, *Between Heaven and Earth*, 31.

77 Cf. J. Duncan M. Derett, "Impurity and Idolatry: John 13:11; Ezekiel 36:25," *Bibbiae Oriente* 172, XXXIV, no. 2 (April-May 1992): 90.

78 This type of Temple-defiling sin appears already in the Priestly Sources (Lev 18:21-30 and 20, 33), which perhaps shares the same basis as Ezekiel's viewing this act as a cause of defilement. Cf. Tova Ganzel, "The Defilement and Desecration of the Temple in Ezekiel," *Biblica* 89, no. 3 (2008): 369-370.

adultery and bloodshed (v. 37), and murderous acts in the Temple courtyards, and the sacrifice of children to idols both within and outside the Temple (vv. 38-39). Another reference to child sacrifice is hinted at 16:20-21. Here Jerusalem is indicted as a prostitute who indulged in cultic offences. Jerusalem sacrificed the children she had borne to Yahweh to idols. The accusation is that Jerusalem slaughtered the children and gave them as food to pagan images (vv. 18, 20). The expression לאכול (lit. for eating) portrays the children as food for idols, along with the fine flour, oil, and honey mentioned in v.19.[79] In verse 21, the pagan view of sacrifice is shown by the expressions: "You have slaughtered (ותשחטי)," and "cause them to pass through (the fire) (ותתנים בהעביר)."[80] This second phrase reflects extreme literary synonymy with sacrifice of children to Molech found elsewhere in the Hebrew Bible.[81] For Ezekiel, the sacrifice of children to idols is a serious cultic crime of Jerusalem and its inhabitants. It defiles the sanctuary.

f. Bloodshed

The use of blood (דם) in Ezekiel is as varied as it is in the other books of the Hebrew Bible. Out of 360 occurrences in the Hebrew Bible, we find it 55 times in Ezekiel.[82] The plural דמים is found in the book used strategically to express the idea of (1) the shedding of female blood, (2) the spilt blood of the slain, and (3) bloodguilt.[83] In Ezekiel, דם is used frequently metonymically for "violent bloodshed" inflicted by one upon another, a notion closely related to the idiom שפך דם (to pour out blood) (16:6, 9, 36; 21:37; 22:2,3,4; 23:45; 36:18). Jerusalem is accused of shedding blood, which led her to become impure before Yahweh.

First, in Ezekiel, blood is a sign of an impure/unclean thing that needs cleansing. When Jerusalem is in her impure state, Yahweh washes the blood off her (16:9). Adultery causes impurity because blood is on their (adulterous) hands (23:45). Goldstein observes that "blood conveys Ezekiel's disgust with the lack of attention to purity issues, while the adultery conveys Ezekiel's critique of the covenant violation."[84] Eating meat with blood is detrimental, in the same manner

79 Block, *Ezekiel 1-24*, 490.

80 שחט usually refers to both profane butchering and sacrificial slaughter, and the phrase בהעביר ותתנים means to pass someone through the fire. For more detail See Block, *Ezekiel 1-24*, 490-491.

81 We find expressions of sacrifice of children to Molech in Lev 18:21; 20:2-5; 2 Kings 23:10; Jer 32:35. Cf. Deut 18:10; 2 Kings 16:3; 17:17; 21:6; 2 Chro 33:6; Ezek 23:39.

82 Ezekiel is second to the book of Leviticus where we find the term 88 times. See John R. Kohlenberger III and James A. Swanson, *The Hebrew English Concordance to the Old Testament (With the New International Version)* (Grand Rapids, Michigan: Zondervan Publishing House, 1998), 412-414.

83 E. W. Goldstein, "By the Blood that You Shed You are Guilty:" Perspectives on Female Blood in Leviticus and Ezekiel," in *Jewish Blood: Reality and Metaphor in History, Religion, and Culture*, ed. Mitchell B Hart, RJSS (London: Routledge, 2009), 58.

84 Goldstein, "By the Blood You Shed You are Guilty," 65.

of shedding blood and worshipping idols (33:25).[85] The prohibition against consuming blood must have been aimed against one element of foreign religious practice which seemed to present a particular danger to the exiles.[86] While the prohibition of blood consumption is evident here, the blood of birds and animals are on one of the menus in the "victory banquet" of Gog (39:17-20).[87] The irony of this banquet with the flesh and blood of birds and animals is hard to explain. It is probably another case reflecting the re-appropriation of purity rules for the exilic community.

Second, Ezekiel connects bloodshed with idolatry and abominations. In the admonition of Jerusalem as "bloody city," the accusation is that "You have become guilty by the blood that you have shed, and defiled by the idols that you have made" (22:4). In 36:18 divine punishment is caused by "the blood that they had shed upon the land, and for the idols with which they had defiled it." Bloodshed accrues divine punishment as it defiles the land. There is yet another example of bloodguilt and defilement in Ezekiel 24 with a metaphor of the filthy pot. This chapter is a cooking song about the pot and the meat. As Block observes, the song confirms in the minds of its hearers the privileged relationship between Israel and Yahweh; the Jerusalemites, and particularly those left in the city after 597, are the good pieces.[88] But verses 6-8 explain why the people possess no special statues before Yahweh ("because her blood is within her"). Verse 6 describes the disease of the pot itself, and the rest of the pericope is particularly concerned with the defilement of the pot itself (vv. 11-13).

Just as in the vocative "city of blood" in v. 6, the blood itself points in several semantic directions: the Jerusalemites have shed blood, thus they have bloodguilt, but also that blood contaminates and defiles in the priestly worldview. The latter recalls the blood of the infant in chapter 16, and the blood of the menstruating woman (22:10), both of which are defiling. As the imagery found in the priestly writings,[89] blood serves as a peculiarly appropriate image for the type of corruption (defilement) that Ezekiel ascribes to the inhabitants of Jerusalem.

85 Cf. Lev. 3:17 prohibits eating of fat and blood. Gen 9:1-7 sanctions animal flesh as food for human, but not its blood.

86 Cf. Eichrodt, *Ezekiel: A Commentary*, 31.

87 Block writes "The literary image sketched here must have been shocking for a person as sensitive to cultic matters as Ezekiel… How the priestly prophet reacted to this horrifying image one may only speculate." See Block, *Ezekiel 25-48*, 477.

88 Daniel I. Block, "Ezekiel's Boling Cauldron: A form critical solution to Ezekiel XXIV: 1-14," *Vetus Testamentum* 41 (1991): 26.

89 Cf. Jacqueline E. Lapsey, *Can These Bones Live? The Problem of Moral Self in the Book of Ezekiel, BZAW* 301 (Berlin: Walter de Gruyter, 2000), 99.

g. Sexual Impurity

There are a number of references to sexual impurity in the book of Ezekiel. As in the other books of the Hebrew Bible, in Ezekiel, the female body represents sexual pollution.[90] This pollution figuratively defines Israel's apostasy and rebellion against her God. There are many terms that describe impurity of Israel such as fornication/harlotry, adultery, incest, and other sexual crimes. The most common form of sexual misconduct in the book of Ezekiel is fornication (תזנה).[91] The usage appears most frequently in the prophetic literature, especially Hosea, Jeremiah, and Ezekiel.[92] The term is used figuratively of Israel's apostasy from Yahweh and its intercourse with other gods. In Ezekiel 16 and 23, the allegorical description of a harlot represents the apostasy of the people. Female pollution is metaphorically employed to explain why Israel suffered exilic catastrophe. As S. Tamar Kamioskowski puts it, "In Chapters 16 and 23 … Ezekiel's preoccupation with gender identity, and in particular with shame-centered emasculation, is found embedded in the text in more subtle ways." [93] Hence, these two chapters are considered as reflections of the trauma of exile.

In Ezekiel 16 there are 9 instances where we find זנה in its different forms. The chapter narrates Jerusalem as an orphan taken care by Yahweh with whom it enters into covenant (v. 8). But Jerusalem (Israel) repaid the kindness of Yahweh with adultery (זנות) (v. 15). It gave itself over to the worship of Canaanite gods (v. 16 cf. v. 3); it played the whore with images (17) and sacrifices its sons and daughters as if its whorings were not enough (20); and entered into relationship with Egypt, Assyria, and Chaldea (vv. 26, 28). It acts like a brazen prostitute, with whom anyone could have sexual intercourse (vv. 25, 31). The price of whoring was given to its lovers for more harlotry (v. 31). Therefore, Jerusalem must bear the penalty of prostitution of women (vv. 40, 41). The metaphor of broken

---

90 For example, in Numbers 5:12-31, the root טמא is used to describe the woman's state of committing adultery (vv. 13, 14, 19, 28), while טהר is used to describe here state if she has not (v. 28).

91 The Hebrew root זנה and its derivatives תזנות/זנות/זנונים are generally translated as commit fornication/be a harlot and hence fornication/harlotry. Most of occurrences of זנה and its derivatives have figurative meaning, referring to Israel's faithlessness toward Yahweh and worship of other gods. Cf. Lev 17:7; 20:5f.; Nu 14:33; 15:39; 25:1; Deut 31:16; Judg 2:17; 8:27, 33:1; 1 Chro 5:25; 2 Chro 21:11, 13; Ps. 73:27; 106:39; Ezekiel 16 & 23.

92 Hos 2:2; 3:1; 4:2, 13, 14; 7:4; Jer 3:8, 9; 5:7; 7:9; 9:2; 23:10, 14; 29:23; Ezek 16: 16:15 (2), 16, 17, 26, 28 (2times), 34, 41 & 23:3 (2 times), 5, 19, 30, 42, 44, 11, 29, 27.

93 She writes: "Shame-centered emasculation refers to the ways in which victimized men express their defeat in terms of female victimization. It is the equation of honor belonging to masculinity and shame to feminity where men experienced behavioral challenge of defeat." See S. Tamar Kamiowskowski, *Gender Reversal and Cosmic Chaos: A Study on the Book of Ezekiel,* JSOT Sup 368 (London: Sheffield Academic Press, 2003), 67. See also discussion about the trauma of the exilic Israelite community in Daniel L. Smith, *The Religion of the Landless: The Social Context of the Babylonian Exile* (Bloomington, Ind: Meyer Stone, 1989).

relationship between Israel and Yahweh, represented as adulterous fornication, describes the defilement of the entire nation.[94]

In Ezekiel 23, there are ten references to זנה (verb) and זנונים/זנות/זנה (nouns). It describes the fate of the two sisters Oholah and Oholibah, an allegorical representation of Samaria and Jerusalem. It emphasizes how Israelites played harlotry with Egypt, Assyria, and Babylonia, and must be punished (27, 35). In verse 29, three impurities signify the apostasy and idolatry of Jerusalem: "the nakedness of your harlotry" (ערות זנוניך), "your lewdness" (זמתך), and "your harlotry" (תנותיך). Harlotry is associated with the nations, and pollution with idols (v.30). The fornication of Samaria and Jerusalem is equivalent to adultery, for which they have to be punished (vv. 43,44, 47).

Ezekiel 22:10-11 listed other aspects of sexual impurity. First, we find the expression "uncovered the nakedness of the father." This implies cohabitation with the father's wife.[95] It may be an allusion to marriage with stepmother or incest with father's wife or concubine.[96] Second, another carnal sin is הנדה טמאת "humbled women in menstrual period" - literally "they defiled one in her impurity." The sexual use of "humiliate, oppress," which occurs here and in v. 11 signifies unwillingness of the woman to acquiesce in the illegal union.[97] In verse 11 we see other instances of sexual misconduct. These include castigating "the inhabitants of the ruins (שבי החרבות)" for their impurity saying, "each of you has polluted/defiled (טמאתם) his neighbor's wife."[98] Another aspect is incest: "defiled

94 Cf. Hosea 5:3b and 6:10b. Here the verse runs as: כי עתה הזנית אפרים נטמא ישראל (For now O Ephraim, you have fornicated; Israel is defiled). In 6:10b we see similar expression: נטמא ישראל שם זנות לאפרים (A fornication of Ephraim (is there); Israel is defiled). As also seen here in Hosea, fornication and impurity (defilement) are two sides of the same coin. Cf. Feinstein, "Sexual Pollution in the Hebrew Bible," "Sexual Pollution in the Hebrew Bible: A New Perspective," in *Bodies, Embodiment, and Theology of the Hebrew Bible* eds. S. Tamar Kamionskowski and Wonil Kim, LBH/OTE 465 (New York: T&T Clark, 2010), 143.

95 The same expression "the nakedness of your mother" is found in Lev 18:7. Deuteronomy 23:1 expresses the illicitness of relations with the wife of one's father as "uncovering the edge of the father's garment."

96 G. A. Cooke, *A Critical and Exegetical Commentary on the Book of Ezekiel Vol. 1*, ICC (New York: Charles Scribner's Sons, 1937), 241. Cf. Lev. 18:7f.; 20:11ff.; Deut 23:1; 22:30; 27:20.

97 Levitical laws laid prohibition of sexual relationships in marriage with a woman during the time of her menstrual period is mentioned in priestly legislation in Leviticus 15. Greenberg, *Ezekiel 21-37*, 455. The verb is used in the same vein in Deut 21:14; 22:24, 29.

98 According to Greenberg "with fellow's wife" cannot be the direct object, as the object marker does not precede it. It means here defilement "on the person of." See Greenberg, *Ezekiel 21-37*, 455. As Feinstein has puts it: "The verb used in each of these cases is in the Piel stem which means to make polluted. Hence, the male is the polluter and the female the polutee. In Numbers 5:12-31 the polluting act is adultery in which the blame is on the woman who has been defiled. See Feinstein, "Sexual Pollution in the Hebrew Bible," 129.

his daughter in law" (את־בלתו טמא).[99] Here defilement falls upon the daughter in law whereas the polluter is the man. It shows the intensity of Israel's sexual impurity. Another term used to refer to sexual misconduct in the book is hmz, which is usually translated as depravity/wickedness/lewdness. It is only in H and Ezekiel that the term occurs in reference to sexual context.[100]

Ezekiel's formulation of strictures against Israel with a picture of sexual wrongs might have close connections with Jeremiah's laments about adultery among his people, Hosea's against adulterous Israel and H's Levitical laws.[101] From the above discussion, it is evident that both male and female are involved in sexual impurity. The metaphor of sexual misbehavior signifies Israel's infidelity and apostasy. The consequence is Yahweh's withdrawal from the land and rejection of its people. Adultery, harlotry, incest, and other sexual misconduct are against holiness, in the simple sense of right order. Here again "the inhabitants of the ruins" are the main culprit, in other words the blame is placed on the Judeans who remained in the land.

h. Holiness, Purity, and Defilement of the Sanctuary

According to the book of Ezekiel and Leviticus, the sanctuary is the holy place where Yahweh dwells. In order to stand at the precinct of the sanctuary, Israel should maintain purity in all aspects of life. Purity and impurity in Israel therefore have their meaning and significance from their relation to the Temple.[102] The main problem with impurity is not the impure state of a person as such, but the danger that impurity poses for the sacred.[103] Levitical laws prescribe a number of laws to keep the holy away from the impure (Lev 10:7; 21:12; Num 9:6-7, 9-12). This is also true for the concept of defilement in the book of Ezekiel.

The sacredness of the sanctuary in the book of Ezekiel is shown by the presence and departure of כבוד יהוה in/from the sanctuary/house (הבית) of the Lord in Jerusalem (8:4; 10:19; 11:16, 22-23; 43:4). The Tabernacle (משק) is called the dwelling place (משכן), and a meeting tent (אהל מעד) in the Torah. The glory of God enters the Tabernacle which shows the presence of Yahweh, which, in turn defined the holiness of the Tabernacle (Exodus 25:8; 29:43-56). In Deuteronomy the name of God dwells in the sanctuary (Deut 12:5, 11; 14:23-24; 16:11). Thus

99 This sexual relationship is prohibited by Leviticus 18:9 and 15 But the case in the stories of Judah and Tamar (Gen 38) and Ammon and Tamar (2 Sam 13) indicate that they are not prohibited.

100 In Ezekiel, the term refers to marriage infidelity (Ezek 16:27, 58; 23:21, 27,29,35, 44, 48, 49 Cf. Jer 13:27). It also refers to having sex with a woman who is ritually impure (Ezek 22:10), and various forms of incest (Ezek 22:11 cf. Lev 18:17; 20:14).

101 Zimmerli, *Ezekiel 1*, 458.

102 Marcel Poorthuis & Joshua Schwartz, "Introduction," in *Purity and Holiness*, 12.

103 Annette Schellenberg, "More than Spirit: On the Physical Dimension in the Priestly Understanding of Holiness," *ZAW* 126, no. 2 (2014): 169.

according to the priestly concept, God's glory (כבוד) and God's name (שם) are the invisible signs of God's dwelling among his people. Strangely enough in Ezekiel, God's glory (כבוד) moves to the unclean land (Ezek 4:13) and dwells among the גולה.[104] Risa Levit Kohn writes:

> The image of God in exile delineates Israel into two conflicting and conflicted groups; namely, those in the land (away from Yahweh) and those in the גולה (in the presences of the כבוד). Most importantly, it provides an opportunity for the prophet to put his own unique spin on the ancient Israelite tradition of wilderness wandering and entry into the promised land. For Ezekiel, the exiles are the wandering Israelites, while the current idolatrous inhabitants of Judah are the sinful Canaanites of the exodus generation.[105]

The presence of the כבוד in exile confirms that the exiles are distant from the land, but not from Yahweh. On the contrary, those in the land are cut off from Yahweh after כבוד יהוה departs from both the Temple and Jerusalem.[106] A pertinent question is: Why does the כבוד יהוה leave Jerusalem and dwell among the גלה? The answer for Ezekiel is: "because Jerusalem and its inhabitants defiled the Temple that is in Jerusalem."

Ezekiel clearly enlists the concept of Temple defilement in the same manner in which it is used in the Priestly Writings. The Jerusalem Temple, or sanctuary, is defiled by the cultic impurities of its people. The first case is found in 5:11a in which Jerusalem is accused of defiling Yahweh's sanctuary (מקדש) with all her detestable things (שקוצים)[107] and all her abominations (תועבת). In Ezekiel the term תועבה is frequently used in connection with cultic offences. It refers either to cultic practices or objects which have no proper place in the cult, or even to idols.[108] Even though there is no clear reference to defilement of the sanctuary by

104 The only other place we see the כבוד appears outside sanctuary is in the wilderness wandering before the construction of the Tabernacle and the ark. Cf. Block, *Ezekiel 1-24*, 84.

105 Risa Levit Kohn, "As Though You Yourself Came Out of Egypt:" The Ethos of Exile in Ezekiel," *Hebrew Bible and Ancient Israel* 3, no. 2 (2014): 193.

106 In the ancient Near East, a deity's departure from the temple means the city is open to destruction; conversely the god's presence guaranteed the city's safety. This text shares the same ancient Near Eastern motif. See discussion in, Yedida Eisenstat, "Sanctification and Shame: Balik's In the City of Slaughter in Light of Leviticus and Ezekiel," in *Purity, Holiness, and Identity in Judaism and Christianity: Essays in Memory of Susan Haber*, eds. Carl S. Ehrlich, Anders Runesson and Eileen Schuller, (Tubingen: Mohr Siebeck, 2013), 273.

107 שקוצים mostly refers to foreign gods or idols, especially in Deuteronomy and Kings. Eg. Dt. 29:16; 1 Kings 11:5, 7; 2 Kings 23:13, 24. Wevers regards Detestable things in Ezekiel referring to idols. See John W. Wevers, *Ezekiel: The Century Bible* (London: Thomas Nelson and Sons Ltd., 1969), 97.

108 Abomination in Ezekiel as an inclusive term used in reference to something repugnant and despicable in either religious-cultic or social-moral sphere. Cf. Tova Ganzel, "The Defilement

idols, reference to prohibition of idol worship that defiles the sanctuary is hinted in Leviticus 20. Thus, in Ezekiel 5:11 defilement of the sanctuary is caused by idolatry and other cultic offences.

We find more examples of defilement in Ezekiel 8:3-17. In this vision, Ezekiel is called to witness the abomination of Jerusalem committed in the sanctuary (vv. 6, 9, 13, 15). Defiling acts in the sanctuary consists of: (1) keeping the image of jealousy, meaning the Canaanite goddess Asherah, in the sanctuary; [109] (2) offering incense by seventy elders inside the sanctuary (vv10-11); and (3) women sitting and weeping for Tammuz, worshipping a foreign goddess and fertility cult.[110] The fourth abomination is in the innermost part of the sanctuary, where "about twenty five men with their backs to the temple of Yahweh, face eastward and bow toward the sun" (v.16). This description points to worship in a sun cult, which is a rejection of Yahwistic cult in favor of another deity.[111] Another case of defiling the sanctuary appears in Ezekiel 23:38. This is the condemnation of adulterous acts of Oholah and Oholibah. Verse 37 tells about the whoring of Israel to idols (גלולים), bloodguilt offering (דם בידיהן), and offering children for sacrifice. Verse 38 connects v. 37 and says: "this they have done to me: 'they have defiled my sanctuary' (טמאו את־מקדשי). Ezek 23:38 could be understood as a general injunction against introducing any type of ritual impurity into the temple.[112]

A case of defilement of the sanctuary is also found in Ezek 9:6-7. The defilement is the murderous act and the laying of corpses in the courts (of the temple). Yahweh says: "Begin from my sanctuary... defile the house and fill the courts with the slain... and they went out and killed in the city," (vv. 6&7). The passage describes the execution in the temple courtyard as commanded by Yahweh. In this text, Yahweh is said to command the defilement. It is presumed that the temple has already been defiled by the people's sinful acts and the כבד יהוה already left the temple.[113] From the above texts, we can infer that the defilement and profanation of the temple involve idol worship, corpse contamination, crimes in the temple precincts, and improper worship and sacrifices in the sanctuary. We could make a note that the main defiling agents in the above texts are Jerusalem itself and its inhabitants.

and Desecration of the Temple in Ezekiel," 371.

109 Cf. 2 Kings 21:7; 23:6; 2 Chro 33:7. See Eichrodt, *Ezekiel*, 1970, 122. Greenberg, *Ezekiel 1-20*, 168.

110 Wong, *The Idea of Retribution in the Book of Ezekiel*, 142.

111 Scholars such as Ackerman, Allen, Dijkstra, and Wong among others follow this idea. See detailed discussion in Wong, *The Idea of Retribution*, 142.

112 Ganzel, "The Defilement and Desecration of the Temple," 377.

113 Cf. 2 Kings 11:15. See also Greenberg, *Ezekiel 1–20*, 177.

i. Purity/Impurity of the Land

Land outside of Israel was considered unclean and contaminated because of the abominable practices of its inhabitants, particularly through idolatry (Josh 22:19; Amos 7:17; Jer 2:7)." In Leviticus 18:24-25 we find a logical connection between the defilement of the people and the defilement of the land.[114] The idea of defilement of the land appears just a few times in Ezekiel, but it plays a very important role in the theology of defilement in Ezekiel. First defilement of the land is found in 36:17-18. In this passage we come across a reference to the defilement of the land by the sinful actions of the house of Israel (בית ישׂראל) in two ways: first, they defiled the land "with their ways and their deeds" (v. 17), the inhabitants of Israel defile the land as they violate the will of the divine sovereign; second, Israel defiles the land by the blood they shed on the land and by their idols (v. 18). Hence, a land could be defiled by both the native population and by a pagan foreigner invading. Ezekiel rhetorically uses אדמה rather than ערץ.[115]

In these two verses major polluting agents of the land in Ezekiel are listed: (1) sexual impurity, "like the uncleanness of a woman in her menstrual period" (Cf. Lev 18:19); (2) bloodshed, which recalls Numbers 35:34 that "blood pollutes the land;" (3) idol worship, including the Molech cult (Lev 18). The expression "as the uncleanness of the woman in her menstrual period" might suggest unrestrained behavior. The second defiling agents, a combination of "bloodshed and idols," alludes to child sacrifices mentioned in 16: 20-21; 20:26 and 23:36-38. The land was full of lewdness and bloody crimes, and the exile of the population remained the only way of purgation.[116] When a promise of purification of the land is announced (36:33-36), Yahweh will cleanse the people of the land, rebuild the wastes, and the desolated land will be cultivated. Only when there is purification, the divine presence my again dwell in their midst (cf. 48:35b).

In Temple vision found in 8-11,[117] we see the withdrawal of the כבד יהוה from Jerusalem. The text tells that the כבוד יהוה departs from Jerusalem (9:18); and now dwells among the exilic group (11:16, 22-23). Ezekiel understands the judgment

114 Andrew Mein states that "…there is in P and other parts of the Hebrew Bible a sense that impurity might get out of control, that much impurity will threaten Yahweh's presence in his sanctuary and even Israel's occupation of the land. See Andrew Mein, *Ezekiel and the Ethics of Exile* (Oxford: Oxford University Press, 2001), 149.

115 The use of the term אדמה rather than ערץ perhaps refers to the preference of national territory not as real estate or political jurisdiction, but as a home, an agricultural land that provide national well-being and prosperity. Cf. Block, *Ezekiel 25-48*, 345.

116 Frymer-Kensky compares the exile with the Flood tradition that exile is the state of purgations of the land. See discussion in Frymer-Kensky, "Pollution, Purification, and Purgation in Biblical Israel," in *The Word of the Lord Shall Go Forth, Essays in honor of David Noel Freeman in Celebration of his Sixtieth Birthday*, eds. Carol L. Meyers and M. O'Connor (Winona Lake, Ind: Eisenbrauns, 1983), 400-414.

117 Ezekiel 8-11 is generally ascribed to temple vision, having distinct materials that have been brought together to form a coherent, rhetorical unit. Odell gives "Abominations and Ethical

experienced by Judah as the result of Yahweh's withdrawal of his presence from the community because of the defilement caused by the impurities of Israel. The nature of defilement of the land is repeatedly expressed in the language "abominations" (תועבה) and violence (חמס).[118] In Ezekiel, both cultic and social sins constitute the basis of divine judgment.[119] They both defile the land. Brad E. Kelle writes: "(For Ezekiel) the people's sins are not simply transgressions against God; they are agents of pollution that create an increasing level of defilement. God cannot dwell in the midst of impurity; such defilement may force Yahweh to withdraw his presence from the community, ensuring its destruction."[120]

Defilement of the land is also alluded to in Ezekiel 22:24 where the land is described as "not purified."[121] The cause of this uncleanness is described in vv. 25-29. It includes the misconduct of every group of leaders: the princes, priests, officials, prophets, and the people of the land. This passage is a comprehensive claim of Ezekiel that Jerusalem's leaders were the source of the violence that finally destroyed the city.[122] Ezekiel's references to the sins of Israel, bloodshed and idol worship in relation to defilement of the land, therefore recall the Genesis flood tradition that the sins of Jerusalem, including its impure acts such as idolatry, bloodshed, and sexual crimes defile the land of Judah.

j. Defilement of the Divine Name

As stated earlier, Deuteronomy tells us that the name of God dwells in the sanctuary (Deut 12:5, 11; 14:23-24; 16:11). The presence of the divine name in the sanctuary is the invisible sign of God's presence among his people. Hence, defilement and desecration of the name of Yahweh is an abomination for the priestly concept of the holiness of God. According to Ezekiel 20, the Israelites repeatedly disobey God's explicit instructions, and God desires to blot them out. However, in "acting for the sake of His name," his reputation, God refrains so that his name is not "profaned" among the nations. (20:8-9, 13-14, 21-22).

While profanation (הלל) of Yahweh (and the name of Yahweh) is found in many instances,[123] defilement (טמא) is used here in Ezekiel 43:7 only in relation to

Abuses" as the title for the vision of the temple. See. Margaret S. Odell, *Ezekiel* (Macon, Georgia: Smith & Helwys, 2005), 101.

118 This is found in 8:6 (2 times), 9, 13, 17; 9:4; 11:18, 21.

119 Cf. Leslie C. Allen, *Ezekiel 1-19*, WBC Vol. 28 (Dallas, Texas: Word Books, 1994), 145.

120 Brad E. Kelle, "Dealing with the Trauma of Defeat: The Rhetoric of the Devastation and Rejuvenation of Nature in Ezekiel," *JBL* 128, no. 3 (2009): 481-482.

121 Zimmerli translates, "You are a land which has not been rained upon, upon which no shower has fallen in the day so wrath." His omission of "not purified" is misleading as the text asserts Israel's lack of purity with the usage of the term לא מטהרה (not being purified). See Zimmerli *Ezekiel 1*, 465.

122 Cf. Odell, *Ezekiel*, 289.

123 See Ezekiel 13:19; 20:9, 14, 22; 22:16, 26; 36:20, 21, 22, 23; 39:7.

the name of Yahweh. The text reads: "never again will they defile again my holy name, neither they nor their kings, with their harlotry (בזנותם) and the funerary offering (פגרי) of their kings at their deaths (במותם)" (43:7). As Block asserts, this account views the return of the deity in the sanctuary with a declaration of Yahweh's intention in entering the temple.[124] The text seems to suggest that defilement of the name of Yahweh is caused by association of the temple with idols (harlotry) and corpses (פגרים) of kings and their deaths. The meaning of the second-defiling factor (פגר) is ambiguous.[125] It is most likely that this verse reflects a regulation for protecting holiness of the temple and the closeness between Yahweh and Israel in the persons of its kings. In the new temple-based community, the position of the king was abolished, and the replacement, the נשיא (chief) was removed far from the sacred area.[126] Cult monuments near the sancta were an abomination to the sanctuary, where the holy name of Yahweh dwells.

k. Defilement of the People

As also expressed in the priestly writings, Ezekiel describes Israel as a nation polluted by her sexual misconduct and idolatry (Cf. Num 5:13; Lev 18:20). In general, the Decalogue prohibits adultery, incest and other sexual misconduct (Ex 20:14; Deut 5:18). Ezekiel indicted the people of the land categorizing them as being in a state of defilement. In chapter 22, we find the accusation that Jerusalem and its inhabitants are practicing many abominations: one with neighbor's wife (22:11a); another defiles a daughter-in-law (22:11b); and another violates (ענה) half sisters (22:11c).[127] The defilement in Ezekiel departs from the priestly concept of defilement of the people in a specific way. As seen in the above case, sexual misconduct defiles not only the offender, but also on others.[128] In the language of Ezekiel, bloodshed, injustices, and other cultic activities cause the defilement of the people. Ezekiel is more concerned that the seriousness of a person's impurity affects the whole worshipping community.

The unique use of the piel טמא is found with the defilement of people in which Yahweh is the subject of defilement. In Ezekiel 20:26 the prophet indicts Israel for her continued rebellion. The indictment is that Israel profaned (חלל) the Sabbath (20:16, 21) and did not obey a command not to defile (טמא) themselves (20:7, 18). Thus, the 'defilement of Israel' in this case is the expression of Yahweh's

124 Block, *Ezekiel 25-48*, 580.

125 For the meaning of פגר see discussion on corpse impurity in the above.

126 For this discussion see Jacob Milgrom and Daniel I. Block, *Ezekiel's Hope: A Commentary on Ezekiel 38-48* (Eugene, Oregon: Cascade Books, 2012), 110-112.

127 Block translates ענה as rape, hence "men rape their half-sisters, their father's daughter. See Block, *Ezekiel 1-24*, 707.

128 See for example in Ezekiel, Babylonians defiles Jerusalem (23:17), sexual misconduct defiles the daughter in law (22:11b), neighbor's wife (18:6, 15), idolatry and fornication defiles the sanctuary, the land and desecrates the Sabbath (23:38).

defense of his honor despite Israel's rebellion. It is not that Yahweh causes them to be 'impure' but rather that Yahweh is justified by their impurity.

Defilement of the people by idols is found in many instances in the book of Ezekiel but it is not as common in the Hebrew Bible.[129] Ezekiel 23 describes the defilement of Oholah (Samaria) and Oholibah (Jerusalem) with their idols (23:7; 13; 30). In the salvation oracle in 36:16-38, the house of Israel is said to be cleansed from its uncleanness and from its idols (36:25). For Ezekiel, Israelites defiled themselves with idolatry and in the future God will purify them from their defilements.

The impurity of the people is the main issue in the regulations regarding Temple service found in Ezekiel 44:3-31. Scholars argue this unit as a later addition which reflects the postexilic struggle between Zadokite and Levite factions within the priesthood.[130] First, there is a concern for temple personnel here. This text suggests that only the Zadokite lineage of Levitical priests are allowed to serve as high priest (44:15) and that the non-Zadokite Levitical priests are not allowed to be in charge of the holy things (44:8). Why are they being rejected? It is plausible that the group belongs to the Shaphanites, who are the Levitical group serving during the exilic period.[131] Ezekiel undermines this group because he views them as breaking the covenant by doing abominations; and therefore profaned the sanctuary (44:6, 7).

Secondly an important issue is the exclusion of foreigners "sons of aliens (בני נכר) and uncircumcised heart and flesh (ערלי)" in the new temple.[132] Zimmerli interprets these people as "heathen surroundings."[133] These people could be those Israelites, who were not part of the exilic group, who had already intermingled with neighboring peoples during the exilic period.[134] Ezekiel perhaps chose the word to identify those individuals who are ritually unfit to participate in cultic

129 In few references such as Psalm 109:39, Jer 2:23; Lev 18:24, 30; 19:31 and perhaps Gen 35:1-4 do we find links between idol worship and defilement of the people.

130 See Eichrodt, *Ezekiel*, 567; Block, *Ezekiel 25-48,* 616; Steven Shawn Tuell, *The Law of the Temple in Ezekiel 40-48*, HSM 49 (Atlanta, Georgia: Scholars Press, 1992), 57-62.

131 These were a certain groups of priests who took control of the political and religious institutions around Mizpah and Bethel after the destruction of Jerusalem. See Jeremiah 29:3; 36:10; 40:7-12 Cf. 2 Kings 22:12.

132 The exact meaning of בני נכר is not known. The expression occurs only here in Ezekiel. Ezekiel consistently uses זרים to refer to foreigners (See Ezek 7:21; 11:9; 28:7, 10; 30:12; 31:12 Cf. Lev 22:25; Gen 17:12).

133 Zimmerli, *Ezekiel 2*, 454.

134 I make this argument because the choice of the word for foreigners in the book of Ezekiel is זרים and not נכר. Hence, they could not be foreigners. Leviticus 22:25 uses the term to refer to offering of food from this group. Hence, they are participating in the cult. In Genesis 17:12 the term implies "slaves" living with families of Israel. Exodus 12:43 prohibits the נכרים to eat the Passover. In Ezekiel and other texts, בני נכר are not foreigners, but people who live with Israel.

activity. They are not qualified to take part in a temple-based community because they are the defiled people. Ezekiel strategically focuses more frequently on Jerusalem and its people when defilement of the people is emphasized.

2.5. Purification

Robert Parker, who develops the concept of purification as the "science of religion," stresses that "without purification there is no access to the sacred."[135] According to the priestly system, impurity should be purged so that it does not threaten the holiness of Israel, the sanctuary and the divine. Purification varies in intensity, complexity, and duration, depending on the nature of the impurity. Modes of purification also vary according to the type of impurities.[136] Severe ritual impurities require complicated procedures of purification like sacrifice, removal from the land, and death. Some impurities need sacrifice whereas some of them could be cleansed by repentance.[137] While purity/impurity is central to the theology of Ezekiel, we do not find complicated procedures of purification in the book, except in chapters 40-48.[138] In other words, they are less systematic in the book of Ezekiel. I will discuss the three ways purification may be traced in the book of Ezekiel.

First, in the oracles of the new Temple and community, we find the purification of the altar, the priests, and the people. Ezekiel 43:20-27 prescribes purification of the altar with a sin/purification offering חטאת. Here various kinds of animals – bulls, goats, and he-goats should be offered (vv. 21-22). The purification involves not only animal sacrifices but also burnt offerings (עולתיכם) and peace offerings (שלמיכם). Here חטאת (vv. 20, 21, 22, 25) and טהרת (v. 26) have the similar meaning of cleansing or purification. This purification offering is part of a larger process of sanctification of the altar in the sanctuary. In this sacrifice, the appeasement comes through purification of the sancta with unique blood rites and the burning of animals on the altar.[139] It is not the purification of the person's body, but to purify its external effects on the sancta (Ezek 43:20-23 cf. Exod

135 Robert Parker, *Miasma: Pollution and Purification in Early Greek Religion* (Oxford: Oxford University Press, 1983, reprint, 2001), 19.

136 In the priestly purity ritual system, modes of purification include the use of water, the passage of time, breakage, and burning. See Jacob Neusner, *Purity in Rabbinic Judaism A Systematic Account: The Sources, Media, Effects, and Removal of Uncleanness* (Atlanta, Georgia: Scholars Press, 1994), 142.

137 See detail description of impurities and their purification in Hannah K. Harrington, "Clean and Unclean," *NIDB* Vol. 1, 684.

138 The general consensus is that Ezekiel 40-48 formed a separate unit as a programmatic vision of the restored temple. It provides a new vision of idealized society for a new Israelite community. The text assumes its present form in the late exilic period of the early Persian period, probably during Darius I. See discussion in Tuell, *The Law of the Temple in Ezekiel 40-48*, 14.

139 For more detail see Wright, "Unclean and Clean," *ABD* Vol. 6, 729-741.

29:36; Lev 8:15). In other words, the purification offering in Ezekiel is meant for purification of the sancta not the worshipper.

Ezekiel 45:13-17 is another example in which we find different sacrifices other than חטאת. The effects of these sacrifices in the context of purification may be described by the verb 'כפר.'[140] Ezekiel uses חטא and טהר along with כפר, as it is used in the priestly literature.[141] The notion of appeasement of God can be construed as "to purify" in some instances in Leviticus.[142] While כפר has an effect on purification of the sancta in the priestly writings, here in Ezekiel, offerings and sacrifices are prescribed to make atonement for the house of Israel. Sacrifices will not only appease Yahweh, but will cleanse the people.

In 44:25-27 we find purification of a priest from corpse contamination. Ezekiel's ordinance concerning contact with the corpse of immediate relatives agrees with the priestly law of purity (Lev 21:1-3; Num 19). Here in Ezekiel, there is no detailed prescribed way of purification. A defiled priest must remain away from the Temple for seven days after purification and then resume his service at the sanctuary. We can assume that here Ezekiel understands the prescription of purification rituals in the priestly system found in Numbers 19:7, 11-12 and avoids the details.[143] Water is the purifying material according to Numbers 19. This passage alludes to the bathing of the body, washing of clothes, and isolation for seven days. Ezekiel might have shared the same procedure in the purification of corpse contamination.

In Ezekiel, the purification of Israel is a divine action. One of the best examples is found in Ezekiel 36:22-34.[144] This text says that Yahweh intends to re-

140 Majority opinion is that כפר refers to "ransom" in the Hebrew Bible. In this sense, it has a meaning of action and its effect. It refers to act of pardon. It generally refers to an aversion of God's wrath or an appeasement of God. Translating the term as to purify or purification is plausible as it is used in the context of ritual cleansing of the Tent of the meeting and the altar and the holiest part of the sanctuary (Lev 16:33a). Also compare with offerings in the new Temple in Ezekiel 45. See detailed discussion about various approaches to the translation of the verb כפר in Sklar, "Sin and Impurity," 18-23.

141 Cf. Leviticus 14:52-53; 16:30. See also discussion in Jay Sklar, "Sin and Impurity: Atoned or Purified? Yes!," in *Perspectives on Purity and Purification in the Bible*, eds. Baruch J. Schwartz, David P. Wright, Jeffrey Stackert, and Natphtali S. Meshel LBH/OTS 474 (New York: T&T Clark, 2008), 22-23.

142 See Lev 4:20, 26, 31, 35; 5:6,10; 16:6, 11-34. Expression such as "he shall purge/purify the holiest part of the sanctuary (וכפר את־מקדש הקדש), and he shall purge/purify the Tent of Meeting and the altar (ואת־אהל מועד את־המזבח וצפר) (Lev 16:33a) shows that כפר functions as purification.

143 Cf. Block, *Ezekiel 25-48*, 643.

144 For the literary unit see different commentaries. The literary characteristics in v. 28 and 31 with the use of אנכי (longer form of I) cf. Jer 11:4; 24:7; 30:22) may indicate 24-32 are a redactional amplification to ascribed to Ezekiel's school and yet to be regarded as fully prophetic in their authority. The overlap of material in vv 24-32 with other parts of the book could certainly point in the direction of later redaction. Cf. Allen *Ezekiel 20-48*, 177-178.

sanctify his holy name by restoring Israel (v. 23), by purifying them from all their defilements (v. 25). Here the language of purity, partly metaphorical and partly literal, is used as a metaphor for forgiveness and cleansing. Purification with water does not imply any ceremonial act; but is reminiscent of priestly legislations.[145] The people will be gathered from exile and brought into their own land (v. 24). Yahweh will cleanse them of defiling filth by means of cleansing water (v. 25). The filth associated with the people is here removed by Yahweh, and by logical extension, their moral incapacity will also be eradicated in the cleansing.[146] Purification will take place with the ingathering of the exilic group from "out of all the lands" "into your land" (v. 24).

This suggests that for Ezekielian authors, restoration and purification will take place with the exilic group. Purification is also alluded to in other restoration prophecies where כפרת implies divine purification like Ezekiel 16:59-63. In this oracle, we find Ezekiel using deliberate words of condemnation along with the promise of restoration: "So you will remember and be ashamed and not be able to open your mouth again because of your shame, when I covered for you (בכפרי לך) all that you have done" (v. 63). Restoration is based solely on the basis of their ancient covenant rather than their own worthiness.[147] Hence, restoration is an act of divine purification.

3. Summary and Conclusion

In the above discussion I demonstrate that purity in the book of Ezekiel is a status required for Israel in order to keep her identity as a people of God. Israel is condemned for the many cases of impurity that affect the sanctity and purity of the sanctuary, the land, and the name of Yahweh. For the prophet, purity and holiness interact each other in Israel's relationship to God and in community life. Sin and impurity are two interrelated concepts but they are not synonymous. In Ezekiel, natural impurities are generally not sinful whereas certain kinds of impurities that defile the sanctuary are known as sinful. Impurity and sin are identical when it expresses the cultic sin of Israel, such as idolatry, bloodshed, and sexual crimes. The impurities that affect Israel's relationship to God are both physical and moral; both cultic and ethical.

Ezekiel's interpretation of purity closely resembles the priestly concept of purity in explaining the impurities of Israel. Impurities such as menstruation, corpse, food, bloodshed, child sacrifice, idolatry, and sexual misconduct lead to defilement of the people, the land, the sanctuary, and the name of God. Ezekiel strongly indicts Israel, particularly Jerusalem and its inhabitants as offenders of the purity regulations. In the description of impurities, the book strategically distinguishes between the exiles and those who remained in Judah during the

---

145 See Num 19:13, 20; Zech 13:1. Cf. G. A. Cooke, *Ezekiel,* 391.

146 Cf. Lapsey, *Can These Bones Live?* 164-165.

147 Tova Ganzel, "Description of the Restorations of Israel in Ezekiel," *VT* 60 (2010): 204.

exile. Jerusalem and its inhabitants suffered heavy indictments. If the impurities and sins of the exiles are ever mentioned, they are connected with purification and restoration. In social identity terms – there is clear ingroup and outgroup differentiation in Ezekiel with a boundary construction of purity rules. While Israel's impurity is a very important issue of the prophetic oracle, there are less systematic procedures of purification rituals in the book. Purification rituals such as sacrifices and offerings are meant for cleansing of the sanctuary rather than the people. Purification is the act of God which will be realized with restoration of the exiles. In other words, purification is the divine action to be realized with the exilic group.

According to the prophet, Yahweh is the holy God, who demands purity in all walks of life. Jerusalem and its inhabitants failed to live up to these demands. In the perspective of Mary Douglas, those who remained in Judah failed to abide with the law of holiness of God and purity of the community because holiness and purity require that individuals shall conform to the class to which they belong.[148] The book of Ezekiel, which is written in the context of the exilic and early post exilic age, demands redefinition of a pure community who would represent the "true Israel." The claim of those who remained in Judah during the exile needs to be reevaluated and reexamined with strict rule of boundary mechanism. The non-exilic group becomes the outgroup whereas those who experienced the exile becomes the ingroup according to the purity rules. As Feinstein argues "purity codes police boundaries of pure and impure by attempting to regulate people's behavior in response to particular stimuli."[149] In response to group conflicts and competition in the sixth century BCE, the book of Ezekiel, which received its final form in the late exilic setting provided strict purity rules as boundary markers to define who is in and who is not in the group. In their response, the Ezekiel's school domesticated the purity system as a boundary marker and to define group norms. I will explore this in more detail with exegetical studies of relevant texts in the next chapters.

148 Mary Douglas, *Purity and Danger*, 53.

149 Feinstein, "Sexual Pollution in the Hebrew Bible," 123.

Chapter 4

Purity and Group Identity in the Book of Ezekiel

General Introduction

The book of Ezekiel covers the period of the fall of Jerusalem and the exile when the Israelite communities were in different geographical locations. The book contains different theological discussions among them, what constitutes purity and group identity. As I have discussed in previous chapters, exilic literatures, including the book of Ezekiel, contain resourceful insights about the life situations of the exilic age when groups of Israelites engaged in intergroup conflicts and went through an identity crisis. In response to this crisis, various theological and ideological discussions emerged in this literature. Certain books of the exilic literature reflect both relationships and conflicts between the community of those who remained in Judah and the exiles. As an ideology, much of this literature advocates ingroup favoritism and outgroup delegitimization. Dalit Rom-Shiloni claims, "....the book of Ezekiel is the voice of the Exiles that created exilic ideology of exclusivity to redefine religio-national identity of the Exiles."[1] Coming from the tradition of the Zadokite priesthood, the book emphasizes holiness and purity as normative for the Israelites as the people of God. As discussed in the preceding chapter, purity is not merely a physical condition and a ritual system in the book of Ezekiel. It

1 Dalit Rom-Shiloni, "Ezekiel as the Voice of the Exiles and Constructor of Exilic Ideology," in *HUCA* LXXVI (Cincinnati: Hebrew Union College-Jewish Institute of Religion, 2006), 41-43. Also see further discussion in Dalit Rom-Shiloni, "Ezekiel and His Book: Homogeneity of Exilic Perspective," in Rom-Shiloni, *Exclusive Inclusivity: Identity Conflicts Between the Exiles and the People Who Remained (6th-5th Centuries BCE)*, (New York: Bloomsbury, 2013), 139-196.

is a relgio-cultural phenomenon that played an important role in social/group relationships. It is a religio-cultural system through which Israel relates to God and identifies who is in the community of Israel and who is not. Impurity as the opposite of purity is a failure to conform to community rules in Israel's worship of Yahweh and in her socio-cultural system. Hence, purity is a boundary marker in social identification in the book of Ezekiel.

These chapters investigate selected passages in the book of Ezekiel to explore how purity plays an important role in group identification. There are a number of passages in the book where we can trace the discussion about purity and its relationship to group identity. I will limit my discussion to four chapters concentrating on selected passages. My choice of four selected passages will represent four main issues of purity and group identification in the book of Ezekiel. (1) First, in the first chapter of the exegesis (Ezekiel 11:14-21; 33:25-29), I investigate how in the book of Ezekiel we find explicit identification of the exiles and those who are in the homeland. (2) Second, the next chapter (Ezekiel 22:1-16) discuses how the book delegitimizes the inhabitants of the homeland. (3) The third chapter of part two (Ezekiel 22:1-16) investigates how the exiles are identified as the restored and purified community. (4) The last chapter (Ezekiel 37:15-28) explores how an exclusive community is envisioned in the new temple-based community. The selected passages are studies in conversation with other relevant texts both from the book of Ezekiel and other books of the Hebrew Bible. My goal is to explore the use of purity ideas and language in the book of Ezekiel as these relate to group identification between the exiles and those who remained in Judah during the exilic period. To identify those who are deported to Babylonia in the exilic age, I employ terms such as the exiles, the *golah*, the deportees, and the exilic group/community. I also employ terms such as the non-exiles, the inhabitants of the land, the survivors in Judah, and the homelanders to identify those who remained in the land. The format of the exegetical study includes investigation of the nature and design, which includes form/genre, structure and socio-historical settings, translation of the chosen passages, and text analysis and comments. I will then explore the implications in relation to purity and group identity with a conclusion.

Explicit Identification of the Ingroup and the Outgroup
(Ezekiel 11:14-21 and 33:25-29)

1. Introduction

Ezekiel 11:14-21 and 33:25-29 can be taken as the texts that illustrate Ezekiel's response to the exilic experience in general and group conflicts between the two communities in particular. In these texts we find purity as a significant concept of group identity in the exilic age. These texts apply purity ideas in order to exclude or include a particular group in the community of Israel. The two texts are both categorized as Disputation Speeches.[2] The genre of prophetic disputation speech is counted among the primary sources.[3] Disputation Speeches are characterized by three-tier literary structures: (a) Accusation/case, (b) Opposing views expressed, and (c) Punishment/oath (prophetic response).[4] It is the general opinion that the two oracles –11:14-21 and 33:23-29 are complementary in that the one in chapter 11 focuses on the exiled Judeans and the one in chapter 33 focuses on those in the homeland.[5] In fact, the texts address both of these communities. The two passages have the same issue: exclusion of the Judahite community of the homeland and advocacy for the exiled Judeans as the 'true Israel.' Hence, Ezekiel 11:14-21 and 33:25-29 are focusing on the same subject yet possibly in different contexts. They answer the question: "who is the true Israel and who is not." For a more in depth evaluation I will discuss the two oracles in succession.

Rom-Shiloni describes these two passages as explicit disputations between the two groups.[6] The disputations are shown by the statements of differentiations such as: ישבי ירושלים (the inhabitants of Jerusalem 11:5) and בני עמך (your fellow country men – fellow exiles 33:30) or בית ישראל (house of Israel 33:10; 37:11). The speeches of those who remained in the land are viewed as baseless (11:3, 15; 33:24) whereas the prophet expresses promise for the future of the exiles (11:17). Ezekiel's response to the claim of those who remained in Judah is negative; he pronounces judgment (33:27-28 cf. 11:1-13) whereas the prophet offers consolation to the exiles (11:16-20). Hence, these two disputation speeches suggest the opposing sides of the controversy, favoring one group and rejecting

2 Daniel I. Block, *The Book of Ezekiel Chapters 1-24* NICOT (Grand Rapids, Michigan: Eerdmans, 1998), 235. & Daniel I. Block, *The Book of Ezekiel Chapters 25-48* NICOT (Grand Rapids: Michigan, Eerdmans, 1998), 262. Rom-Shiloni, *Exclusive Inclusivity*, 142.

3 See Adrian Graffy, *A Prophet Confronts His People: The Disputation Speech in the Prophets*. An Bib 104 (Rome: Biblical Institute, 1984), 42-44.

4 Block, *Ezekiel 25-48*, 258.

5 See Leslie C. Allen, *Ezekiel 1-19* WBC Vol. 28 (Waco, Texas: Word Books, 1990), 133.

6 Other disputation speeches are: (a) Refutations of Jerusalemite assertions (11:1-13, 14-21; 12:21-25; 18:1-20; 33:23-29) and (b) refutations of Exiles' pronouncements (12:26-28; 20:1-38; 33:10-20; 37:1-14). See Rom-Shiloni, *Exclusive Inclusivity*, 142.

the other group. These two speeches may suggest opposing sides, but they are still both represented by the author(s) of Ezekiel who is obviously biased towards the exiles. Thus, purity is domesticated as an ideology and a norm for group identity.

2. Ezekiel 11:14-21: Choice of the Exilic Group

2.1. Nature and Design

Scholars are of the opinion that Ezekiel chapters 8-11 is organized into a single visionary experience whose complexity indicates a considerable literary effort.[7] Allen asserts that the framework of the vision is firmly set within Ezekiel's prophetic ministry to the Judean prisoners of war in Babylonia.[8] But in the pericope of chapters 8-11, 11: 14-21 is considered originally to be an independent oracle, which is integrated in to a larger whole of the vision account.[9] The identification of a prophetic word formula in v. 14 and the prophetic utterance formula at the end of v. 21 gives a hint of an independent unit.[10] However, the words in this unit are a response to Ezekiel's expression of alarm in 11:13. Though independent in structure, thematic connection with the preceding unit is obvious.[11] The oracle is framed in a pattern of disputation speeches. Whatever the history of this text, its present literary form follows the structure of a modified disputation speech. The unit may be structured as: (a) Preamble (v. 14), (b) the Thesis (v. 15), (c) the Refutation (v. 16), (d) the Counter thesis (vv. 17-20), and (e) Epilogue (v. 21).

2.2. Setting

Regarding the setting, some scholars attribute this entire section to post-Ezekiel scribes, or at least to a post-587 period in Ezekiel's career.[12] M. E. Andrew argues that the ill-founded confidence in possessing the land while the exiles are far away suggests a post- 587 BCE.[13] Walter Eichrodt considers this unit as a postscript to

---

7 See Greenberg, *Ezekiel 1-20*, 192.

8 Allen, *Ezekiel 1-19*, 129.

9 Greenberg and Allen argue so. See Greenberg, *Ezekiel 1-20*, 192; Allen *Ezekiel 1-19*, 129. Some includes v. 13 within the unit, which is the vision report and the death of Petaliah son of Benaiah. See Steven S. Tuel, *Ezekiel* NIBC Vol. 15 (Peabody, Massachusetts: Hendrickson, 2009), 57.

10 Thus Hals affirms 11:14-21 as an independent unit. See Ronald M. Hals, *Ezekiel* FOTL Vol. XIX (Grand Rapids, Michigan: Eerdmans, 1989), 69.

11 Cf. Margaret S. Odell, *Ezekiel*, Smith & Helwys Bible Commentary (Macon, Georgia: Smyth & Helwys Publishing, Inc., 2005), 123.

12 Hence, William H. Brownlee, *Ezekiel 1-19*, WBC Vol. 28 (Waco, Texas: Word Books Publihser, 1986), 163. Allen, *Ezekiel 1-19,* 133, G. A. Cooke, *A Critical and Exegetical Commentary on the Book of Ezekiel Vol. 1*. ICC (New York: Charles Scribner's Sons, 1937), 121.

13 M. E. Andrew, *Responsibility and Restoration: The Course of the Book of Ezekiel* (Dunedin, New Zealand: University of Otago Press, 1985), 56. Block also argues that there are sound reasons for post-586 date for the parallel nature of the prophecy with 33:24. See Block, *The Book of Ezekiel Chapters 1-24,* 333.

the Temple Vision (8-11) and that it does not belong to the vision experienced by Ezekiel.[14] While some scholars attribute a late (post 587) setting, the original setting may be before the fall of Jerusalem in 587. The vision is considered to originate in the prophet's own setting in Babylonia.[15]

We assume that Ezekiel's audience was the exilic group; even his severe judgments directed against Jerusalem are intended to bolster the self-confidence of his actual audience (the exiles).[16] Greenberg concedes that vv. 14-21 appear to have been an originally independent oracle and its dating before the fall is defensible, even likely.[17] Zimmerli's argument is persuasive when he says that the oracle undoubtedly goes back to the period when the Jerusalem sanctuary was still standing, i.e. before the year 587 BCE.[18] I argue for the period between 597 and 587 for two reasons: (1) the inhabitants of Jerusalem are referred to here while 33:23-29 speaks of the inhabitants of the waste places, (2) it appears that the situation of the land was better than that of the exiles at this time.[19] Hence, the period between 597 and 587 seems to be the original setting of the unit. However, a later redaction or addition is also possible, probably in the late exilic period.[20]

2.3. Text Analysis and Comments

2.3.1. The Thesis – False Claim of the Homelanders (vv. 14-15)

v. 14. The word of Yahweh came to me saying,

v. 15. "Son of man, your brothers, your brothers, your own kind[21] *and all the house of Israel, all of them who are the inhabitants of Jerusalem have said to them, "They have gone far*[22] *from Yahweh; to us this land is given for a possession."*

This section is introduced by the preamble, a prophetic introductory formula "The word of the Lord came to me." (v. 14), and Yahweh's addressing Ezekiel as "mortal" or "human" (בן־אדם). The thesis or the claim of the homelanders is found in verse 15. The central focus of the thesis is the exiles. The exilic community is

14 Walter Eichrodt, *Ezekiel: A Commentary* (Philadelphia: The Westminster Press, 1970), 142.

15 Allen, *Ezekiel 1-19*, 129.

16 Cf. John W. Wevers, *Ezekiel* NCB (London: Thomas Nelson and Sons Ltd., 1969), 96.

17 Moshe Greenberg, *Ezekiel 1-20* AB Vol. 22 (Garden city, New York: Doubleday & Company Inc., 1983), 204.

18 Zimmerli compares the passage with 33:24 "inhabitants of the ruins" which for him refers to the land after 587BCE. See Zimmerli, *Ezekiel 1*, 263.

19 Paul M. Joyce also shares this idea. See Paul M. Joyce, *Ezekiel: A Commentary*, LHB/OTS 482 (New York: T&T Clark, 2007), 110.

20 A later redaction is likely with the addition of promise of restoration with giving one heart and new spirit in vv. 17-20, that points to second-generation exiles. Cf. Odell, *Ezekiel*, 124.

21 LXX and Syriac have "fellow exiles." See the meaning of this phrase below.

22 Literally "go away" as implied by the qal imperative. Greenberg translates "remove yourselves from Yahweh." As suggested by textual emendation of the BHS, it is to be read as perfect 3rd common plural – "They have gone far/away."

addressed with different designations. (1) "Your brothers, your brothers" (אחיך אחיך). This indicates the prophet's involvement in the exilic community. The term is also used for the non-exiles in a contest of judgment.[23] (2) "Your kindred" (אנשׁי גאלתך). This designation literally means 'the men of your redemption (גאל) suggesting that Yahweh's thoughts of the exiles are the next-kin to be redeemed.[24] It can also refer to the circle of relatives referring to Ezekiel's family.[25] (3) "The whole house of Israel" (כל בת ישרעל). This designation is an unusual stress on the exiles as the whole people. It indicates the prophet's belief that the future of Israel now lies entirely with the exilic group.[26] It also suggests that the exiles are the remnant of Israel, to whom the city and the land belong.[27] This designation is ironic, as the exiles did not represent the whole house of Israel. With self-categorization, Ezekiel identifies the exiles as the only legitimate people of Israel.

The quotation, "they have gone far from the Lord; to us this land is given for a possession (למורשה)," is undoubtedly the claim of the inhabitants of Jerusalem and Judah. The inhabitants of Judah claimed that the land now belonged to them. This statement (separated far from God) represents the traditional view that God and the land were so associated that separation from the land means separation form God.[28] They invoked the right to redeem property granted under Levitical law. The Jubilee year stipulated redemption of property, within the family and tribal group (Lev 25:25-35).[29] Throughout Deuteronomy, an important refrain is that the people are about to enter the land that Yahweh is giving them as a possession (Deut 4:38; 15:4; 32:4). The implication is that just as Yahweh dispossessed the previous inhabitants of the land in order to give it to the Hebrews, God has now dispossessed some of the Judahites and given the land to others.[30] The inhabitants of Jerusalem obviously thought of themselves as such, for the promise to Abraham was bound up with the possession of 'the land,' and now they alone were in possession although under the imperial rule of Babylonia.[31] The thesis is clear – Those who remained in Judah during the exilic

23 Wevers, *Ezekiel*, 96.

24 Cf. S. Fisch, *Ezekiel: Hebrew Text & English Translation with an Introduction and Commentary* (London: The Soncino Press, 1950), 60.

25 Block, *Ezekiel 1-24*, 347.

26 Keith W. Carley, *The Book of the Prophet Ezekiel* (London: Cambridge University Press, 1974), 70.

27 Robert W. Jenson, *Ezekiel*, Brazos Theological Commentary on the Bible (Grand Rapids, Michigan: Brazos Press, 2009), 97.

28 See 1 Sam 26:19; Ruth 1:16; 2 Kings 5:17-19; Hos 9:3.

29 Lamar Eugene Cooper, Sr., *Ezekiel*, NAC Vol. 17 (USA: Broadman & Holman Publishers, 1994), 142,

30 Nancy R. Bowen, *Ezekiel* AOTC (Nashville: Abingdon Press, 2010), 56.

31 D. M. G. Stalker, *Ezekiel: Introduction and Commentary* (London: SCM Press Ltd, 1968), 113.

age claimed for themselves possession of the land and hence the true heirs of Abrahamic promise.

2.3.2. The Refutation - Yahweh's Sanctuary Among the Exiles (v. 16)

v. 16. Therefore, says the Lord Yahweh, "though[32] I have removed them among the nations and that I have scattered them in the lands, yet I have became a little[33] sanctuary for them in the lands where they have gone there."

The prophet refutes the claims of those who remained by asserting Yahweh's choice of the exiles. Yahweh is present among the exilic group in spite of their expulsion from the land. Ezekiel affirms that it is among the exiles that the Lord's presence is manifested, albeit in small measure. The exiles were scattered among other countries (Babylonia and Egypt), yet, it does not mean that Yahweh abandoned them. To the contrary, Yahweh pitched his sanctuary among them. Yahweh has not gone away from the exiles as Jerusalem's inhabitants claim. Instead the Lord has abandoned Jerusalem.

The exact meaning of the saying, "I was to them as a little sanctuary" (ואהי להם למקדש מעט) is debated.[34] It could be translated in many ways. Zimmerli understands it to mean "the limited forms of a worship practiced far from the sanctuary."[35] The phrase generates several possible meanings. It may imply the presence of the Lord in the person of Ezekiel, that Ezekiel himself becomes an intermediary between God and his people.[36] William A. Tooman translates it "I will be a temporary sanctuary" insisting that מעט can be translated as an adjective of time and 11:17 indicates that Yahweh will gather them to the land of Israel in the future.[37] One possible implication is the concept of sacred space. It indicates

32 כי has a causal meaning of "because," "that" "since." It is to be taken as assertive sense with a meaning of "although." Allen argues that since it has a positive meaning in this verse, it cannot be causal. See Allen, *Ezekiel 1-19*, 128.

33 מעט can have a substantive meaning of "little" "small," appositional meaning as "of little help," or "the least of all," and temporal meaning as "short time," "brief moment." See *HALOT* Vol. 2, 611.

34 מקדש is usually translated "sanctuary" or "tabernacle." In the Pentateuch, Yahweh tells Moses to make a מקדש so that he may dwell among them. (Exodus 25:8-9). Yahweh made his abode the מקדש on the mountain when Israelites were in their journey (Exodus 15:17). It may connote a temporary abode associates with a nomadic lifestyle and tents other than a temple or a specific place of cultic installation. See more discussion in, Rannfrid I. Thelle, *Approaches to the "Chosen Place:" Accessing a Biblical Concept*, LHB/OTE 564 (New York: T&T Clark, 2012), 97-100. The term occurs 30 times in Ezekiel mostly referring to the temple and temple area.

35 Walther Zimmerli, *Ezekiel 1*, 262.

36 So thus Tuell, *Ezekiel*, 58; Bowen, *Ezekiel*, 56. Stalker writes that Yahweh was a sanctuary because they had Ezekiel to make them known the will of God." See Stalker, *Ezekiel*, 114.

37 William A. Tooman, "Covenant and Presence in the Composition and Theology of Ezekiel," in *Divine Presence and Absence in Exilic and Post-Exilic Judaism*, FAT 61, eds. Nathan MacDonald and Izaak D. de Hulster (Tubingen: Mohr Siebeck, 2013), 160-161.

that God's presence is not limited to Jerusalem's Temple, or to Jerusalem, or even to the territory of Israel.[38] In the writings of the prophets, except in Ezekiel 40-48, we do not find the temple as a particularly significant feature.[39] But for Ezekiel, the significance of מקדש is explicitly mentioned. Yahweh now abandoned the Jerusalem temple and he moved to the land of the exiles.[40] This is also implied by the following verses that the כבוד יהוה moved to the east (11:22-23).

This verse echoes chapter 10 where the cherubim moved to the Temple's east gate, moving away from the city abandoning Jerusalem (10:19). This verse implies that Yahweh will offer no such sanctuary to the homelanders. God's כבוד goes with the people in Babylon as a comforting presence.[41] In the same way, the prophet beholds the return of the כבוד יהוה to his Temple and his reenthronement (Ezek 43:4,7). For the prophet, Yahweh is not confined to the Temple in Jerusalem.

Divine presence and absence in the Temple is an important theological theme in the Hebrew Bible. In the monarchic Israel, Yahweh is understood to be enthroned and present in the Temple (1 Sam 4:4ff; 1 King 8:10-11; 2 King 19:14f., Cf 2 Chro 7:1-3.) In contrast, Deuteronomy emphasized on the conception of the dwelling of a שם (name) of Yahweh in the Temple (Deut 12:11;14:23f., 16:11cf. 1 King 8:16, 18ff.). The theology was replaced in P by the dwellings of the כבוד in the ark, of the holiest place of the Temple (Exo 25:22; Num 7:89). In Ezekiel we find Yahweh's presence and absence in the temple and among his people. Von Rad points out that Ezekiel represents a theological shift beyond P's representation describing the appearance of the כבוד יהוה not only in

---

38 Carley, *The Book of the Prophet Ezekiel*, 70. In Deuteronomy we find the centrality of the Temple yet less detailed description of cultic norms. The Deuteronomistic history also suggests that the Temple is the place where the name of God is to be found (1 Kings 8:29 Cf. Deut 12:4). Solomon's prayer indicates that Temple cannot contain God (1 King 8:27). For discussion on the Temple in Jerusalem see Jon D. Levenson, "The Temple and the World," *Journal of Religion* 64 no. 3 (1984): 275-298.

39 Robert R. Carroll insists that due to the paucity of detail and generality of reference to the temple in the prophets, whether the first or second temple is at best a textual one. See Robert P. Carroll, "So What Do We know about the Temple? The Temple in the Prophets," in *Second Temple Studies 2: Temple Community in the Persian Period*, JSOTSup 175, eds. Tamara C. Eskenazi and Kent H. Richards, (Sheffield: Sheffield Academic Press, 1994), 37.

40 This is implied by God's comments about the Judahites in 8:6. "Do you see what they are doing-great abominations, which the house of Israel is doing in order to be far from my sanctuary?" Yahweh is now far from the Jerusalemites and his presence is now with the people in diaspora.

41 This idea is questioned on the ground that there is little indication that in Ezekiel that יהוה כבוד goes to be with the exiles. But, this text suggests that perhaps God also goes into exile, not to Babylon, but away from the covenant community (of Judah). See discussion in Bowen, *Ezekiel*, 57. See also further discussion in Nathan Macdonald and Izaak K. De Hulstler (eds), *Divine Presence and Absence in Exilic and Post-Exilic Judaism* (Tubingen, Germany: Mohr Siebeck, 2013).

the Temple, but to the restored people.[42] John T. Strong reflects von Rad's idea that "Ezekiel's innovation was the revival of an older *kabod* tradition that inserted and element of mobility and impermanence in to the conception of Yahweh's presence."[43] Ezekiel, therefore, represents a middle ground that Yahweh's glory is not confined to a particular place. Thus, the presence of the כבוד יהוה among his people indicates an effort to recognize the presence of Yahweh through all of creation and to explain the significance of Yahweh's destruction of Jerusalem and the Temple itself.[44]

The presence of the divine in the temple along with the rationality of the cult in ancient Israel was an issue of contention in the prophetic literature. Pre-exilic prophets such as Amos, Micah, Isaiah I, and Jeremiah denounced cultic acts due to their corrupt practices.[45] However, we do not find direct rejection of Temple worship or the cult per se. Isaiah 66:1 seems to reject the Temple in the manner of the pre-exilic prophets.[46] Post-exilic prophets such as Haggai and Zechariah are presented as being in favor of rebuilding the Temple. As shown in this text and other prophetic texts, it appears that the cult per se is not rejected; just those practices polluted by crimes and injustices.[47]

As stated in chapter 3, the sacredness of the sanctuary in the book of Ezekiel is shown by the presence and departure of the hwhy dwbk in/from the sanctuary/house of the Lord (הבית) in Jerusalem (8:4; 10:19; 11:16, 22-23; 43:4). In the Exodus tradition, Yahweh meets his people at the dwelling place (משכן),

42 See detail in G. von Rad, "Deuteronomy's 'Name' Theology and the Priestly Document's 'Kabod' Theology," in *Studies in Deuteronomy*, trans. David Stalker (Chicago: Henry Regnery Company, 1953), 37-44.

43 John T. Strong, "God's Kabod: The Presence and Absence of Yahweh in the Book of Ezekiel," in *The Book of Ezekiel: Theological and Anthropological Perspectives,* SBL Symposium Series 9, eds. Margaret S. Odell & John T. Strong (Atlanta: SBL, 2000), 71 (69-95).

44 Cf, Marveen A. Sweeney, *TANAK: A Theological and Critical Introduction to the Jewish Bible* (Minneapolis: Fortress Press, 2012), 322.

45 See Amos 5:21-22; Mic 6:6-8; Isa 1:11-13; Jer 7:22.

46 The text says, "Heaven is my throne, and the earth is my footstool; what is the house that you would build me, and what is the place of my rest?"

47 John Barton argues that the prophets of ancient Israel sought for true religion, who not only concerned observance of ritual stipulations, but also sought right social relationship. They were against the wrong practices both by cultic officials and the worshippers. This is also the conclusion of Ronald Hendel who stresses that "the anti-ritualism of the prophets is wedded to their theory of ideal society." Barton and Hendel apply Mary Douglas' ritual symbolism that interprets both ritualism and anti-ritualism as characteristics of religious cultures of society. See discussion in John Barton, "The Prophets and the Cult," in *Temple and Worship in Biblical Israel*, ed. John Day, LHB/OTE 422 (London: T&T Clark, 2005), 11-122; Ronald Hendel, "Away from Ritual: The Prophetic Critique," in *Social Theory and the Israelite Religion: Essays in Retrospect and Prospect*, ed. Saul M. Olyan (Atlanta: SBL, 2012), 60-79. See also Mary Douglas, *Natural Symbols: Explorations in Cosmology* (London: Penguin Books, 1970).

and at the tent of the meeting (אהל מעד).[48] The כבוד יהוה is manifested in these places (Exo 25:8; 29:43-56). Yahweh's כבוד makes the meeting places sacred.[49] In Deuteronomy the name of God dwells in the sanctuary (Deut 12:5, 11; 14:23-24; 16:11). Thus, God's glory (כבוד) and God's name (שׁם) are the invisible signs of God's dwelling among his people. The moving of כבוד יהוה from Jerusalem to the land of the exiles has a significant meaning for Ezekiel. While Yahweh turned away from the homelanders who are represented as polluting the cult, he moved his presence to the exiles. The exiles are not far from Yahweh; there is great hope for them. It also indicates that if the God of Israel is present anywhere, that God can only be with the exiles. In other words, the exilic group is the chosen group with whom the holy God is present. Any future for Israel can only realistically proceed from the exile.[50] Thus, exile itself can be a sacred space when God is there. Two things are clear here: (1) the sanctuary is no longer a place of meeting for Israel with God, and (2) God's presence has withdrawn from the sanctuary in Jerusalem due to their pollution and now dwells among the exiles.[51] The author of this passage portrays Yahweh's choice and rejection in terms of withdrawal of divine presence from Jerusalem and dwelling with the exiles in Babylonia.

2.3.3. The Counterthesis (vv. 17-20)

(a) Promise of the Land and Purification of the Land by the Exiles (vv. 17-18)
v. 17. Therefore declare, the Lord Yahweh said, I will gather you[52] *from the nations and I shall assemble you from the lands where you were scattered among them.*
v. 18. I will give you the land of Israel. And when they come there they will remove all its detestable things and its abominations from it.

These verses continue to address the exiles with the promise of restoration and purification. It is also a kind of reply to the Jerusalemites who are viewed as having false claim of landownership. The promise is that Yahweh will gather them and assemble them - "I will gather you and assemble you" (וקבצתי אתכם ... ואספתי אתכם), and grant the land of Israel - "I shall give to you the land of Israel"

48 Van Seters argues that meting for religious purpose at the Tent of the Meeting was already practiced among the Jewish exiles in Babylonia. See more discussion in John Van Seters, "The Tent of the Meeting in the Yahwist and the Origin of the Synagogue," *SJOT* 29, no. 1 (2015): 1-10.

49 See discussion in John I. Durham, *Exodus* WBC, Vol. 3 (Nashville: Thomas Nelson Publishers, 1987), 354-355, 396-397.

50 Cf. Andrew, *Responsibility and Restoration*, 57-58.

51 See detailed discussion of the absence and presence of God in Ezekiel in John F. Kutsko, *Between Heaven and Earth: Divine Presence and Absence in the Book of Ezekiel, BJS* Vol. 7 (Winona Lake, Ind: Eisenbrauns, 2000).

52 The LXX has third personal pronouns (αυτοις) throughout verse 17 to harmonize verse 18 "when they come there..." It is not necessary to translate as "them" as the address is the exiles here.

(לכם את־אדמת ישראל). The Septuagint normalizes the text by changing all the 2nd personal pronouns to 3rd plural thereby suggesting the Jerusalemites are being addressed.[53] As suggested by some scholars, these verses could be later insertions, probably from second-generation exiles.[54] These verses indicate that a the promise of restoration was addressed to a community not in Jerusalem, but to the exiles as also attested elsewhere.[55] When the exiles return, the Lord will return the land now claimed by Jerusalem's arrogant inhabitants to its rightful owners.

When the deportees return they will purify the land.[56] Purification will include "removing all its detestable practices (כל־שקוציה) and abominations (כל־תועבתיה) from it." שקוצים is always associated with idolatry (Jer 16:28; Dan 9:27; 12:11; Hos 9:10; 2 Chr 15:8; Ezek 5:11; 14:6; 16:36; 18:12). The verb שקץ is used in Lev 11:11, 13, 43; 20:25 of unclean animals and those who eat them.[57] In Ezekiel the term תועבה is frequently used in connection with cultic offences. It refers either to cultic practices or objects which have no proper place in the cult.[58] When the returnees become the owners of the land their first act will be purification of the land from the defilement of idolatry. The people in Jerusalem are presented as unfit to be the possessors of the land because they had maintained the vile and abominable practices, which the returning exiles would have to remove.

(b) The Purified Community (vv. 19-20)

v. 19. And I shall give them one[59] heart and I will put a new spirit within them,[60] and I shall remove a stony heart from their flesh and I shall give to you a heart of flesh. v. 20. In order that they may walk in my statutes and keep my judgments and they shall do them. And they shall be my people and I will be their God.

53 See discussion in Wevers, *Ezekiel*, 97.

54 Zimmerli, *Ezekiel 1*, 263. Wevers, *Ezekiel*, 97. In the same way Odell argues that the audience is neither the actual Jerusalemites not Ezekiel's audience, but a second-generation exiles (restored remnants). See Odell, *Ezekiel*, 124. Also see Thomas Renz, *The Rhetorical Function of the Book of Ezekiel*, VTSup 78 (Leiden: Brill, 1999).

55 We find examples in 20:33-44; 36:16-38; 37:1-14.

56 Verse 18 along with verse 21 reflects the period of the return from exile and renewed interest in worship purified of former faults. Carley, *The Book of the Prophet Ezekiel*, 71.

57 For a discussion about שקוצים "detestable things" see "idol worship" in the previous chapter.

58 Abomination in Ezekiel as an inclusive term used in reference to something repugnant and despicable in either religious-cultic or social-moral sphere. Cf. Tova Ganzel, "The Defilement and Desecration of the Temple in Ezekiel," 371.

59 LXX has ετεραν "another" so "another heart." Vulgate and Syriac read as "new." If we compare with 18:31 and 36:26 - new (חדש) spirit is likely. But one heart implies "undivided heart" which is not tainted by idolatry. Hence, the MT may be retained.

60 The MT has "in your midst." As suggested by many readings including LXX, Syriac, Targum and Vulgate, third person plural "in their midst or within them" is taken here.

When the people cleansed the land, God will transform the people by giving them undivided hearts and putting a new spirit in them. "I will give to them one heart" (ונתתי להם לב אחד) would imply an obedient heart to God. As the context implies, it could mean that their heart will no longer be divided between worship of God and images.[61] Putting a new spirit (רוח חדשה אתן בקרבכם) refers to a new vitality of life. A new heart and a new spirit also occur together in 18:31 and 36:26. As in 18:31 where Ezekiel calls on the people to make for themselves a new heart and a new spirit, this could imply transformation of the human spirit.[62] In 36:26-27 the new spirit is associated with God's Spirit, which he promises to put in Israel. רוח is God's empowering agency for Israel.[63] The usage of רוח as divine being (רוח יהוה) indicates that purification is the initiative of the divine in association with humankind.

When Yahweh's act of renewal is manifested, a heart of flesh would replace a heart of stone. The parallel reference is found in Jeremiah 32:36-41 which possibly shows Jeremiah's influence.[64] Ezekiel never uses the actual words 'new covenant' as in Jeremiah. But, this is implied in this verse as "they shall be my people and I will be their God" in v. 20 which is the covenant formula (cf. Ezek 14:11; 26:28; 37:23, 27; 34:30). The stony heart (לב האבן) refers to the disposition of the Israelites, also expressed as hard-hearted (הזקי־לב 2:4) and stubborn-hearted (לב־וקשי 3:7). In 14:3 & 20:16 we find that the hearts of the Israelites have pursued idols. Hence, this phrase could mean God would remove a heart defiled by idols by giving a heart of flesh, which is tender, yielding and responsive.

The purpose of purification is that "they will be my people, and I shall be their God" (v. 20). The covenant relationship would again be God's gift to the renewed people. Purity in Israel's religious system is linked with relationship with God. Purity is a requisite to be in the community of Israel and to become the people of God. By purification, the exiles will continue to receive divine favor. The exiles are not far from Yahweh; there is great hope for them. In contrast to those living in Jerusalem, Yahweh is near to them. They are not forsaken; they are the recipients of restoration, which is a response to their particular situation.

61 Fisch, *Ezekiel*, 61. Israel had attempted to follow both the Lord and idols (cf. 1 Kings 11:4; 15:3, 14; 2 Kings 20:3).

62 Cf. Block, *Ezekiel 1-24*, 353.

63 רוח occurs 52 times in Ezekiel. Out of these 52 occurrences, about 14 times is to be read as the רוח of God. See Ludwig Kohler and Walter Baumgartner, "רוח," *HALOT* Vol. 2, 1197.

64 Tuell, *Ezekiel*, 59. Block contends that Ezekiel expands Jeremiah's words further by describing the covenant renewal in terms of a heart transplant. See Block, *Ezekiel 1-24*, 353. There are a significant number of points of contact between Ezekiel and Jeremiah in many instances. These are particularly strong where the sayings concerning future hope and restoration from exile appear. Cf. R. E. Clements, "Chronology of Redaction in Ezekiel 1-24," in *Ezekiel and His Book: Textual and Literary Criticism and their Interrelation*, ed. J. Lust (Leuven: Leuven University Press, 1986), 285.

For the prophet, renewal is available to the exiles, not to those who remained in Jerusalem who were condemned as unclean.

2.3.4. Epilogue - The Charge Against the Impure Community (v. 21)

v. 21. And to those[65] *whose heart is going to their detestable things*[66] *and whose heart is going to their abominations, I will give their ways on their heads, says the Lord Yahweh.*

The unit is closed with indignation against the disobedient people whose heart turned towards abominations and detestable things. The punishment is vividly mentioned. "I will give their way (דרכם) on their heads (בראשם)."[67] Here again the charge against Jerusalem and its inhabitants is recapitulated. It is their impurities that cause them to face continued disaster.

2.4. Summary - Divine Presence and Purification

Ezekiel 11:14-21 is a disputation speech directed against the Judahite community who remained in their homeland. It is also a counter thesis that affirms the choice of the exiles who are in Babylonia. The non-exiled Judeans console themselves with a theological claim to the land. But, Ezekiel denounces the claim by pronouncing judgment upon them due to their impurities (11:21). In contrast to judgmental prophecy, Ezekiel affirms the choice of the exiles as his people by dwelling among them in the exile. When the exiles are restored in the land, they will have one heart and a new spirit with which they will purify the land.

There are three important things here: First, we see the presence of the divine sanctuary – a sign of Yahweh's holy presence is in the midst of the exilic group. This narrative confirms that the divine glory now departs to Babylonia, where it will be experienced by the exiles as a "sanctuary." (11:16). According to this text, the exiles though deported in a foreign land were Yahweh's chosen Israel. Choice of the exilic group is represented in the form of the holiness of God who is present with them. The deportees are distant from the land, not from Yahweh. Secondly, the exilic community will purify the land and the people will be purified through the acts of God. The text indicates that when the exiles return to the land, they will abolish all kinds of impurities by removing all detestable

65 The אל here could mean "concerning" or "about" which can be equivalent to על (upon/unto). The two often are used interchangeably in Ezekiel. Cf. Horace D. Hummel, *Ezekiel 1-20* (St. Louis: Concordia Pub. House, 2005), 311.

66 Literally "and unto the heart of detestable things…" The *BHS* proposes emendation to "and after the heart of…" Greenberg believes the MT a corrupt reading and proposes to read as ואשר בקוציהם לבם הלך "But as for those whose hearts follow their loathsome…" See Greenberg *Ezekiel 1-19*, 191. Block translates as "But as for those whose heart is committed to their detestable…" Bock, Ezekiel *1-24*, 342.

67 "Putting their heads upon their deeds" is a no pity formula, a statement of irrevocability of the punishment. This echoes 9:10.

things and abominations. The heart and spirit of the people will be renewed. A new heart and spirit will cleanse the worship of idolatry. While newness of life is promised to the restored community, the fate of the impure people – whose heart goes to detestable things and abominations, is a disaster. Finally, there is a radical representation of Yahweh's move from the temple of Jerusalem to the foreign land. It is quite revolutionary as prior to the exile, Yahweh was viewed as a national god, bound to the land and people of Israel; with special ties to Jerusalem and the Temple. What Ezekiel is presenting is a radical view. The text represents that the holy God dwells with the exilic group manifesting his presence with them whereas as the non-exilic group is rejected due to their impurities.

3. Ezekiel 33:23-29: The Non-Exilic Group as the Outgroup

3.1. Nature and Design

Ezekiel 33 is placed at the opening chapter of the third oracle of Ezekiel known as the 'oracle of hope and salvation' or 'the message of consolation' (33:1-48:35).[68] This chapter forms a bridge between the oracle of judgment (1-32) and restoration (33-48). Block asserts that this chapter laid an oracle of judgment by commissioning of the prophet with a moral and spiritual foundation for a new order.[69] Scholars generally recognize five individual units in this chapter, which are delineated by prophetic formulae and thematic emphases such as: the charge for the prophetic watchman (1-9), the appeal of the prophetic watchman (10-20), the report of a fugitive (21-22), the final disputation (23-29), and the final vindication (30-33).[70] Commentators agree that vv. 23-29 is a separate unit.[71] The oracle bears the structural marks of the classic disputation oracle. This includes (a) the thesis (v. 24), expressed as a quotation of a popular saying, (b) the refutation (vv. 25-26), and (c) the counter thesis (vv. 27-29). The unit is marked by the introductory formula in v. 23 "you son of man" and the recognition formula in v. 29, "They shall know that I am Yahweh." The oracle aims to refute the opinion of those who remained in the land. It refutes the claim that Yahweh judges the exiles since they were deported to Babylonia. The main subject is an accusation against

68 The other oracles are: The Message of Judgment (1:1-24:27) and the Prophecies against foreign nations (25:1-32:32). See Hals, *Ezekiel* FOTL, 3. R. E. Clements treats this chapter as the first chapter of the message of hope in Ezekiel 33-37 in which the chapter carries back readers to the events recorded in chapter 24 (the fall of Jerusalem). See R. E. Clements, *Ezekiel* (Louisville, Kentucky: Westminster John Knox Press, 1996), 150. See also Wevers, *Ezekiel*, 249.

69 Block, *Ezekiel 25-48*, 235.

70 See Block, *Ezekiel 25-48*, 236. Cf. Odell, *Ezekiel*, 413. Some have three main sections by combining vv. 23-29 & 30-33; thus 33:1-20, 21-22, 23-33. See structural patterns of the chapter in Zimmerli, *Ezekiel 1*, 183-200; Hals, *Ezekiel*, 233, 239-240, 242; Greenberg, *Ezekiel 21-37*, 687-688.

71 The unity of vv. 23-29 is maintained by critics such as Greenberg, Block, Allen, Zimmerli, Hals, and others. See Greenberg, *Ezekiel 21-37*, 687; Block, *Ezekiel 25-48*, 258; Zimmerli, *Ezekiel 2*, 198; Allen, *Ezekiel 20-48*, 153; Hals, *Ezekiel*, 242.

the population left behind in the homeland. However, the rhetorical audience is the exilic community. Instead of using the names Jerusalem and Judah, the prophet addresses them as "the people living in the ruins," a stereotypical name for the non-exilic inhabitants of Judah.

3.2. Setting

The setting of this oracle is likely post-587 BCE since the 'inhabitants of these ruins' (v.23) are victims of 587 destruction.[72] 586-585 BCE (in the twelfth year of the exile) is most likely.[73] But this date may not be accurate either since fixing a date could be an editorial gloss to find a suitable introduction for the third division of the book.[74] The date given when compared with the actual date of the fall and destruction of the city given in Jeremiah 39:2; 52:6-7; 52:12 seems to be too late.[75] Sometime must have elapsed between the report of the fall of Jerusalem and this revelation. The text implies some interval, suggested also by the change of mood between vv. 22 & 23.[76] It can be seen elsewhere that Ezekiel had knowledge of remarks that were circulating among those who had been left behind.[77] It could be immediately after the catastrophe of 587.[78] The designation "inhabitants of the ruins (ישבי החרבות) points to those who were left in Judah by Nebuchadnezzar in 587/6 BCE. It is possible that the oracle was the original reply to 11:15 where the survivors of the earlier exile of 597 laid a similar claim to the land involuntarily abandoned by its owners.[79]Thus, it reflects the continuing tension between the inhabitants of Jerusalem and the exiles over inheritance right.

72 Zimmerli, *Ezekiel 2*, 198.

73 The preceding section (vv. 21-22) tells the fugitive from Jerusalem came to Ezekiel in "the twelfth year of our exile, in the tenth month, on the fifth day of the month." This could be 586-585 BCE.

74 So the Greek and the Hebrew traditions alternate between the two numbers (11th year and 12th year) See Eichrodt, *Ezekiel*, 457.

75 In Jeremiah the day of the capture of Jerusalem is in the fourth month of the eleventh year of Zedekiah; that is 587-586 BCE. (Jer 39:2; 52:5-7). Cf. Wevers, *Ezekiel*, 253.

76 Cf. Cook, *Ezekiel*, 366.

77 See Ezek 33:21-22; Cf. Jer 40:10; 52:16.

78 Eichrodt, *Ezekiel*, 461. It is probable that information was about Gedaliah's attempt to repopulate deserted villages with displaced and landless persons in the country (cf. 2 Kings 25:12; Jer 40:9).

79 Wevers, *Ezekiel*, 254. Cf. Block, *Ezekiel 25-48*, 258.

3.3. Text Analysis and Comments

3.3.1. The Thesis – Claim of the Non-Exilic Group (v. 23-24)

v. 23. The word of Yahweh came to me saying,

v. 24. "Son of man, the inhabitants of these ruins[80] *in the land of Israel are saying*[81] *"Abraham was one and he possessed the land; but we are many, the land is given to us for a possession."*

Just as the people of Jerusalem claimed landownership after the 597 deportation (Ezekiel 11), the survivors of Jerusalem's fall in 587 assume that their presence in the land is a sign of divine approval. They claimed the land by mocking the deportees saying:

Abraham was one, and he possessed the land;	אהד היה אברהם ויירש את־הארץ
but we are many; the land is given to us	ואנהנו רבים לנו נתנה הארץ
for a possession.	למורשה:

The Jerusalemites looked down on their deported kin (11:14-21). They were neither concerned for the welfare of their compatriots nor have any anticipation of their return. The people in the devastated land recollect the promise to Abraham, which promised that he should have Canaan as his possession (Gen 12:1-2; 13:14-17). This is one of the seven references to Abraham in the prophets.[82] In fact, the citation and representation of Abraham is inaccurate in this quotation.[83] This promise had been asserted over and over again (Deut 1:8; 6:10; 9:5; 30:20; 34:4). In Isaiah 41:8, Israel is addressed as the "seed of Abraham," In Isaiah 51:2, Israel is summoned to look to Abraham, her father, who was called as an individual and then richly blessed and multiplied.[84] Hence, prophets of the exilic age (Deutero Isaiah & Ezekiel) applied the promises to the patriarch to their own struggle over

---

80 חרבות implies a dislocated land or ruins of cities. See *BDB*, 352.

81 לאמר is qal infinitive construct which marks direct discourse, somewhat a quotation mark in English. The same form is used in the first line of v. 23. See the use of Infinitive construct in Page H. Kelly, *Biblical Hebrew: An Introductory Grammar* (Grand Rapids, Michigan: Eerdmans, 1991), 179-183.

82 Other references are Isa 29:22; 41:8; 51:2; 63:16; Jer 33:26; Mic 7:20.

83 First, Abraham had indeed had a large household when he broke up the Mesopotamian alliance (Gen 14). Second, he never actually possessed the land; he even had not a place to bury his wife (Gen 23). See more detail in Block, *Ezekiel 25-48*, 259-260.

84 The saying is probably based on Genesis 15 in which Abraham, still childless, is promised innumerable descendants and possession of the land. For the homelanders, if one man (Abraham) is enough to establish title to a land, and they are many and it is secure to have the title of "owners of the land." In Isaiah 51:1-2, the prophet alludes to Abraham and Sarah, in order to assert that the exiles will receive Yahweh's blessings, thrive, and grow in number. In this text, God sides with those exiles who have remained faithful to Yahweh an who will accept the Lord's invitation to return. See detailed discussion in Katheryn Pfisterer Darr, "The Book of Ezekiel: Introduction, Commentary, and Reflections," in *NIB* Vol. VI, 1458.

land ownership. Eichrodt paraphrases the self-evaluation of the survivors in Judah as:

> So if God had already shown how great his power was in his dealing with one man, how much more would he do so by replanting the many who had escaped the sword of the enemy in the land and making them grow up again into a new Israel in order to fulfill his promise that the seed of Abraham would become an innumerable multitude! [85]

According to Ezekiel, those who "dwell in the ruins of the land of Israel" claim the land for themselves. But, they were not the owners of the land before; nor are they now. The inhabitants of the homeland based their claim on the patriarchal promise. But for Ezekiel, the survivors have no right to claim the patriarchal promise as their actions show that they have less in common with Abraham than with the foreign nations whom God displaced so that Israel could take possession of the land (cf. Lev 20:22).[86] The reasons for rejection of this claim are listed in the next verses.

3.3.2. The Refutation and Accusation – They are Impure People (vv. 25-26)

v. 25. Therefore say to them, "Thus says the Lord Yahweh; you eat blood[87] *and you lift up your eyes towards your idols, and you shed blood. Shall you possess the land?*
v.26. You stand on your sword, you did abominations and a man defiles himself[88] *with his neighbor's wife. And shall you possess the land?"*

The refutation is introduced by "therefore say to them," (לכן אמר אלהם) and the messenger formula "thus says the Lord Yahweh" (כה־אמר אדני יהוה). These counter their claim by condemning their character. The six specific accusations fall into two groups, each group ending with the rhetorical question, "shall you possess the land?"

You eat (on) the blood,	על־הדם תאכלו
and you lift your eyes up to your idols,	ועינכם תשאו אל־גלוליצם

85 Eichrodt, *Ezekiel*, 462.

86 Cf. Tuell, *Ezekiel*, 231.

87 Literally you eat upon the blood (על־הדם תאכלו). Some have proposed to amend it as "upon the mountains." See commend below.

88 Many translations including NRSV, REB, NAB, and JB among others have "defiles his neighbor's wife," taking the wife as an object. But the particle את in some of its occurrences has an intensive/emphatic and reflective force corresponding to the English pronoun 'self.' For example in cases like "He, himself (nom) kept the law," "He kept the law itself (accusative). Thus, "a man defiles himself" is a sound translation. See discussion of את in Bruce K. Walkte and M.O 'Connor, *An Introduction to Biblical Hebrew Syntax* (Winona Lake, Ind: Eisenbrauns, 1990), 177-178. את as a marker of direct object usually has (a) the article that precedes the subject noun (b) the proper noun and (c) followed by a genitive or suffix pronoun. It rarely precedes an undetermined noun such as this את־אשת. See *HALOT* Vol. 1, 100-101.

and you shed blood.	ודם תשפכו
And shall you possess he land?	הארץ למורשה:
You stand on your sword,	עמדתם על־חרבכם
you do abominations,	עשיתן תועבה
and each of you defile his neighbor's wife.	ואיש את־אשת רעהו טמאתם
And shall you possess the land?	הארץ למורשה:

The accusations against the surviving inhabitants (vv. 25-26) have significant parallels with chapters 18, 22, and the Holiness Code in Leviticus.[89] Repeating parts of the indictment of Jerusalem in chs. 18 and 22, the accusations of the homelanders are represented by three cardinal sins: idolatry, bloodshed, and sexual crimes. The first accusation – "eating (on) the blood" emphasizes bloodguilt. Some translate this as "eating upon the mountains," by comparing with 18:6.[90] MT literally reads, "you eat upon the blood" (הדם) rather than mountains (ההרים). Lev 19:26 also has the same formulation: "Do not eat upon the blood." This may reflect the priestly law of Gen 9:4, prohibiting the consumption of blood in the belief that it contained the life force of the animal and should be offered to God. Eating meat with blood was as detrimental in the same manner as shedding blood and worshipping idols (33:25). Eichrodt writes: "The prohibition against consuming blood must have been aimed against one element of differing religious practice which seemed to present a particular danger to the exiles." [91] The second accusation is worship of idols (גלולים). As I indicated in chapter 3, the most common mode of defilement in Ezekiel is idol worship.[92] In most of the cases it is connected with impurity. In Ezekiel, the term is used frequently to express the charge against the people in Judah. It usually denotes a sin of idolatry committed by Israel in both the past and the present.[93] The third accusation is shedding blood (ודם תשפכו). The plural דמים is found in Ezekiel to express the idea of (1) the shedding of female blood, (2) the spilt blood of the slain, and (3) bloodguilt.[94] דם is used frequently for "violent bloodshed" inflicted

89 In chapter 18 Ezekiel speaks about the character of a righteous people. This includes those who refrain from idolatry, sexual misconduct, and bloodshed. In chapter 22 we find the sins of different groups of the inhabitants of Jerusalem such as rulers, priests, and the people of the land.

90 If we compare with 18:6 we see characteristics of the righteous – "… does not eat upon the mountains" (אל־ההרים לא אכל). In 18:6, 15 "looked for help to your idols" (לא נשא אל־גלולי ועיניו) is preceded by "eat on the mountains," as here in v. 25, "eating on the mountains' may be a possible translation. Hence Greenberg understands so. See Greenberg, *Ezekiel 21-37*, 684.

91 Eichrodt, *Ezekiel*, 31.

92 The most common term for idolatry in Ezekiel is גלולים. The noun גלולים occurs 39 times in Ezekiel out of 48 occurrences in the Hebrew Bible. See Kutsko, *Between Heaven and Earth*, 32.

93 It is most commonly found in judgment oracles. See Ezek 6:2-10, 11-14; 16: 36; 20; 23; 36.

94 E. W. Goldstein, "By the Blood that You Shed You are Guilty:" Perspectives on Female Blood in Leviticus and Ezekiel," in *Jewish Blood: Reality and Metaphor in History, Religion, and Culture*,

by one upon another, a notion closely related to the idiom שפך דם (to pour out blood).[95] Here, inhabitants of Judah are accused of shedding blood, which led her to become impure before Yahweh. The fourth accusation is another form of violence. The accusation: עמדתם על־הרבצם literally means "you stand on your sword," or "you rely upon your sword." This may simply be an extension of the accusation of bloodshed (v. 25). It may have the specific meaning of addressing the inhabitants as rebels against Babylon. This may also explain the reference to "those in strongholds and caves" (v. 27), an insurgency group.[96] Zimmerli agrees that this refers to the lawlessness of a land that had been laid waste by a long war after 587 BCE.[97] The fifth accusation is committing abominations (תועבה עשיתן). In Ezekiel תועבה indicates various kinds of sins, including idolatry (e.g. 6:9; 8:6,9) and sexual misconduct (eg. 22:11; Lev 18:26-30). Finally, their impurity is explained by "defiling neighbor's wives."[98] This is an illicit act of intercourse (cf 18:6, 15; 22:11). The term defile (טמא) appears here which is repeatedly used for impurity of the inhabitants of Judah. Here את signifies reflective force. We may translate as: "each one defiles (himself) with or on the person of his neighbor's wife." The Hebrew plainly means a man who violates (usually commit adultery with) his fellow's wife.

The rhetorical question "should you possess the land," appears two times, each after three types of accusations. This expression appears once in the Holiness code (Lev 20:24), where Israel's possession of the land is conditional upon their avoidance of those customs that had caused the land to vomit out the nations before them. In Deuteronomy, obedience to God's commands is a requisite for possession of the land (Deut 1:8, 21; 3:20; 4:1; 6:1; 30:16). In contrast, the survivors have no legitimate claim to the land due to their sin and impurity (as given in v. 25). Ezekiel establishes his claim that the remnant through whom God will work to give birth to a new Israel is "the remnant of scattered exiles whose only proof of acceptance with God was their penitent trust in the divine word."[99] Ezekiel delegitimizes the claim of the homelanders with a rhetorical question which expects the answer "no."

The accusations make it clear that the survivors who remained in the land of Israel forfeited their privileged position to be the faithful remnant of Israel. Instead, this privilege and opportunity now lies at the feet of those who were in Babylonia and whose faithfulness to God was ministered to by prophets and priests like Ezekiel. Evidence of this radical shift of focus is provided by the

---

RJSS, ed. Mitchell B. Hart (London: Routledge, 2009), 58.

95 See Ezek 16:6, 9, 36; 21:37; 22:2,3,4; 23:45; 36:18.

96 Tuell, *Ezekiel*, 231.

97 Zimmerli, *Ezekiel 2*, 199.

98 The MT literally means "wife of his friend" or his companion.

99 Clements, *Ezekiel*, 152.

shameless lives and indifference to holiness and purity demonstrated by those who survived in Jerusalem.

3.3.3. The Counterthesis - Punishment of the Homelanders and Desolation of the Land (vv. 27-28)

v. 27. Therefore say to them,[100] *"Thus says the Lord Yahweh, "As I live surely those in the ruins shall fall by sword and those in the field I will give them to beasts for food*[101] *and those in the stronghold and in the caves shall die by pestilence.*
v. 28. And I shall make the land a desolate and a waste and her mighty exaltation shall come to an end. The mountains of Israel shall be desolated, no one shall pass through the land."

Not only are the homelanders denied of land ownership due to what is presented as their blasphemous life, the land and the inhabitants will be punished. The land will be destroyed, the inhabitants will be punished with three plagues: war, beasts and pestilence, which are familiar instruments of judgment in Ezekiel.[102] Those who remained in Judah thought that they had escaped judgment as they were left in the land as "survivors." On the contrary, those in the ruins shall fall by the sword (בחרב יפלו), those in the open spaces shall be given to beasts (נתתיו לחיה), and those in the forts and the caves shall die by plague (בדבר ימותו). The three great instruments of punishment unmistakably reflects the actual situation of the period immediately after 587, in the struggle against Babylonia.[103]

Not only will the people of the land be punished, but the land itself will be devastated (ונתתי את־הארץ שממה) and no one will cross it again. Why was desolation of the land a necessity for Ezekiel? It is inevitable because of the idolatry and impurity of the inhabitants. It is likely that Ezekiel has the same idea as the Holiness Code and the Chronicles concerning the Sabbatical year and the healing of the land through the exile (Lev. 26:34-35, 43; 2 Chro. 36:21). As we earlier indicated, the land was never really emptied; people did remain in the land.[104] This ideological claim of the empty land may be viewed as a rejection of those who remained in the land. During the exile these are forms of delegitimization by which the inhabitants of the land were denied ownership of the land as well as true membership in the Israelite community.

100 Many ancient manuscripts read אלהים "God."

101 Following Vulgate, Syriac and LXX, the MT לאכלו (to eat him) should be emended to לאצלה (for food).

102 They occur in 5:1-3, 12; 6:11; 7:15; 14:12.

103 Cf. Zimmerli, *Ezekiel 2*, 199; Block, *Ezekiel 25-48*, 262.

104 See the discussion in the second chapter. The book of Lamentations also shows occupation of the land.

3.3.4. Epilogue - Purpose of Desolation of the Land and Punishment (v. 29)

v. 29. Then they shall know that I am Yahweh where I have made the land a desolation and a waste, because of all their abominations which they have done.

In the final verse (v. 29) we find the purpose of desolation of Judah and punishment of its inhabitants. The statement makes it clear that the purpose is that those who remained in Judah will know that Yahweh destroyed the land, and punished them in order that they might know him. In other words, Judah's punishment is for the knowledge of the true nature of Yahweh, who is the holy God. The reasons for destruction and punishment is clearly mentioned. It is "because of all their abominations."

3.4. Summary - The Non-Exilic Group is Rejected Due to Impurities

Ezekiel 33:24-29 is a disputation speech that reflects controversy between the two groups of Israelites post-587 BCE. Ezekiel denies the claim of land ownership of the surviving inhabitants of Judah for their impurity. The survivors have disqualified themselves (because of their impurity) to possess the land as Yahweh charged them. Ezekiel does not dispute that Abraham was promised that his descendants would inherit the land of Canaan. But he rejects any notion that those who remained in Judah can be heirs of the land. Rather, Yahweh will inflict punishment upon them. They would face a three-fold form of punishment – war (killed by sword), beasts in the open field, and death. The land itself would be desolated as it had been defiled by various impure acts of the inhabitants. The punishment of the inhabitants and the ultimate desolation of the land has one consequence; that it will lead people to know the true nature of the Holy God.

4. Conclusion

Exegetical studies of Ezekiel 11:14-21 and 33:21-29 demonstrate that the identity crisis between the exiles and the non-exiles was a major issue in the period following the fall of Jerusalem and deportations. The claim of landownership was a controversial issue between the exiles and those who remained in the land. The population in Judah and Jerusalem are accused as impure by virtue of their idol worship, bloodshed, and sexual misconduct. Though the exilic community is not singled out as the holy people and the pure community, Yahweh became a sanctuary to them, whose indwelling marks them as a people who are the chosen group. In contrast to the accusation of the inhabitants of the homeland, they are in a state of purification. Through them a new Israel will be established with the indwelling spirit of God.

In the aftermath of the fall of Judah, the surviving remnant constituted thousands of people. The land was not empty. The elite group including the king and his nobles, priests, and prophets were taken to Babylonia and went to Egypt. Hence, ownership of real estate had become a crucial issue. Ezekiel favors the exiles as the real owners of the land and denies the inhabitants of Judah. As the two passages in these exegetical studies illustrates, the two communities of Israel receive negative evaluation and positive remark respectively. While the inhabitants had the opportunity to rebuild the nation they are represented as continuing to worship their old idols, and practice their licentious impurity and their violence towards their weaker neighbors. Hence they are doomed to punishment. By contrast, the exiles are in divine favor in spite of their deportation to the land of Babylonia. Yahweh is present with them as a little sanctuary.

The text reflects class struggles in the exilic period. As found in the Deuteronomical history, those who remained in the land are "the poor of the country" and the deported group consisted of the elite group. Ezekiel and the priests who authored the book were high-class citizens who judged those who remained in the land as their subordinate. As illustrated in the theory of group identity, in order to maintain the status quo, the dominant group (Ezekiel's school) created a category of differentiation. As Tajfel and Turner propose, by means of constructing purity as group norm the inhabitants of the homeland were identified as morally and ritually impure.

It is difficult to determine the accuracy of Ezekiel's portrayal of the homelanders. One thing is clear, the author(s) of the book of Ezekiel was among the exiles, who were at odds with the claim of those non-exiles. These texts are pro-exilic group propaganda, favoring the exiles and condemning those remained on the land. These texts reflect a biased crisis of identity and for Ezekiel only the exilic community (not the Judean remnant) represents the true community of Israel. By identifying who is and who is not the true Israel, Ezekiel employs purity as a criterion for group membership. The non-exilic group is portrayed as doomed to punishment due to their impurities. This I will further elaborate in the next chapter.

Chapter 5

Judgment of God on the Inhabitants of the Homeland (Ezekiel 22:1-16)

1. Introduction

There are a number of passages in the book of Ezekiel that tell about the judgment of God upon Jerusalem and the inhabitants of Judah. Some scholars attribute such oracles to the whole of Israel.[1] A closer look at the oracles of judgment show that, in many instances, there are traces of group identification and rejection of a particular group of the Israelites. In the book we find a number of references that disenfranchise the people of Jerusalem and the inhabitants of Judah whose impurity resulted to judgments. Many oracles denigrate Jerusalem (Judah) accusing them as practicing all kinds of sins and impurities.[2] Among them, Ezekiel 22:1-16 contains a series of diatribes against Jerusalem and its inhabitants. The majority of critics agree that the oracle pertains to the historical situations of 597 and 587 BCE.[3] The oracle may originally have come from the prophet Ezekiel himself. It is plausible that the Ezekiel's school may have logically arranged it

1 For this argument see discussion in Brian Neil Peterson, *Ezekiel In Context: Ezekiel's Message Understood in Its Historical Setting of Covenant Curses and Ancient Near Eastern Mythological Motifs*, PTMS 182 (Eugene, OR: Pickwick Publications, 2012), 173-225.

2 Examples of these types of oracles are found in Ezekiel 6:1-14; 7:1-27; 11:1-13; 16:1-43; 21:1-32; 22:1-31; 24:1-14.

3 See Leslie C. Allen, *Ezekiel 20-48*, WBC Vol. 29 (Dallas: Word Books, 1990), 34; Peter Craigie, Ezekiel (Philadelphia: Westminster Press, 1983), 165.

in the late exilic or postexilic period.[4] The systematic presentation of the case against Jerusalem, and particularly her political leaders, indicates rulers such as Jehoaichim and Zedekiah, or perhaps Gedaliah and the Shaphanids who are the ones rejected.[5] Jerusalem, her rulers, and her inhabitants are charged for their cultic and moral sins. The oracle of judgment in this chapter provides a rationale for the exilic group to exclude the inhabitants of Jerusalem and Judah during the exilic period. Rom-Shiloni rightly points out that "Ezekiel's intensive references to Jerusalem (those who remained in Judah) and its fate are a response to both his immediate audience in exile and to the need to redefine the religio-national identity of the Exiles."[6] The immediate audience could be the exilic ones though the main focus is the residents of Jerusalem and those who remained in the land. In short, for Ezekiel, the impurity of those who remained in Judah alienated them from the community of Yahweh.

2. Nature & Design

Chapter 22 is one of the most astounding oracles of judgment in the book of Ezekiel. It may roughly be divided into three sections, consisting of three separate oracles.[7] The three oracles consist of: (1) Judgment of the bloody city (vv. 1-16), (2) meltdown of the house of Israel (vv. 17-22); and (3) the land defiled through corruption of the inhabitants (vv. 23-31). The oracles are clearly distinguished by formulae, style of presentation, and agenda. These oracles contain numerous links.[8] They are three discrete but interlocking oracles; each of them focuses upon Jerusalem and its inhabitants with disputation speeches.[9] In this exegetical study, I will limit my scope to the first oracle (vv. 1-16), which is about judgment of God

4 Block argues that the logical arrangement may be occasioned by the need to address the postexilic community to explain the rationale for judgment on Jerusalem. See Daniel I. Block, *The Book of Ezekiel Chapters 1-24*, NICOT (Grand Rapids: Eerdmans, 1997), 700.

5 Allen, Ezekiel 20-48, 36. G. A. Cook, *A Critical and Exegetical Commentary on The Book of Ezekiel Vol. 1*, ICC (Edinburgh: T&T Clark, 1937), 241.

6 Dalit Rom-Shiloni, "Ezekiel as the Voice of the Exiles and Constructor of Exilic Ideology," in *Hebrew Union College Annual LXXVI* (Cincinnati: Hebrew Union College, 2006), 41-43.

7 The three-fold division according to Block runs as: (a) The indictment of Jerusalem (1-16); (b) The Judgment of Jerusalem (17-22); and (c) The rationale for the judgment on the land (23-31). See Block, *Ezekiel 1-24*, 699. The three clear division of the oracle is attested by most of the Ezekiel commentators. See discussion in Allen, *Ezekiel 20-48*, 33.

8 These include common geographical focus, many semantic links, common motifs and themes. See more detail in Block, *The Book of Ezekiel 1-24*, 699 ff.

9 Cf. Margaret S. Odell, *Ezekiel*, Smith & Helwys Bible Commentary (Macon, Georgia: Smyth & Helwys Publishing, Inc., 2005), 281. Thus Greenberg observes that the object of God's wrath complements one another: in A (1-16) the city, bloody and impure; in B (17-22) the house of Israel is all dross; in C (23-31) the land unpurged of the corruption of its inhabitants. A ends with God's threat to "purge the impurity" of Jerusalem, anticipating as it were the figure of smelting in the next oracles. The smelting crucible of B is identified with Jerusalem-the bloody city of A, while the base elements gathered into it for fiery liquefaction foreshadow the

on the homelanders. The unity of vv. 1-16 is generally accepted. The prophetic word formulas in vv. 1 and 17 "The word of Yahweh came to me saying" (יהוה אמר ויהי דבר) make it plain that this oracle is to be seen as a unit. The oracle announces judgment against the bloody city that violates a series of laws. In this oracle, Ezekiel accuses Jerusalem of shedding the blood of its own people. On account of her impurities, Yahweh judges Jerusalem and its inhabitants. All of its citizens from high to low classes are committing various cultic and moral impurities that lead them to face furious judgment.

The oracle (vv. 1-16) is generally known as a judgment speech. The genre of the prophecy is obvious from Yahweh's opening charge to Ezekiel: את־עיר הדמים התשפט התשפט (will you judge, will you judge the bloody city?) which is a special form of judgment speech, known as the *rib* (ריב).[10] Israel's guilt is demonstrated by the violation of its own legal constitution and tradition. Hals describes the logical arrangement of the passage as prophetic proof saying, accusation, announcement of punishment, and recognition formula.[11] There is a close connection with apodictic laws of the Holiness Code (H).[12] This is demonstrated by the accusation of sin (of Israel/Jerusalem), which takes place quite simply according to the divine law set out without any mention of the dimension of historical depth.[13] Hence, the prophecy has an accusation motif, which is defined as ריב, which is closely related to the priestly code of purity and impurity, particularly found in the Holiness Code. The oracle may be divided into three subsections: (a) A general indictment (vv. 1-5); (b) an indictment detailing the sins of the inhabitants grouped in three clusters, (vv. 6-8, 9-11, 12) (vv. 6-12), and (c) the announcement of judgment upon the inhabitants for their impurities (vv. 13-16).

---

corrupt ranks of C, destined to destruction in outpoured rage, "in the fire of my wrath" (vs. 31). See Moshe Greenberg, *Ezekiel 21-37*, AB (New York: Doubleday, 1997), 465.

10 ריב (Rib) is often identified with a lawsuit, which involves three parties, the judge, a plaintiff, and the defendant, and the judge is called upon to adjudicate a dispute between tow contending parties. In prophetic oracles that use the term rib involves only two parties: Yahweh as plaintiff, and Israel, as defendant. The picture in a rib is thus not that of a judicial process before the courts, but of two contending parties arguing their cases between themselves) whose tone and style derives from the court setting. See detailed explanation of the ריב form of speech in Block, *The Book of Ezekiel 1-24*, 459-460.

11 Ronald M. Hals, *Ezekiel*, FOTL Vol. XIX (Grand Rapids, Michigan: Eerdmans, 1989), 156.

12 Cf. Walther Zimmerli, *Ezekiel 1: A Commentary on the Book of the Prophet Ezekiel 1-24*, trans. Ronald E. Clements, eds. Frank Moore Cross, Klaus Blatzer and Leonard Jay Greenspoon. Philadelphia: Fortress Press, 1979), 455. Stalker argues that here in Chapter 20 catalogues of contemporary sins are stated in apodictic form and the verses have close affinity with the Holiness Code. See D.M.G. Stalker, *Ezekiel: Introduction and Commentary* (London: SCM Press Ltd., 1968), 184.

13 Chapters 18 & 20 present the same accusation of Israel's sin. However, it is mentioned in relation to the history of Israel in the past and present.

3. Setting

There are two main arguments for a possible setting of Ezekiel 22, along with its authorship, date and composition.[14] The most commonly accepted idea is that the chapter is an outcome of three separate oracles reflecting the situation between 597 BCE and 587 BCE combined editorially in the later part of the exile.[15] This view holds that while the original oracles may go back to the prophet himself, the school or schools of Ezekiel composed it later. Some scholars challenge this view, stating that the entire chapter is the outcome of a single hand – the prophet himself. In line with this thesis, Block argues "obviously the prophet probably delivered these three oracles at a different time, though all are to be dated before 587 BCE."[16] The unit vv. 1-16 obviously looks back to 597 events and looks forward to the fall of Jerusalem in 587. According to Allen, the oracle reflects particularly well the midpoint historical position peculiar to Ezekiel's first period of prophesying. It looks back to the catastrophe of 597, and forward to the further, final one of 587. The prophet hereby offers the exiles an explanation for the severity with which Yahweh is about to judge the land of Israel. Thus, this idea represents a single hand, delivered and composed by the hand of the prophet himself. It has a geographical setting in Babylonia.[17]

Another argument puts forth a post-587 BCE compilation. While a pre-587 setting of the original texts is presupposed, there is strong support for a late composition by the Ezekiel's school.[18] There is evidence of an editorial hand of the three separate oracles from the exilic period, probably by Ezekiel's disciple(s). One argument for the late composition is the literary dependence of the third section (vv. 23-31) on Zephaniah 3:3-4, 8 which tells the fourfold sequence of Jerusalem's civil and religious authorities.[19] The punishment of the land is portrayed as already having taken place in vv. 30-31. This text possibly refers to a post 587 BCE. Block who claims the original words of the prophet, also maintains the possibility of an editorial hand. He states, "... having recognized the interconnections (of different oracles), the compiler of Ezekiel's prophecies arranged them in a logical order,

14 For example, Schulz has argued that a number of passages depend on established sets of laws, which are to be attributed to a post-exilic Deutero-Ezekiel. Holscher, Herntrich and Bertholet believe that Ezekiel must himself have spoken in Jerusalem. For some critics vv. 13-16 are secondary. For Allen, together with form critical factors the tight bonding gives the impression of compositional – rather than redactional unity. See discussion in Zimmerli, *Ezekiel 1*, 454; Allen, *Ezekiel 20-48*, 34.

15 Horace D. Hummel, *Ezekiel 21-48* (Saint Louis: Concordia Pub. House, 2007), 679.

16 Block, *The Book of Ezekiel 1-24*, 700.

17 See Allen, *Ezekiel 20-48*, 34.

18 Cf. Gerhard Fohrer, *Die Hauptprobleme des Buches Ezechiel*, BZAW 72 (Berlin: Topelmann, 1952), 130. John W. Wevers, *Ezekiel*, The Century Bible (London: Thomas Nelson and Sons, 1969), 172. See also Zimmerli, *Ezekiel 1*, 467; Eichrodt, *Ezekiel*, 316.

19 See detail in Allen, *Ezekiel 20-48*, 35.

beginning with the general indictment of Jerusalem, followed by an announcement of judgment, to which was added a postexilic reflection on the need and rationale for that judgment."[20] The late compilation theory is more convincing as the texts indicate the "already" shattered situation of the exilic period. The texts respond and confirm chapters 11 & 33 that reject the claim of the inhabitants of Judah as the "true Israel." The text as a whole therefore, is an exilic composition, a core of which should be Ezekiel's original sayings. We may conclude that the judgment oracle of vv. 1-16 probably originally came from the mid-point between 597 and 587 BCE. It received its final compilation with other two oracles (vv. 17-22 and 23-31) in the late exilic period.

4. Text Analysis and Comments

4.1. A General Indictment - Jerusalem the Bloody City (vv.1-5)

vv. 1-2. The word of Yahweh came to me: You, son of man will you judge, will you judge[21] *the bloody city? Make her known all her abominations.*
v. 3. You shall say, thus says the Lord Yahweh;[22] *the city sheds blood in her midst, and her time comes as she makes idols for herself to defile herself.*
v. 4. By your blood that you shed you became guilty and by your idols, which you have made, you became unclean. And you have brought your days; a time of your years[23] *have come. Therefore, I made you a reproach to the nations and a mockery to all the lands.*
v. 5. Those who are far and near from you shall mock you O defiled of name,[24] *abounding in tumult.*

Ezekiel chapter 22:1-16 is an oracle that contains indictment and charges against Jerusalem. In this oracle, vv. 1-5 explain why Jerusalem is named "the city of blood." The oracle is introduced by the call and summons – the customary word-event formula, followed by double direct address of the prophet, 'Now you, son of man' (ואתה בן־אדם). Ezekiel is invited to transmit a message of the crime and punishment of Jerusalem. There are three logical arrangements of the indictment here.

20 Block, *Ezekiel 1-24*, 700.

21 The repetition "will you judge" התשפט is missing in ancient versions such as LXX and Syriac. However, it may be retained here as it shows emphasis on the arraignment of Jerusalem.

22 Some versions insert אָן "O" or "behold" instead of יהוה. REB and NAB read as הוי "Alas" or "Woe" here, emphasizing the severity of the indictment.

23 עד־שׁנותיך literally means "until your years." עד could refer to a degree of time and can be translated as "until," "as far as," "even to," and "to the point of." See "עד" *BDB*, 723-725. This phrase would be translated as "the appointed time" of judgment.

24 טמאת שׁם "defiled of name" is the title given to Jerusalem. In Syriac version, "and they shall say" preceded this phrase. The preceding verse as well as sexual and social offence listed in vv. 6-12 indicates how the name of Jerusalem will be a mocking for other nations.

First, we find a call to indict Jerusalem for her bloodshed (vv. 1-4a). The indignation begins with a rhetorical question: "Will you judge the bloody city? (v. 2a)"[25] The plain meaning of this question and answer is: "Why would the city be judged? The answer is "because of her bloodshed." Indictment of Jerusalem is clearly shown by identifying her as the "bloody city" (את־עיר הדמים).[26] Nahum called Nineveh 'the bloody city,' thinking of the Assyrians' power politics and cruelty (Nah 3:1). And Isaiah said of the people of Jerusalem, 'Your hands are full of blood' (Isa 1:15), having in mind social sins. The idea of bloodshed and impurity are essentially connected in the book of Ezekiel.[27] The connection of blood and cultic matters is apparent in the priestly writings too. Ezekiel here combines moral and cultic offences under the term 'bloodshed'- the keyword of the entire passage is blood.[28] The accusations against ritual offences are expressed in a priestly-legal language.[29] Hence 'bloodguilt' in the priestly understanding, becomes a comprehensive category of guilt. This appears to be a guiding principle of Ezekiel's style, accusing the inhabitants of Judah by presenting their sin. As Julie Galambush writes, "Ezekiel's use of the identical phrases to address Jerusalem as "bloody," gives Jerusalem a quasi-personified status in 22:1-5."[30] As the imagery found in the priestly writings, blood serves as a peculiarly appropriate image for the type of corruption (defilement) that Ezekiel ascribes to the inhabitants of Jerusalem.

Jerusalem is not only involved in bloodshed, but also practices abominations. The prophet is commanded to "make known her abominations." (v. 2b). The Hebrew תעבה in v. 11 as a key term to express the sin of Jerusalem. This term is used frequently by Ezekiel to refer to the radical nature of sinful acts. תועבה in Ezekiel is an inclusive term used in reference to something repugnant and despicable in either religious-cultic or social-moral sphere. [31] Zimmerli defines it

---

25 MT repeats התשפט (will you not judge?), which is absent in Greek and Syriac readings. But the same doubling is found in 20:4 which is also retained in LXX.

26 Literally it means "city of blood." Ezekiel repeats the shocking epithet in 24:6, 10.

27 See discussion in chapter 3 about bloodshed as one type of impurity. The book indicates that flow of blood, bloodshed, and offering of blood to idols are things that are impure.

28 Stalker, *Ezekiel, Introduction and Commentary*, 184.

29 Zimmerli contends that the connection of blood law, sins of social oppression, and ritual disorder is found in Priestly thinking in Gen 9:4f. See Zimmerli, *Ezekiel 1*, 456. According to Michael A. Lyons, Ezekiel here draws on H's regulations in Lev 18-20 to accuse the inhabitants of Jerusalem to justify the imminent destruction of the city. See Michael L. Lyons, *From Law to Prophecy: Ezekiel's Use of the Holiness Code*, LHB/OTS 507 (New York: T&T Clark, 2009), 115.

30 Julie Galambush, *Jerusalem in the Book of Ezekiel: The City as Yahweh's Wife*, SBL Dissertation Series 130 (Atlanta, Georgia: SBL, 1992), 136.

31 The term is found 117 times in the Bible, and 45 of theses occurrences are found din Ezekiel. The combination of תובות רות (evil abomination), תובות גדוסות (great abominations) and תובובם זלמי (images of their abominable things) are more frequently used by Ezekiel in the context

as a "comprehensive term for all sins of cultic impurity."[32] The question "will you judge the bloody city?" is identical to Yahweh's call to judge Oholibah, Yahweh's unfaithful marriage partner, in 23:36. Similarly, "make known her abominations" recalls chapter 16:2 which portrays Jerusalem as Yahweh's wife who became a harlot. These verbal parallels indicate the sexual impurity of Jerusalem and its inhabitants. In short, Jerusalem is in an impure state, just as a harlot and an adulterous woman are stained by blood.

The general indictment is further clarified by addressing Jerusalem as the place where bloodshed is "in her midst (בתוכה) (v. 3)." This address conveys the impression of the city as a receptacle, a sink of impurity.[33] The bloodguilt of Jerusalem consists of two intertwining crimes, belong fundamentally together: idol worship and bloodshed. Greenberg comments that the expression "shedding blood in her midst" (שפכת דם בתוכה), a perfect consecutive participle, denotes indefinitely repeated, frequent, continuous action."[34] By idol worship the city became defiled (טמאת), and by shedding blood she was guilty (אשמת) (v. 4). As indicated in chapter 3, idol worship in Ezekiel is a cultic crime that defiles the land, the temple and the people. Bloodshed is further explained as "guilt" (אשם). The term ~va is most commonly used for trespasses that involves bloodshed.[35] It is also used for trespasses against sancta.[36] For Ezekiel and the priestly legislations, bloodshed defiles the land as it poses a threat to the maintenance of the presence of God in the midst of Israel.[37]

Secondly, the indictment of the city is followed by "Her days of judgment, the appointed time of punishment for her years of sin has come."[38] Defilement of the city leads to reproach and doom. The impurity of the city with its double crimes led to shortening the days of Jerusalem, and mocking by the neighboring nations. These two sentences predetermined the time of Jerusalem's doom. "Those

---

of idolatrous practices. See Tova Ganzel, "The Defilement and Desecration of the Temple in Ezekiel," *Biblica* 89, no. 3 (2008): 371.

32 Zimmerli, *Ezekiel 1*, 190.

33 "In her midst" is repeated in vss. 7 and 13 and together with reiterated "in you" in vss. 6-7, 9-12, 16. According to Katheryn Pfisterer Darr, This epithet suggests that "the city is, in effect, a defiled vessel filled with blood and consequently rife with bloodguilt." See Katheryn Pfisterer Darr, "The Book of Ezekiel: Introduction, Commentary, and Reflections," in *NIB* Vol. VI, 1307.

34 Greenberg, *Ezekiel 21-37*, 452.

35 Cf. Gen 42:41; Num 5:6; 35:31. LXX has "in their blood which your have shed, you have transgressed."

36 Cf. Lev 4:13, 22; 5:5; Ezr 10:19. See discussion in Jacob Milgrom, *Cult and Conscience: The Asham and The Priestly Doctrine of Repentance*, SJLA 18 (Leiden: Brill, 1976), 1-21.

37 Cf. Num 35:30-34. Klawans explains this type of defilement as moral defilement. See discussion in Jonathan Klawans, "Pure, Violence: Sacrifice and Defilement in Ancient Israel," *Harvard Theological Review* 94, no. 2 (April 2001): 133-155.

38 This is the paraphrase by Darr. See "*The Book of Ezekiel*," 1308.

who are near and those who are far" will mock it. Yahweh will inflict judgment upon the city because of her impurities such as bloodshed and sexual misconduct.

The city is addressed as "O defiled of name, abounding in tumult," (v. 5).[39] In Old Testament thought, a name is more than a mere identification. It is a representation of the whole entity of a person.[40] Jerusalem is now named a defiled city with bloodshed, idolatry and sexual impurities, and is mocked by the other nations, whose days will be shortened. It is noteworthy that, for Ezekiel, the name of Jerusalem itself was so bound to impurity that in his vision of the restoration of the city, it is renamed – יהוה שמה (Yahweh is there) (48:35). The intensity of the city's defilement and its consequence is further explained by רבת המהומה "abounding in tumult."[41] The evaluation of the homelanders, put in the mouth of neighboring nations by the prophet, conveys the idea of serious crime committed by the inhabitants of Jerusalem.

4.2. A Detailed Indictment - Various Cases of Impurities of the Homelanders (vv. 6-12)

v. 6. Behold! The rulers of Israel, in you everyone by his own strength[42] *have involved in blood shed.*
v. 7. In you they have dishonored father and mother, they treat aliens in your midst with extortion; they oppress orphans and widows in you.
v. 8. You despised my holy things, and you profaned my Sabbaths.
v. 9. In you are men of slander who shed blood; among you are those who eat on the mountains; they do wickedness in your midst.
v. 10. In you one has uncovered the nakedness of the father; in you they uncovered the impurity of the defiled one.[43]
v. 11. One commits abomination with the wife of his companion, and in you a man defiles his daughter-in-law in wickedness; in you a man defiles his sister, the daughter of his father.

39 In Syriac, this is preceded by "and they shall say," showing that, the two epithets – "impure of name" and "abounding in tumult" as hurled at Jerusalem by the deriding gentiles. See Greenberg, *Ezekiel 21-37*, 453.

40 Cf. Exo 3:14; 2 Sam 12:25; Isa 7:14; 9:5.

41 The literal meaning of the phrase is great/many in confusion. The same phrase is used in Amos 3:9 which explains Israel's guilt and punishment due to her oppressions, robbery, and violence in the land.

42 LXX has προς τους συγγενεις "each one with his kindred" emphasizing conflicts within the house of princess of Israel. The MT may be retained here as it indicates the personal power one has at his disposal. The literal meaning of לזרעו "according to his arm" indicates so. Cf. Greenberg, *Ezekiel 21-37*, 453. Also see Block, *Ezekiel 1-24*, 706.

43 טמאת נדה literally means "impurity of defiled one." It refers to impurity by menstruation. This combination in many instances refers to menstrual woman. See Lev 12 & 15; Num 19.

v.12. In you they have taken a bribe in order to shed blood; you have taken interest and usury; you have gained your friends violently by extortion, and you have forsaken me, says Yahweh the Lord.

These verses express detailed indictments upon Israel. The expression, "Behold! the rulers of Israel" (v. 6) signals the commencement of a new phase of threats to Jerusalem, particularly her political leaders. The New Jerusalem Bible translates the accusation of princess of Israel in verse 6 as follows: "Look! In you the princess of Israel, one and all, have furthered their own interests at the cost of bloodshed." The series of offences cited recalls the lists of moral-religious obligations encountered earlier in 18:5-8 and 15-17, though this set displays closer correspondences to the Decalogue, and to Lev. 19 in particular.[44] Jerusalem's sin is catalogued in a series of intertwined cultic, sexual and social abuses. Three roughly parallel sections of indictments are found in connection with the indignation "you have shed blood." (שׁפך דם) found in vv. 6, 9, and 12. There are three specific groups indicted here: (a) the princes of Israel (vv. 6-8), (b) slanderers (vv. 9-11) and, (c) bribe-takers (v. 12).

In vv. 6-8, the princes of Israel cause bloodshed in two ways: (1) by their failure to maintain social order and (2) by violating cultic purity rules. The princes of Israel are indicted in that "they shed blood (v. 7), they dishonor father and mother (v. 7) and they oppress aliens, widow and orphans (v. 8)."[45] The rulers of Jerusalem were involved in bloodshed, which is followed by other unjust practices against the citizenry. In other words, the social dislocation begins with the royal abuse of power. They are involved in bloody crimes and undermine the most basic social unit, the family. They also endanger those on the margins of the society.[46] Far from maintaining justice they set an example that undermined the norms of their society by ignoring the tradition of honoring the father and mother, and caring for aliens, orphans and widows. In his exegesis of this passage, Greenberg compares the sentiment in Ezekiel to a Sumerian text.[47] As also indicated by the

44 While Zimmerli argues that the Decalogue may indeed have inspired this list, Block advocates the text's greater dependence on the holiness code; which for him betrays Ezekiel's priestly background See Zimmerli, *Ezekiel 1*, 457 & Block, *Ezekiel 1-24*, 708.

45 The Greek reading has "house of Israel" for "princess of Israel." Though the king might be held responsible, here, it is more likely that 'they' signifies undefined person; it may imply people in general. Honoring father and mother is emphasized in the Deuteronomic law. See Deut 27:16 – "Cursed be on who dishonor his father or his mother."

46 Cf. Odell, *Ezekiel*, 283.

47 The Sumerian text contains illuminating passages for these in Ezekiel. In the prologue of his law, King Lipit Ishtar of Isin (early second millennium BCE) records how he rectified social wrongs in his city which includes making children and fathers support each other. A reform instituted by Urukagina of Lagash (mid-third millennium BCE) also reads about making a covenant with god not to commit injustice against an orphan or widow. Israel shared the ancient Near Eastern law of social order that upholds social justice. See Greenberg, *Ezekiel 21-37*, 454.

Deuteronomic law, Ezekiel claims that these social orders have been violated in the land of Judah in the oppression of aliens, widows and orphans.[48] According to Allen, the accusation of royal house in these verses (6-8) has readily come to the mind of Ezekiel as well as in the mind of Jeremiah who denounced the activities of Jehoiakim in 22:13-19 for causing human suffering and death.[49] Hence, it is an accusation of the rulers of the homelanders during the exilic age.

The princes of Israel also commit sin by their cultic impurities: In verse 8 we find the accusation in a word pair:

You have despised my holy things	קדשׁי בזית
And you have profaned my Sabbaths	ואת־שׁבתתי חללת

The offences attributed to the city here are ascribed to the priests in vs. 26. If the city is the offender it could be offenses of consuming sacrificial meal in an impure state, or beyond the time allowed for it, or violation of the Sabbaths.[50] Holy things could indicate the Temple and its various accessories. Zimmerli holds a view that קדשׁי in Ezekiel is limited to a general command to reverence for holy things (sanctuary, sacrifice, temple vessels as also found in chs 40-48).[51] Despise (בזית) is the word used in 16:59 for Jerusalem's attitude towards her vassal oath, a marriage metaphor between Israel and her God.[52] The pair קדשׁי־שׁבתתי "holy things-Sabbath" recalls מקדשׁי ־שׁבתתי "Sabbath-sanctuary" in Lev 19:30. Cultic sin is directly intended here.

Secondly, another group called slanderers shed blood by their cultic crimes and various types of sexual misconduct (vv. 9-11). Who the slanderers (רכיל) are, is not mentioned here.[53] The Hebrew term for slanderers אנשׁי רכיל could be understood in the sense of "robbers," "men of gossip," or "informers" mostly in combination with הלך (go around) in an evil sense.[54] In Jeremiah, the term is used to express a form of contaminating contact with harmful people that makes

48 Cf. Deut 14:29; 16:11, 14; 24:17, 19-21; 27:19. See also Jer 7:6; 22:3.

49 Allen, *Ezekiel 20-48*, 36. Cooke interprets 'princes' as Zedekiah and his immediate predecessors. See Cook, *Ezekiel Vol. I*, 241.

50 See Lev 7:20; 7:15-18; 19:6-8 and Jer 17:21ff.

51 Zimmerli, *Ezekiel 1*, 458.

52 Here despising the holy things parallels defilement of the sanctuary in 23:38. Hence the two passages could be written in the same context. See Galambush, *Jerusalem in the Book of Ezekiel*, 136.

53 The word רכיל occurs in six places in the Hebrew Bible. Six of them are noun forms (Lev 19:16; Jer 6:28; 9:3; Prov 11:13; 20:19). Only in Ezek 22:9 it is used as an adjective. The word may originally relate with "trader" and then go from there to "tale-bearer" and "slanderer." The root רכל occurs sixteen times in Ezekiel out of 22 occurrences in the Hebrew Bible. The See discussion in Ellen van Wolde, "A Cognitive Linguistic Study of the Concept of Defilement in Ezekiel 22:1-16," in *Biblical Interpretation and Method: Essays in Honour of John Barton*, eds. Katharine J. Dell and Paul M. Joyce (Oxford: Oxford University Press, 2013), 260-264.

54 See "רכיל," *BDB*, 940. LXX renders the term referring to "treachery" "deceit" and "crookedness."

good people less pure (Jer 6:27-29; 9:3). The noun רכלה/רוכלים/רכל in Ezekiel usually refers to "traders" who trade with other nations (27:13,15; 26:12; 28:5). For the prophet, the city-dwellers of Jerusalem exchange trade with other nations that causes them to be impure. Here the expression "slanderers" is followed and defined by בך למען שפך דם (in you to shed blood) which shows that a lying slanderer incurred bloodguilt.

The bloodguilt of slanderers involves two kinds of impurities: Firstly, the cultic offence of "eating on the mountains" (אל־ההרים אכלו) (v. 9a). In Ezekiel, mountains are mentioned as the site of idolatrous sacrifices on which meals were eaten (6:13; 20:28; 34:6). Since the expression is peculiar to Ezekiel (cf. 18:6; 11, 15; 22:9), it has been proposed to emend it in accord with 33:25, to the more familiar cult offence of "eating the blood." But this may not be implied here. As proposed by Zimmerli, this cultic crime could indicate worship in tribal locations such as Bethel and Mizpah that had been carried over since the days of Josiah.[55] It is a condemnation and rejection of worship at the northern part of Judah, rather than Jerusalem during the exilic age.

Sexual misconduct is another focus in the accusation of slanderers (vv. 9b-11). Jerusalem is portrayed as the arena of sexual wrongs. This is summarized with the expression: "They do wickedness in your midst"(בך זמה עשו בתוכך).[56] In the following verses (vv.10-11), the sexual sins of the slanderers are listed:

In you one has uncovered the nakedness of the father;[57] ערות־אב גלה־בך
in you they uncovered the impurity of the defiled one.[58] טמאת הנדה ענו־בך:
A man has done abominations with his fellow's wife;[59] את־אשת רעהו עשה תועבה
and a man defiled his daughter-in-law in wickedness;[60] ואיש את־כלתו טמא בזמה

55 Zimmerli proposes to explain in connection with the pre-Josianic struggle, which came to a decisive point in the reform of Josiah. See Zimmerli, *Ezekiel 1*, 458.

56 זמה (wickedness) refers to a generality covering all forbidden sexual unions, followed by some particulars. Ezekiel's use of this term (16:27, 58; 22:9, 11; 23:21, 27, 35, 44, 48f) may have connection with priestly usage in the Torah (Cf. Lev 18:17; 19:29; 201:14). Cf. Greenberg, *Ezekiel 21-37*, 455.

57 This implies intercourse with father's wife. Cf. Lev 18:7; Deut 23:2. It may also be an allusion to marriage with stepmother or incest with father's wife of concubine. Cf. Lev 20:11ff.; Deut 23:1; 22:30; 27:20.

58 This is sex with a menstrual woman. This is a type of immoral sex according to the priestly laws of impurity. Levitical laws laid prohibition of sexual relationships in marriage with a woman during the time of her menstrual period is mentioned in priestly legislation in Leviticus 15. Cf. Deut 21:14; 22:24, 29. The use of ענה (humbled/oppressed) with menstrual woman (נדה) here and in vs. 11, which signifies unwillingness of the woman to acquiesce in the illegal union.

59 This is adultery committed by men. According to Greenberg "with neighbor/fellow's wife" cannot be the direct object, as the object marker את does not precede it. See Greenberg, *Ezekiel 21-37*, 455.

60 This is incest. Sexual union with one's daughter in law was forbidden by Lev 18:5; with one's sister, similarly (Lev 18:9). These sexual crimes involve excommunication (Lev 20:17 Cf. 2

In you a man has defiled his sister, ואיש את־אחתו בת־אביו
his father's daughter.[61] ענה־בך׃

As noted here, these sexual offences have parallel references to the priestly legislations. Particularly sex with a menstruating woman is a taboo because it defiles the whole community of Israel (Lev 15:19-24). Embodiment of menstrual impurity טמאת הנדה is found here and in Ezekiel 18:6 and 36:17. In another text, the situation in the homeland is described as an impure state with the expression כטמאת הנדה היתה "like the uncleanness of a woman in her menstrual period" (36:17). The sexual wrongs combined in these verses illustrate the sins of the homelanders as sexual offences.

Ezekiel's formulation of criticisms against Israel with a picture of sexual wrongs might have close connections with Jeremiah's laments about adultery among his people, Hosea's against adulterous Israel and Levitical laws of the Holiness code.[62] The influence of the priestly writings may also be felt.[63] However, it is evident that Ezekiel clearly goes his own way. This is shown by the use of the idiom עשה תועבה "commit abomination with" in the context of sexual impurities in Ezekiel, which is not found elsewhere in the Hebrew Bible.[64] The metaphor of sexual misbehavior signifies Israel's infidelity and apostasy. Adultery, harlotry, incest, and other sexual misconduct are against holiness, in the simple sense of right order. Ezekiel employs these accusations to categorize a particular group - the people of the land of Judah. As rules of sexual morality presuppose, incest adultery, and other sexual misconduct are against holiness and purity, in the simple sense of right order. As Mary Douglas observes, the homelanders fail to conform to the class to which they belong as the people of God.[65]

The third group of statements found in verse 12 concerns those people called bribe-takers. The sins in this category are disorders in the sphere of property and money. It is to be noted that unjust gain and extortion mentioned in this verse are set in the context of bloodshed and violence. First, bribe-takers strike down the

---

Sam 13:13).

61 Prohibition of sexual union with paternal sisters is found in Lev 18:9 and with maternal sisters in 18:11. Sibling incest is a taboo in the morality of the priestly legislations.

62 Zimmerli, *Ezekiel 1*, 458.

63 Block advocates the influence of Holiness code, particularly Lev 18 and 20. See Block, *Ezekiel 1-24*, 710.

64 See discussion in Hummel, *Ezekiel 21-48*, 668.

65 In the perspective of Mary Douglas, holiness/purity requires that individuals shall conform to the class to which they belong. It requires that different classes of things shall not be confused. It therefore involves correct definition, discrimination, and order. See Mary Douglas, *Purity and Danger: An Analysis of Concepts of Pollution and Taboo* (New York: Oxford University Press Inc., 1966), 53.

life of innocent people.[66] This is indicated by the phrase, "in order to shed blood." Second, they have taken interest (נשך) and increase (תרבית).[67] As suggested by D.H. Muller, "interest" and "increase" are unitary concepts.[68] Cooper explains this sin as exacting of exorbitant interest rates because of greed.[69] Thirdly, they (lit. you) have gained (תבצעי) friends/neighbors by extortion.[70] The Syriac translates this phrase, "they defrauded their friends unjustly." Since the address in this oracle is Jerusalem, "friends/neighbors" could also imply Jerusalem's neighboring nations such as the Ammonites.[71] Instead of making good relationship, they extort their own neighbors and surrounding people. Lastly, "they have forgotten the Lord." By doing those unjust acts, they involved in bloodshed and forgot the meaning of divine law that protects the poor. Forgetting Yahweh is the climax and summary of these sinful acts, which is the real failure of Jerusalem's royalty and its citizens. By disobedience and dishonoring the law, the bribe-takers, violate the will of Yahweh. In vv. 6-12, Ezekiel pictures a situation in Jerusalem in which rulers, slanderers, and bribe-takers, the representatives of the homelanders, get involved in various cultic and moral crimes. Those behaviors infect the whole community, which demands Yahweh's righteous acts in order to purify the land and the people. The next verses elaborate this theme.

4.3. Jerusalem's Sentence - Purging the Impurities (vv. 13-16)

v. 13. Behold I have struck my hand against your unjust gain which you have made, and upon the blood which has been in your midst.
v. 14. Can your heart stand or can your hands be strong for the days when I shall deal with you? I Yahweh have said, and I will do it.
v. 15. And I will scatter you among the nations and I will disperse you in the lands; I will purge[72] your impurity from you.
v. 16. And I shall be profaned[73] in you in the sight of the nations, and you shall know that I am Yahweh.

---

66 Relating passage found in Deut 27:25 says: "Curse be one who takes a bribe to strike down the life of an innocent person." The prohibition against accepting a bribe, which brings about miscarriage of justice and bloodguilt, was current in the older laws of Israel (Cf. Ex. 23:8; Deut 10:17; 16:19; 27:25).

67 The distinction between "interest" and increase" is not clear. Ezek 18:8 have the same expression saying, "he does not lend at interest or collect with increase."

68 Cited in Lamar E. Cooper Sr. *Ezekiel* NAC Vol. 17 (United States of America: Broadman & Holman Publishers, 1994), 219.

69 Cooper, *Ezekiel*, 219.

70 תבצעי piel form of בצע has a meaning of 'violently make gain of.' See *BDB*, 130.

71 Cf. Ezek 21:18-20. See discussion in Odell, *Ezekiel*, 284.

72 The Hebrew והתמתי – literally means I will "finish," "destroy" or "cease doing." Hence it denotes purging or doing away with their impurities.

73 Literally ונחלת - niphal perfect second person feminine singular means, "you shall be profaned." This is taken by NJB, NIV, NASB, and ASV. As emended by LXX, Syriac and Vulgate certain

These verses contain the announcement of the sentence or judgment inflicted upon Jerusalem. The announcement is opened with the call for attention והנה "and behold." Since the content of the unit is somewhat repetitious of vv. 4b-5, a later addition of the verses is plausible.[74] A summons to attention is followed by a sign act: The prophet claps his hands in anger for Jerusalem's social injustices and bloodshed.[75] Two rhetorical questions are asked here: "Can your heart stand (היעמד), or can your hands be strong (תחזקנה), in the days that I shall deal with you."[76] (v.14). These rhetorical questions express the intensity of Yahweh's judgment that the inhabitants of Jerusalem cannot endure.

The sentence on Jerusalem is found in vv. 15-16 directly addressing Jerusalem with a pronoun "you" (ך) a second person feminine singular, but referring to the residents. The last clause in verse 15, "I will purge your impurities from you" could have different meanings. With the first clause in verse 15, it may be translated: "When its inhabitants, whose wicked conduct defiled it, will be exiled, then the city will be purged of its (your) impurity."[77] The sentences include two things: "scattering and dispersing the inhabitants and purging their impurities." In short, those spared exile in the first deportation of 597 BCE would now encounter the judgment, and so Jerusalem was to fall again.[78] Yahweh will purge the city's filthiness from her by removing them from the land. Exile is the punishment for defiling the land both in Ezekiel and the priestly writings. Impurity of the people defiles the land and as a result the land will spew out its inhabitants (Lev. 18:24-28). In other words, when Yahweh judged the inhabitants by removing them from the land, the city will be made clean.

The impurities of the inhabitants not only affect the people, but also Yahweh himself (v.16). Impurities resulted not only in the expulsion of the people from their land, but Yahweh has also abandoned the sacred space and has given the

---

translations such as NRSV, NAB, among others take fist person "I shall be profaned."

74 Zimmerli proposes it to be added by Ezekiel himself or his disciple somewhat later. Wevers suggests the problem of putting 13-16 within 1-16 as v. 13 has another introductory formula "behold" and two conclusions in v. 14 &16 and assigns some part of it to be the work of later traditionist. See Zimmerli, *Ezekiel 1*, 459 and Wevers, *Ezekiel,* 171.

75 Hand clapping seems here literally refers to gesture of a hostile reaction profiteering and murder, examples that span the foregoing, from v 12 back to v 3. See Allen, *Ezekiel 20-48*, 37. The accusation here literally reads "blood that are in your hand." Here the MT has singular noun and plural verb. LXX has plural noun and plural verb. Syriac has singular noun and singular verb. The accusation seems to reflect bloodshed in the hands of rulers of Jerusalem.

76 The meaning of his phrase may be clarified by its opposite in 21:12 "heart will melt" (נמס). Similarly in the next clause חזק "be strong" is the opposite of רפה "be slack" (hands) in 21:12. Thus, this rhetorical question declares that in the time of judgment hearts will quake and hands will be slackened.

77 Cf. Greenberg, *Ezekiel 21-37,* 457.

78 Allen, *Ezekiel 2*, 37.

people over to experience the consequences of their actions."[79] This sentence is confirmed by the declaration that not only Jerusalem, but also Yahweh himself shall be profaned among the nations by their impurities.[80] Zimmerli rightly interprets the passage:

> This event means the scattering of people, through which it perishes in its uncleanness (טמאה) and the terrible act occurs that Yahweh himself, who has committed his name to his people, is set in the forum of the nations as one who is dishonored...[81]

Thus, exile is a dishonor for Israel and for her God, which is caused by Israel's pollution. The oracle ends with the concluding formula "and you shall know that I am the Lord." In the state of defilement and humiliation in the sight of their enemies, they will at last learn something of the God they had forgotten. Thus, for Ezekiel the harsh destruction of an unclean Israel will serve as purgation that will let Yahweh's name to be known.

5. Summary and Conclusion

Ezekiel 22:1-31 portrays Israel's (Jerusalem's) sin, judgment of God, and crimes committed by leaders of the land of Judah with harsh accusations. Within this larger pericope of the oracles, scholars emphasize the uniqueness and the unity of Ezekiel 22:1-16 which has a literary form of a judgment speech. The oracle is named "judgment of the bloody city" connected by the repeated phrase שפך דם "shedding blood." Putting the text in the setting of the period between the first deportation (597BCE) and the fall of Jerusalem (587), the author(s) condemn inhabitants of Jerusalem for their cultic and moral impurities. The oracle in this passage enumerates various crimes against all members of society. There are vital theological and ideological points upon which the prophecy is built. The report of the sins of Jerusalem and divine judgment exhibits certain rhetorical strategies and sociological significance. The oracle needs to be examined in the light of group relationships and ideological responses to group conflicts. Questions may be raised concerning the central claim of the oracle in its portrayal of Jerusalem's sin.

From the above analysis one may conclude that Israel's sin is explicated in the context of purity and impurity. This is demonstrated by the repetitive use of

---

79 Cf. Gordon H. Matties, *Ezekiel 18 and the Rhetoric of Discourse*, SBL Dissertation Series 126 (Atlanta, Georgia: SBL 1989), 204.

80 LXX, Syriac and Vulgate Emend the Phrase: "You Shall be Profaned," which for the Hebrew reading is "I" referring to Yahweh. The MT is to be retained that when Jerusalem is defiled, Yahweh's reputation might suffer among the nations. Cf. Darr, "The Book of Ezekiel," 131. Profanation of Yahweh or Yahweh's name is found in many instances (Ezek 20:9, 14, 22, 39; 36:20, 21, 22, 23; 39:7).

81 Zimmerli, *Ezekiel 1*, 459.

the term "impure" (טמא) and the portrayal of Israel's sin as an abomination (תועבה). The serious crime everyone commits is bloodshed. Moreover, the reason for the great catastrophe (the mocking of the nations) is their idol worship. Profanation of the Sabbath and the holy things are strongly denounced, which are cultic offences. Other indictments also include impurities such as sexual crimes. Moral disorders such as injustices are again defined in the context of bloodshed, which is not only violent action, but a reversal of priestly legislation of bloodguilt. Everyone in Jerusalem commits sin as they are involved in bloodshed, social injustices and sexual misconduct. Rulers failed to keep traditional values of the social system. For Ezekiel, slanderers are those traders who make alliance with other nations, which is defiling the people of Israel before their God. In their alliance with idol worshippers, they practice various kinds of sexual wrongs. Bribe-takers shed blood for unjust gains. The crime of the inhabitants of Jerusalem and Judah are so severe that even Yahweh himself is being profaned. Only through purging the impurity of the city by scattering the citizens among the nations will the land be purified and people will know who Yaḥweh is. Judgment of God on the inhabitants of the homelanders is inevitable because of their lack of purity. This includes profanation of the holy, defilement of the human body with idolatry, bloodshed, sexual misconduct, and failure to keep human dignity. The extension of concept of purity is found here as all of Israel's offenses, moral or cultic are accounted as defiling. The portrait of Jerusalem and its inhabitants in this oracle shows that they are in no way worthy of possessing the land. For the author(s), the homelanders are responsible for the final destruction of Jerusalem due to their lack of purity.

The depiction of impending destruction in this chapter reflects the horrors of war and subsequent exiles. Ironically, Ezekiel does not primarily deploy this language against the perpetrators of violence, but rather "against insiders who supposedly pose the most profound danger to the survival of the community."[82] We have to note that the impending destruction found in this chapter is not a future event. The author and his audience have already seen these events. The portrayal of Jerusalem as a violent and cold-blooded city can hardly be treated as sober and objective reportage. Accusation of such serious crimes could hardly reflect the real social situation of the land of Judah during the exilic period. David J. Halperin rightly argues: "Surely sixth century Jerusalem was a home of violence and lawlessness. But no other biblical writer seems to react quite so vehemently to the city's misdeed. His (Ezekiel's) peculiar psychic bent refracted and distorted that reality."[83] In other words, Ezekiel's indignation of the wicked

82 Louis Stulman, "Ezekiel as Disaster/Survival Literature: Speaking on behalf of the Losers," in *The Prophets Speak on Forced Migration, Ancient Israel and Its Literature 21* (Atlanta: SBL Press, 2015), 138.

83 David J. Halperin, *Seeking Ezekiel: Text and Psychology* (University Park, Pennsylvania: The Pennsylvania University Press, 1993), 161.

city as an impure city is a sociological tool for drawing boundaries between the exilic group and the inhabitants of Judah during the exilic age. The whole oracle is written from a pro-Babylonian or *golah* perspective of the exile that condemns the homelanders. As an ideological discussion, the author of Ezekiel categorized the non-exilic group who remained in the land as committing moral and cultic crimes. In the context of intergroup conflicts and competition in the exilic age, the extreme negative evaluation of Jerusalem and its inhabitants served as a tool for rejecting the claim of ownership of the land by the homelanders. By contrast, the exilic group is presented as the remnant, the only hope for the future of Israel, the community that emerges out of the fire of the exilic refinement.

Looking from the perspective of group identification, this oracle is a systematic representation of a particular group as a secondary or marginalized group. With the criterion of purity as a social norm, the homelanders are portrayed as too disreputable to be included in the ingroup. Their impurities are presented in familial, socio-cultural and religious systems. Their contact and trade with other nations led them to various kinds of moral, economic and cultic impurities. This oracle is a description of the Jerusalemite community during the exilic period by the exilic group. Viewed from the perspective of a priestly group in exile, the author(s) of this oracle assesses the city's behavior in the past and its situation at the present with category of purity and impurity.[84] They delegitimized the claim to the land by those who are in the homeland. They rejected worship carried out by the homelanders disproving them as impure and corrupt. The whole system of the society of the land was viewed as failure. Divine judgment is impending for those who lived in Jerusalem and Judah during the exile. What is the fate of the exiles who are living in Babylonia while the homelanders face the judgment of God? This is a crucial issue in the book of Ezekiel, which I will discus in the next chapter.

84 Wolde, "A Cognitive Linguistic Study of the Concept of Defilement in Ezekiel 22:1-16," 269.

Chapter 6

Restoration and Purification of the Exiles (Ezekiel 37:15-28)

1. Introduction

Restoration is one of the most important theological themes in the book of Ezekiel, particularly in the later part of the book. In the previous chapter, I argue that the book of Ezekiel contains several accounts of the judgment of God on Jerusalem and its inhabitants for their sins and impurities. There is a shift of direction from judgment to message of hope and restoration. The oracles of salvation and restoration scrupulously avoid mention of Jerusalem.[1] There are a number of announcements of deliverance, which are a meager hope to the Judahites, or the exiles of the first *golah*, and hope for the whole diaspora after the fall of Jerusalem.[2] There is more focus on restoration of the exiles in the latter part of the book. Ezekiel 37:14-28 is one of the best examples of restoration of the exiles which contains unique features. This oracle pertains to a more inclusive restoration of the exiles of the whole diaspora.

---

1 Cf. Julie Galambush, *Jerusalem in the Book of Ezekiel: The City as Yahweh's Wife*, SBL Dissertation Series 130 (Atlanta, Georgia: SBL, 1992), 147.

2 Cf. William A. Tooman, "Covenant and Presence in the Composition and Theology of Ezekiel," in *Divine Presence and Absence in Exilic and Post-Exilic Judaism*, eds. Nathan MacDonald and Izaak J. De Hulster, FAT 2, Reihe 61 (Tubingen: Mohr Siebeck, 2013), 159. According to Tooman, The first type of hope may be found in Ezek 5:13; 6:8-9; 12:16; 14:11, 22-23; 20:33-39. The second type may include 11:14-21; 16:53-63; 17:22-24; 20:40-44; 28:25-26; 34:11-22, 23-24; 36:1-15; 36:16-38; 37:15-29.

Scholars are not of the same opinion in identifying the chapter where a thematic shift from oracles of judgment to a message of hope is found. In general, chapters 33-48 are named the "message of consolation/hope" or "oracles concerning the restoration of Israel."[3] Chapters 1-32 conceive the remnant in Judah as the outgroup, representing them of being rejected by Yahweh. Many passages in this section portray the land, the people and the sanctuary defiled, and the people doomed to punishment. In the meantime, languages of hope for the exiles are also found in the oracles of judgment.[4] Chapters 33-48 mainly focus on gathering of the exiles and restoration in the land of Israel. Various features including new life, new ruler, new covenant, purification/sanctification, and the establishment of the sanctuary in the land mark restoration of the exiles.[5] In these passages, the languages of purity are found in connection with restoration. Yahweh condemns the inhabitants of Judah saying, "When the house of Israel lived in their own land, they polluted it by their ways and actions" (36:17). By contrast, when Yahweh gathers the exiles, Israel no longer defiles the land as Yahweh has purified her (37:23, 28). The relation between restoration and purification of the exiles are interconnected in the restoration oracles. In this chapter, I investigate how restoration and purification of the exiles are portrayed in Ezekiel 37:15-28. I will also investigate how group identity is constructed in the portrayal of restoration and purification of the exiles in this passage.

2. Nature and Design

Ezekiel 37 portrays Israel's restoration and purification in two symbolic forms – one in the form of resurrection from death (vv. 1-14) and another in the form of two sticks fitting together (vv.15-28). While there are significant links between vv.

3 Most commentators follow this structural division. Some have divided the message of consolation into two parts: 33-39 (message of hope), and 40-48 (vision of the new temple and the new community). See Ronald M. Hals, *Ezekiel*, FOTL Vol. XIX (Grand Rapids, Michigan: Eerdmans, 1989), 3; Moshe Greenberg, *Ezekiel 1-20*, AB (New York 1983), 6, Daniel I. Block, *The Book of Ezekiel Chapters 1-24*. NICOT (Grand Rapids: Eerdmans, 1997), 23; John W. Wevers, *Ezekiel*, The Century Bible (London: Thomas Nelson and Sons, 1969), 9.

4 A change in perspectives from judgment oracle to oracle of hope is probably brought about by a change in historical circumstances. This also may be occasioned by redaction of the original message of the prophet in the book itself. It is hard to draw a hard and fast line between the two themes. In the arrangement of the book of Ezekiel, some passages of a more hopeful nature are found in the midst of oracles of judgment (cf. 11:14-21; 16:53-63; 17:22-24; 18:30-44; 20:33-44; 28:25-26; and 29:21). See discussion in, Werner E. Lemke, "Life in the Present and Hope for the Future," in *Interpreting the Prophets*, eds. James Luther Mays and Paul J. Achtemeier (Philadelphia: Fortress Press, 1987), 200-202.

5 We find promise of life when Israel turns her ways to God (33:10-20). Israel's restoration under one shepherd, a new Davidic king is promised (34:11-31). Yahweh intends to re-sanctify his holy name by restoring Israel (36:22-24), by purifying them from all their defilements (37:25). Yahweh revives the lifeless exiles (37:1-14). An everlasting covenant will be made with them (37:26); the sanctuary of God will be established in Israel when they are sanctified (37:27-28).

1-14 and vv. 15-28, different thematic content and the citation formula suggest the division into two literary units. The literary unit is demarcated by its own introductory formula, ויהי דבר־יהוה עלי "the word of the Lord came to me," (v.15). This unit (vv. 15-28) discusses how the dispersed people of the two kingdoms would participate in the restoration. It is plausible that vv. 15-28 became a unified text that was subsequently amplified with several literary units. The unity of the two parts is likely an editorial one, provided by Ezekiel himself or his close disciples.[6] In this oracle, the first part (vv. 15-24a) completes the salvation oracles (chaps 33-37) by promising the unity of Judah and Israel, and the second part (vv. 24b-28) provides a summary of the salvation oracle by relating it to the temple vision (chaps 40-48). The oracle is marked by a repetitive use of אחד "one" which occurs ten times. Restoration and Purification of the exiles are interconnected features in the oracle. The restored community in Israel will no longer defile the land as Yahweh purifies the people from their apostasy. When Yahweh moves his presence back into the land the sanctification of Israel will be complete. Scholars generally label this unit, "a re-union and restoration of the people of Israel."[7] Zimmerli calls it "repurification of the two parts of Israel."[8] We may also entitle it "restoration and purification of the exiles."

Ezekiel 15-28 takes the form of a symbolic or sign-act, but with a loose form.[9] This oracle is the only sign-act with a primarily positive message. The oracle has a systematic function as a salvation oracle updated perhaps at a later date.[10] In this oracle, Yahweh's directive for a sign act (vv.16-17) is followed by a kind of interpretation (vv. 18-19). From verse 21-28 we find lengthy divine speeches which can be considered as interpretation. Verses 21-24a discuss the restoration of Israel emphasizing the unity of the Israelites scattered by Assyria and Babylonia. Verses 24b-28 tells permanent restoration with the catch-word עולם "everlasting/forever," such as (a) everlasting dwelling in the land (v. 25) (b) David's everlasting prince

6 Cf. Lesile C. Allen, *Ezekiel 20-48*, WBC Vol. 29 (Dallas, Texas: Word Books, 1990), 192; also see Millard C. Lind, *Ezekiel* (Scottdale, Pa: Herald Press, 1996), 302.

7 See Katheryn Pfisterer Darr, "The Book of Ezekiel: Introduction, Commentary, and Reflections," in *NIB* Vol. VI, 1504; Walther Eichrodt, *Ezekiel: A Commentary*, trans. Cosslett Quin, OTL (Philadelphia: Westminster Press, 1970), 512; Moshe Greenberg, *Ezekiel 21-37*, AB (New York: Doubleday, 1997), 752.

8 Walther Zimmerli, *Ezekiel 2: A Commentary on the Book of the Prophet Ezekiel 25-48*, trans. James D. Martin, eds. Paul D. Hanson and Leonard Jay Greenspoon (Philadelphia: Fortress Press, 1983), 271.

9 Symbolic or sign-act form (*Symblischge Handlung*) of prophetic oracle has three parts: (1) Yahweh's instruction to perform the action, (2) the report of its execution, and (3) a word of interpretation. See Hals, *Ezekiel*, 355. See also Block, *Ezekiel 1-24*, 164ff. Other form of sign-acts are found in chaps 4-5; 6:11-12; 12;1-16, 17-20; 21:11-12, 13-22, 23-29; 24:15-24. See Block, *Ezekiel 25-48*, 393.

10 Hals argues that the original report of a symbolic action has been updated that the text in its final form has become a kind of summary collection of Ezekiel's message of hope. See, Hals, *Ezekiel*, 274.

(v. 25); (c) everlasting covenant (v. 26); and (d) everlasting presence of Yahweh's sanctuary in their midst (v. 28). Due to repetition, thematic development and expansion of contents, scholars find it difficult to divide this oracle into sections.[11] The oracle may be divided roughly into three sub units, viz: (1) vv. 15-19- a sign action of joining the two sticks; (2) vv. 20-24a - interpretation of the sign act – A nation purified and restored by Yahweh; and (3) vv. 24b – 28 – Promise of everlasting covenant and establishing divine sanctuary in the land.

3. Setting

Scholars generally agree that the oracle grew with editorial expansion of the original text. While most critics attribute the sign-act account in vv. 15-19 to Ezekiel, the authorship of vv. 20-28 has been much debated. There is an argument for a single authorship that the salvation promises of vv. 20-28 echo many of Ezekiel's prior promise of salvation. But there are hints of later additions with expanded forms. There is evidence to suggest that in addition to clarifying glosses interpreted here and there, the original sign-act account was subsequently expanded by vv. 20-24a (a contribution either of Ezekiel or of a redactor) and, at a later stage, by vv. 24b-28 (probably the product of another hand)."[12] Zimmerli considers vv. 20-28 as a redactional addition to the basic text of vv. 15-19, which emanated either from Ezekiel or from his school.[13] The term נשיא "prince/ruler" in v. 25b differentiates from מלך "king" in vv. 22, 24a, and seems to be a later correction (cf. 34:24).[14] Ezekiel never uses "Israel" for the northern kingdom. The use of Joseph representing the northern tribes here indicates a later traditionist's hand who feared that Joseph might not be understood and hence added "the stick of Ephraim."[15] Rom-Shilloni dates this chapter with other consolation prophecies (chaps 34-37) to a late period within the sixth century, probably earlier than the Edict of Cyrus.[16] As shown by the text's development and expansion, it is likely that the redactors of Ezekiel in the late exilic period arranged the oracles in this form. In the context of social instability and crisis of identity, this oracle envisions a restored community of Israel scattered by the Assyrian and Babylonian

11 For example, v. 20 indicates continuity with what preceded; v. 21 intended to answer the exile's question concerning the symbolic action which is not expressed in v. 20. v. 22 is an interpretation of the symbolic action originally linked with v. 19. See also discussion in Allen, *Ezekiel 20-48*, 191.

12 Cf. Darr, "The Book of Ezekiel," 1505. Tooman observes that vv. 24-28 is a late addition to the book which addresses the diaspora after the destruction of the temple in 587 BCE. See Tooman, "Covenant and Presence," 169.

13 Zimmerli, *Ezekiel 2*, 273.

14 See the meaning and usage of נשיא in the book of Ezekiel in Ian M. Daguid, "Kings and Princes," in *Ezekiel and the Leaders of Israel*, VTSup 56 (Leiden: E.J. Brill, 1994), 10-57.

15 Cf. Wevers, *Ezekiel*, 280.

16 Dalit Rom-Shiloni, *Exclusive Inclusivity: Identity Conflicts Between the Exiles and the People Who Remained (6th-5th Centuries BCE)* (New York: Bloomsbury, 2013), 196.

deportation. Purification and eternal presence of the holy God with them shall be a sign of Israel's new identity.

4. Text Analysis and Comments

4.1. Sign Action of Joining the Two Sticks (vv. 15-19)

v. 15. The word of Yahweh came to me saying,
v. 16. "You, Son of man, take one stick and write on it, "Judah and the people of Israel associated with it;"[17] *then take another*[18] *stick and write on it, "Joseph, the stick of Ephraim and all the people of Israel*[19] *associated with it.*
v. 17. And bring them together for yourself to be one stick so that they may become one in your hand.
v. 18. When your people say to you, "Will you not declare to us what are these?"
v. 19. Say to them, "Thus said the Lord Yahweh, behold I am taking the stick of Joseph which is in the hand of Ephraim and the tribes of Israel associated with it; and I shall put (join) them with the stick of Judah, and I will make them to become one stick and they shall be one."

After an introductory oracular formula (v. 15), Yahweh commands the prophet to perform a symbolic action. Yahweh commanded the prophet to bring the two pieces of wood/stick inscribed respectively with the names of Judah and the sons of Israel, and Joseph and the people (lit. sons) of Israel associated with it. He is told to bring the two sticks together. When people ask the meaning of the sign-act, the prophet has to tell them that the tribes of the northern kingdom represented by Ephraim will be joined with Judah, the representative of the south. It is a message of restoration of a united Israel represented with a sign act. However, further questions arise. What is meant by עץ in this context? What does the sign-act symbolize?

17 Many manuscripts have חבריו (associated with them) instead of חברו (singular) probably referring to the two nations in their separate locations. But here "Judah and the people of Israel" could indicate a one nation – Judah or the exilic group. The emendation is not necessary. Fisch interprets this phrase to mean the tribe of Benjamin which joined the tribe of Judah. See S. Fisch, *Ezekiel: Hebrew Text and English Translation with and Introduction and* Commentary (London: Soncino Press, 1950), 250.

18 The MT has אחד (one). As rendered by LXX, Vulgate, and Syriac אחר (another) is a better rendering.

19 MT has "house of Israel." LXX and Syriac read it בני ישראל instead of בית ישראל which are more likely correct readings. This is also seen in 3:1b. We have to note the difference between these two designations. See discussion about the scribal additions or alterations of Ezekiel's texts in Timothy P. Mackie, *Expanding Ezekiel: The Hermeneutics of Scribal Addition in the Ancient Text Witnesses of the Book of Ezekiel*, FRLANT 257 (Gotingen: Vandelhoeck & Ruprecht, 2015). The prophet had consistently used the name the "whole house of Israel" to refer to reunited Israel, not a particular tribe. See Ezek 3:1b; 11:15; 36:10. Cf. Jer 3:18.

4.1.1. The Sign Act - The עץ *of Judah and Joseph (v. 16)*

To interpret the meaning of the sign-act, we have to investigate the use of עץ in the Hebrew Bible. First, the term עץ can refer, depending on the context, to a stick, wood, timber, a tree or trees.[20] The Greek term for עץ is ραβδος which is variously translated as "stick," "twig" "rod" "shepherd staff," "royal scepter."[21] There are differing views concerning the meaning of the term עץ in this text. One possible implication is a royal scepter that represents the kings of the Northern and the Southern kingdoms.[22] Another proposal is a shepherd staff. This argument suggests that the two staffs represent clans or tribes. In Hebrew, the words for staff (שבת and מטה) can also mean "clan" or "tribe."[23] Hence, two sticks could imply rulership of the two kingdoms of Judah and Israel that have to be united into one.[24] Ezekiel objects to these two implications. One clear example is that the unification of the northern and the southern kingdom is found nowhere else in the book.[25] It can also mean, "tablet, which was also used in ancient times as a writing material."[26] Another idea is that עץ is a flat piece of wood, smoothed with hardened wax, on which rough messages could be written."[27] As suggested by many places in the book, עץ in this text probably is a small wooden writing-tablet, that can be used as a wooden stick.[28] It is likely that Ezekiel took two sticks of manageable size just to represent the tribes of the former two kingdoms. The sticks, therefore, represent the two groups of Israelites formerly divided into two nations.

---

20 See *HALOT* Vol. 2, 863-864. In Ezek 6:13; 31:8; 34:27 it has a meaning of trees (cf. Exo 7:19; Hos 4:12; Isa 40:2).

21 See Schneider, "ραβδος," *TDNT* Vol. VI, 966-971.

22 Sirach 47:21 understood the division of the kingdoms as a separation into two scepters. See discussion in Zimmerli, *Ezekiel 2*, 273.

23 See *BDB*, 641 & 986. The head of a tribe or a clan bear a staff as a symbol of authority (Num 17:1-11).

24 The book of Zechariah 11:7ff develops the idea of the staff representing the kingdoms of the south and the north. Odell observers that "the two sticks signify Yahweh's sovereign prerogative to rule and protect these people. See Margaret S. Odell, *Ezekiel*, Smyth and Helwys Bible Commentary (Macon, Georgia: Smyth & Helwys), 456.

25 See discussion in E. Power, "The Shepherd's Two Rods in Modern Palestine and in Some Passages of the Old Testament," *Biblica* 9 (1928): 434-442. See also Block, *Ezekiel 25-48*, 398-399.

26 Targum translates so. Block defends this translation by comparing with similar tools of writing found in ancient writing tablets. See Block, *Ezekiel 25-48*, 400.

27 Cf. Christopher J. H. Wright, The Message of Ezekiel: a New Heart and a New Spirit (Downers Grove, Ill.: InterVarsity Press, 2001), 399-401.

28 So it is translated as "stick" See chapters 17, 21,.31. Eichrodt, Zimmerli, and Odell are among others who translate it so. NRSV, NEB, ASB, NJB render as "stick." See Eichrodt, *Ezekiel* 511ff. Zimmerli, *Ezekiel 2*, 267ff., and Odell, *Ezekiel*, 455ff.

4.1.2. Uniting Judah and Joseph – Restoration of the Exiles (vv. 16-19)

When the prophet is commanded to bring the two sticks, he was also told to inscribe on it "Judah and the people of Israel associated with it and for Joseph, the stick of Ephraim, and the people of Israel associated with it" (v.16). The MT attached ל (for/regarding) before Judah and before Joseph. The force of the preposition ל before Judah and Joseph could signify different meanings. The most meaningful usage in this context may be "for/in regard to."[29] Ezekiel appends חברו to Judah and Joseph, which indicates "its companion," or "its associate." Ezekiel now takes the two sticks, one in each hand, and bring them together until it appears they are one in his hand. The symbolic meaning of "the two sticks and their associates" is a controversial issue.

From a close study of the historical and political development of ancient Israel, opinion among scholars remains significantly divided over the question of the two kingdoms and the tribes that made up the kingdoms.[30] According to Deuteronomistic history, the twelve tribes of Israel developed into two clusters. One was in the north, with Ephraim and Manasseh (the two Joseph tribes) dominant in this region. Another cluster was in the south, with Judah as the dominant force with the tribes of Benjamin and Simeon.[31] Following the death of king Solomon in 922 BCE, the two kingdoms of Israel and Judah had been established (1 King 12).[32] Israel with its capital at Samaria fell to the Assyrians under Sargon II (722/1 BCE) and Judah with its capital at Jerusalem fell to Babylonia in 587 BCE. Joseph sometimes designated the northern kingdom in some prophetic books, but most commonly known by Joseph's two sons, Ephraim and Manasseh.[33] The history of the Northern tribes after Assyrian domination was

---

29 Here ל should be taken as lamed of specification rather than of possession. Hence I omit "regarding" in the translation simply translating "Judah" and "Joseph." See the use of ל in *BDB*, 510-518.

30 See further discussion in Megan Bishop Moore and Brad E. Kelle, *Biblical History and Israel's Past: The Changing Study of the Bible and History* (Grand Rapids, Michigan: Eerdmans, 2011), 266-333.

31 See Josh 19:1-9; 1 Kings 12:23; 2 Chro 11:10, 12.

32 Clements who summarizes the challenge against the Deuteronomic history expresses that "in the earliest period the group of southern clans that make up the tribe of Judah and the group of northern clans that constituted Israel (Joseph) were really separate. Only the shared worship of the Lord as God and the success and leadership of David brought them briefly together to form a united people of Israel." See R. E. Clements, *Ezekiel* (Louisville: Westminster Jon Knox Press, 1996), 167.

33 See I Kings 11:28; Psalms 77:17; 80:1-2; Amos 5:15; Obadiah 18. The founder of the Northern kingdom Jeroboam I was an Ephraimite (1 Kings 15:25). Ephraim has become a popular designation of the tribes in the northern kingdom under the leadership of Jeroboam I (Hos 4:16-17). Ezekiel uses elsewhere only in tribal sense in 47:13 and 48:32.

scanty in the biblical record. There are numerous theories to explain the history of the Assyrian exiles; particularly after the fall of Assyria to Babylonia.[34]

Researchers demonstrate that the Israelites of the northern tribes who were scattered in the Assyrian empire retained their ethnic identity in spite of the assimilation policy of the Assyrians.[35] Some have argued that the remnant of the northern Israel emigrated to the south after the fall of Samaria.[36] William Rosenau argues that "the house of Joseph and the tribes associated with it," points to those people of the northern kingdom who formed a separate group at the time of temple construction at Jerusalem in 516 BCE.[37] This group could be those who refused to take part in the construction of the temple at Jerusalem as narrated in the book of Ezra-Nehemiah. It is plausible that the remnant of the northern tribes of the Assyrian exiles were absorbed in Babylonia. It is also probable that a few of them were mingled with those who remained in Judah during the sixth century BCE. The exact locations where the exiles of the northern kingdom lived following their deportation remain a subject of debate.

The idea of Israel as a unity was clearly a very important issue in the prophets, including Ezekiel. However, unity of the two kingdoms is not the focus in the book of Ezekiel. The use of Israel in v. 16 and 19 "Judah and the tribes of Israel associated with it," and "Ephraim and the tribes of Israel associated with it," shows Ezekiel reserves the use of the name Israel for the entire people of God,

---

34 One argument is that the people of the Northern kingdom were absorbed with the rest or the population when Babylonia conquered Assyria in 625 BCE by Nabopallassar. Another idea is that they scattered everywhere. Descendants of the ten tribes are said to have found in Europe (Anglo-Saxons), China, Japan, North America, and in India. See discussion in Allen H. Godbey, *The Lost Tribes A Myth: Suggestions Towards Rewriting Hebrew History*, Library of Biblical Studies (New York: KTAV Pub House, 1974; Tudor Parfitt, *The Lost Tribes of Israel: The History of a Myth* (London: Weidenfeld & Nicholson, 2002); Zvi Ben-dor Benite, *The Ten Lost Tribes: A World History* (Oxford: Oxford University Press, 2009). More than a thousand people from Mizoram and Manipur (NE India) who belong to Mizo tribe recently migrated to Israel claiming that they are descendants of Manasseh. See discussion in Zaithanchhungi, *Mizo-Israel Identity* (Aizawl, Mizoram: L. N. Tluanga, 2008).

35 For example, Gehard Maier maintains that archaeological evidences indicate the ethnicity of the northern tribes after the fall of Samaria until the time of Ezekiel. See Gerhard Maier, *Des Prophet Hesekiel Kapitel 25 bis 48* (Wuppertal: R. Brockhaus Verlag, 2000), 212. The presence of distinctive Israelite names in Samaria also suggests that many retained their ethnic identity in the North. See further discussion in Block, *Ezekiel 25-48*, 412.

36 From the Israelite material culture in Judah after the fall of Samaria, Israel Finkelstein maintains that "many of the new settlers in Jerusalem, the highlands of Judah and the Shephelah emigrated from the territory of Israel, mainly form the southern Samaria highlands." See Israel Finkelstein, "Migration of Israelites into Judah after 720 BCE: an Answer and an Update," *ZAW* 127, no. 2 (2015): 204.

37 See detail discussion in William Rosenau, "Ezekiel 37:15-28: What Happened to the Ten Tribes," in *Hebrew Union College Annual* 1925, Special Issue (Cincinnati: Hebrew Union College, 1925), 79-88.

not referring to the former northern kingdom.[38] Since the use of Joseph is less common in Ezekiel, it appears that the northern kingdom is not a legitimate kingdom for Ezekiel.[39] Ezekiel uses the term "Israel" for Judah, sometimes for the "entire house of Israel." (11:15); and makes no distinction between the North and the South.[40] Ralph W. Klein writes: "Ezekiel never uses the term "Israel" in the sense of the northern kingdom as opposed to Judah."[41] Israel therefore could mean Judah itself or the descendants of the twelve tribes of Israel scattered everywhere during the seventh-sixth century BCE.[42] For Ezekiel, Israel and Judah refers to the twelve tribes of Israel, who are now in exile. It refers to the Babylonian exiles and the remnant exiles of Assyria, who will participate in the restoration.

The prophet is commanded to bring the sticks together into his hand to become one. When his compatriots ask him the meaning of the sign-act, he says that Yahweh is about to take the two sticks together so that they may be one (stick). Here is a key word אחד "one" occurring ten times. This term suggests unification of the divided people for nearly two centuries. The interpretation remains a matter of debate.[43] While unification of the people of the North and the South are found in some prophetic texts, it appears that Ezekiel goes on his own way.[44] Ezekiel here refers to the diaspora groups of Israelites under Assyria and Babylonia. Though the existence of people in the homeland (Judah) was attested

38 Cf. Werner E. Lemke, "Life in the Present and Hope for the Future," in *Interpreting the Prophets*, eds. James Luther Mays and Paul J. Achtemeier (Philadelphia: Fortress Press, 1987), 213.

39 Cf. Block, *Ezekiel 25-48*, 402.

40 This is particularly seen in chapter 20 where Israel's history is narrated. See Discussion in Joseph Blenkinsopp, *Ezekiel: Interpretation*, A Bible Commentary for Teaching and Preaching (Louisville: John Knox Press, 1990), 175.

41 Ralph W. Klein, *Ezekiel the Prophet and His Message*, Studies in the Personalities of the Old Testament (Columbia, South Carolina: University of South Carolina Press, 1988), 152.

42 Wright agrees this idea that though the northern kingdom hijacked the name "Israel" for itself, the term still applied to the original ideal concept of the twelve tribes of Israel. See Christopher J. H. Wright, *Message of Ezekiel: A New Heart and A New Spirit* (Downers Grove, Ill.: InterVarsity Press, 2001), 313; Cooke also endorses this opinion. See G. A. Cooke, *A Critical and Exegetical Commentary on The Book of Ezekiel Vol. II*, ICC (New York: Charles Scribner's Sons, 1937), 401.

43 The most likely implication is that Yahweh is bringing the exiles of the two nations back into Israel as one nation. But, this interpretation may be challenged for two reasons: (1) If the inhabitants of Israel/Samaria were scattered throughout the Assyrian Empire, is there any prospect of their descendants being literally brought back with the exiles of Judah into the promised land. (2) Since the term Israel was used freely to describe the southern kingdom of Judah when the Assyrians had overrun the north, its use could have been ambiguous. See more discussion in John B. Taylor, *Ezekiel: An Introduction and Commentary* (Downers Grove, Ill., InterVarsity Press, 1969), 239-240.

44 Restoration of the exiles with an inclusive tone of embracing the "house of Judah," "house of Israel," and "house of Jacob," is found in the book of Zechariah 8:13 and Isaiah 40:227; 41:14; 44:21, etc.

in the time of Ezekiel, they are not mentioned in the promise of restoration. Those designations, "Israel" "house of Judah/Israel" and "Joseph," are terms used by the exiles to designate themselves as the legitimate heir of the land.[45] Hence, Ezekiel envisions a new united Israel of diaspora groups restored to the land of Israel. The restored nation is a new nation rooted in the dispersed group of exiles.

4.2. The Nation Restored and Purified by Yahweh (vv. 20-24a)

v. 20. When the sticks you write upon your hand are before their eyes,
v. 21. Then say to them, "Thus said the Lord Yahweh, Behold I will take the sons of Israel from the nations where they have gone, I shall gather them from every side, and bring them to their own land.
v. 22. And I will make them to one nation in the land, on the mountains of Israel. There shall be one king[46] *over all of them; and they shall never again be divided into two kingdoms.*
v. 23. And they shall never again defile themselves with their idols and their detestable things; nor with any of their transgressions. I will save[47] *them from all the sins of their apostasies*[48] *and I will purify them. They shall be my people and I will be (to them) their God.*
v. 24(a). My servant David shall be king over them; there shall be one shepherd to all of them.

The symbolic act of taking the sticks together is interpreted in this way. When Israel is taken from the land of the nations they will be brought back to their own land (v. 21). They will become one nation in the land, on the mountains of Israel with one king. This is what Jeremiah also foretells in 3:18: "In those days the house of Judah join the house of Israel, and together they shall come from the land of the north to the land that I gave your ancestors for a heritage." (NRSV). In another passage restoration and transformation of Israel is seen as a new covenanted people in Jeremiah (Jer 31). In Ezekiel, restoration not only involved covenant renewal or transformation, but endowment of the רוח יהוה "spirit of God" and purification of the people. As Block comments, restoration

45 Cf. Rom-Shiloni, *Exclusive Inclusivity*, 196.

46 The MT has "king to be king over them." Greek and Syriac rightly omit the gloss מלך "to be king" as it may be a copyist's dittograph of לכלם, "for all of them."

47 Ezekiel is the only prophetic book where we find ישע in the context of saving from impurities. Cf. Lind, *Ezekiel*, 304. Wevers writes, "Restoration, not salvation (appears only here and 34:22; 36:29) was the hope of the Ezekiel school." See Wevers, *Ezekiel*, 282.

48 Symachus Greek renders "dwellings." Many manuscripts following LXX read this as "backslidings or apostasies." The MT has מושבתיהם (dwellings) for משבותיהם (their turning-back). Apparently, a scribe reversed ש and ו in the MT. Cf. Steven S. Tuell, *Ezekiel: New International Biblical Commentary* (Peabody, Massachusetts: Hendrickson Publishers, 2009), 262.

involves (a) ethnic and territorial integrity (v. 21), (b) political integrity (v. 22), and (c) spiritual integrity (v. 23-24a).[49]

Restoration of the ethnic integrity is shown by the use of בני ישראל "sons of Israel." There is a shift from Judah and Joseph (Ephraim) in vv. 15-20 to the one designation of the ethnic unity of Israel from verse 21. Here the whole population of Israel is named בני ישראל "sons/descendants of Israel." Not only the Babylonian and Assyrian exiles, it probably includes those who voluntarily immigrated to Egypt because Yahweh will "gather them from every side (מסביב) where they have gone."[50] Crane observes that "gathering them from every side into their own land" is a message applicable to all in the Diaspora whether their 'entering' was forced or voluntary.[51] It indicates that restoration will involve a much wider Diaspora.[52] Hence, Ezekiel's vision of the remnants include the dispersed group in the upper Mesopotamia who had been dispersed and assimilated since 722 by the Assyrian power, the exiles of Babylonia who lived in the area around the banks of river Tigris and Euphrates, and the exiles in Egypt. Israel's reunification has a new shape with unity of the exilic groups and returning the exiles into their homeland. Formerly, Ezekiel portrays the land as devastated (Ezek 33:24; 36:3 Cf. Lev 36:43). The returning exiles will form a new community (11:16; 36:2-36). The expression "I will make them one nation in the land, on the mountains of Israel" (v. 22) signifies restoration of territorial integrity. It is a reversal of judgment on the land and its people.

Restoration of the political integrity is mentioned in verse 22. The political ends of Israel in 722 and Judah in 587/6 were lingering in the mind of the exiles. Here Ezekiel envisions restructuring of political integrity of separate nations into one nation with one king. The key words in this verse are – אחד (one) and לא לשני (not two) mentioned twice respectively. Israel will be constituted a single nation (גוי), under one ruler when they return to their own land – at the mountains of Israel.[53] The use of מלך (king) not נשיא (ruler) in this context (also in v. 24) puzzles us because the term mostly signifies foreign kings, and נשיא is used more

49 See further discussion in Block, *Ezekiel 25-48*, 410-415.

50 Another exilic prophet Deutero-Isaiah uses the term "the nations" (הגוים) used five times to refer to all displaced, survivors, and known nations who will be restored (Isa 40:17; 42:1; 43:9; 45:20; 52:10). It is plausible that Deutero-Isaiah addresses the entire community - the Babylonian exiles, Judeans who remained in the land, and the Egyptian exiles. See discussion in the whole house of Israel in prophetic literature in chapter 2.

51 Ashley Crane, *Israel's Restoration: A Textual-Comparative Exploration of Ezekiel 36-39*, VTSup 122 (Leiden/Boston: Brill, 2008), 115-116.

52 Cf. Horace D. Hummel, *Ezekiel 21-48*, Concordia Commentary (Saint Louis: Concordia Publishing House, 2007), 1089.

53 The mountains of Israel is one of Ezekiel's favorite phases used 16 times referring to the homeland. See Ezek 6:2,3; 19:9; 32:28; 33:28; 34:13,14; 35:12; 36:1(2), 4; 36:8; 38:8; 39:2,4,17.

frequently for Israel's ruler.[54] The LXX prefers αρχων (ruler) instead of βασιλευς (king) here and in v. 24. This is explained in various ways.[55] John W. Olley notices that "in the LXX, David is a 'ruler in their midst,' as part of the people, unlike MT's 'king over them.' It is a spiritual and political leadership, with no military aspects."[56] Block rightly concludes that "the present choice of מלך highlight the restoration of Israel to full nationhood. To the prophet's audience, the use of נשׂיא would have signified less than complete restoration."[57] The promise assures the exiles a reunited nation with political stability in their land.

In addition to the nation's reunification, restoration also involves the spiritual integrity of Israel (v. 23), which is purification of the exiles. The exiles were assured that they would never again defile themselves with their images and detestable things. These practices led the two kingdoms to destruction (Ezek 16, 20). The exiles are told that "Yahweh will save them from their apostasies." The MT renders these words of promise: והושעתי אתם מכל מושבתיהם אשר חטאו "I will save them from the dwelling places of their sins."[58] To save from apostasy is equivalent to cleansing the defiled (cf. Ezek 36:25-28). Yahweh's great promise is sealed by וטהרתי אותם "and I will cleanse/purify them." Thus, restoration of the exiles goes together with purification. As found in the oracles of judgment, the reason for punishment of the homelanders is explicitly mentioned that they defiled themselves with idols and detestable things. Idolatry led to the divine abandonment of Jerusalem and the Temple. By looking back to the period of defilement, the text predicts the restoration and purification of the exiles. The final chapters of Ezekiel (40-48) also predict the restored and purified Jerusalem as well as a series of regulations to ensure a holy environment that would secure the deity's continued presence.[59] Thus, in a new community of a one nation,

54 For example, the kings of Babylon (17:12; 19:9; 21:23-25; 26:7), Egypt (29:2-3), Tyre (28:12), Edom (32:29), the earth (28:17), and the coastlands (27:23). The use of נשׂיא is found in many places such as19:1; 32:29; 34:24; 38:2f.; 39:1; 44:3; 46:2f., among many.

55 For example, Johan Lust argues that LXX and its vorlage downplay the role of the expected human leader enhancing the royal messianic character of the expectation. Van der Kooij argues that the use of נשׂיא legitimized the Maccabean rulers who were also high priests. See discussions in Johan Lust, "Messianism in LXX-Ezekiel: Towards a Synthesis," in *The Septuagint and Messianism*, ed. M. K. Knibb, BETL 195 (Leuven: Peeters, 2006), 430; Van der Kooij, "The Septuagint of Ezekiel and Hasmonean Leadership," in *Interpreting Translation: Studies on the LXX and Ezekiel in Honour of Johan Lust*, eds. F. Garcia Martizes and M. Vervenne, BETL 192 (Leuven: Peeters, 2005), 437-446.

56 John W. Olley, *Ezekiel: A Commentary Based on Iezekiel in Codex Vaticanus.* Septuagint Commentary Series (Leiden: Brill, 2009), 495.

57 Block, *Ezekiel 25-48*, 414.

58 Following the rendering of LXX, NRSV and NAB translate it "apostasies." REB and NIV have "backsliding" and the NJB translates as "infidelity." The suggested root משובתיהם has a meaning of "turn," suggesting backsliding or disobedience (Cf. Jer 8:5; Hos 11:7).

59 See Jill Middlemas, "Divine Presence and Absence: Aniconism and Multiple Imaging in the Prophets," in *Divine Presence and Absence in Exilic and Post Exilic Judaism*, eds. Nathan

there will be no defilement among them. The identity of the restored community is described as different from that of the defiled people in the homeland. As in 36:15-28, inner renewal of the people will be an essential aspect or their return to the land. Inner renewal will be complete when they restore their relationship with God. This restored relationship is summarized by a covenant formula." "They will be my people, and I will be their God." It is the purified community who will settle in the land as the people of God.

In verse 24(a) restoration of political integrity is recapitulated with the establishment of Davidic rule. The term מלך is used again here. Block notes, the use of this term in this context indicates restoration of full nationhood.[60] But, the new king is named עבדי דוד "David my servant." This emphasis reflects the relationship of a new king with Yahweh. David is the only person except Jacob who is referred to in Ezekiel as "my servant."[61] The use of the designations עבדי "my servant" and רועה עליהם "shepherd unto them" explains the nature of an anticipated new ruler who will have an intimate relationship with God and the people.[62] Lemke writes, "Ezekiel and his disciples were not necessarily looking forward to restoration of the Davidic monarchy. David in this passage is more of an ideal symbol of Israelite unity than a specific past or further historical future."[63] This new ruler will embody the ideals of a shepherd-king who will take care of the people after the model set out in chapter 34.[64] In this oracle, there are various titles for a ruler such as king, prince, and shepherd. These might reflect the historical situations in which the book took its shape.[65] This section of the oracle (vv. 20-24a) offers a new hope for the exiles who were scattered by the Assyrians and the Babylonians. Yahweh is going to restore them in their own land to be a united nation and purify them to regain their status as covenanted people. Blenkinsopp summarizes this section as follows:

> Yahweh proposes to reunite the twelve tribes now dispersed in foreign countries, bring them back to their own land, and constitute them as a purified people under a single ruler. How, given the fate of the northern tribes, this was thought to be possible, we do not know. Perhaps Ezekiel

---

Macdonald and Izaak J. De Hulster, FAT 61 (Tubingen, Germany: Mohr Siebeck, 2013), 186.

60 Block, *Ezekiel 25-48*, 414.

61 Bruce Vawter and Leslie J. Hoppe, *A New Heart: A Commentary on the Book of Ezekiel* (Grand Rapids: Eerdmans, 1991), 204.

62 עבד "servant" is a title of great honor in the ancient Near East and in the biblical literature. Great leaders of the Hebrew Bible are named "servant of the Lord."

63 Lemke, "Life in the Present and Hope for the Future," 213.

64 See discussion on the shepherd motif in the book of Ezekiel in Ignatius M. C. Obinwa, *The Shepherd Motif in Ezekiel 34: Its Theological Import and Socio-Political Implications*, FZB 125 (Wurzburg: Echter Verlag GmbH, 2012). Also See James A. Durslesser, *The Metaphorical Narratives in the Book of Ezekiel* (Lewiston, New York: Edwin Mellen Press, 2006), 9-38.

65 Cf. Clements, *Ezekiel*, 168.

had in mind the survivors of the mixed population to the north or whom we hear from time to time (e.g. Jer 41:4-8)… Some of these may be who profess to worship Yahweh or Jewish settlers at Elephantine who return from captivity. But is seems likely that Ezekiel is acting out and proclaiming an eschatological goal the fulfillment of which would be brought about by God.[66]

4.3. Everlasting Covenant with the Restored Community (vv. 24b-28)

v. 24b. They shall follow my ordinances; they shall keep my statutes.
v. 25. And they shall dwell in the land which I gave my servant Jacob[67] *where your ancestors lived in it.*[68] *And they shall dwell in it; they and their children and the children of their children forever. And my servant David shall be their prince forever.*
v. 26. And I will make with them a covenant of peace; it shall be an everlasting covenant
with them. And I will bless them[69] *and will multiply them. I will set my sanctuary in their midst forever.*
v. 27. And my tabernacle shall be with[70] *them; I will be their God and they shall be my people.*
v. 28. Then the nations shall know that I am Yahweh who sanctify Israel when my sanctuary is among them forever.

This section (vv. 24b-28) summarizes restoration prophecies of chapters 34-37. It also looks forward to the new community in chapters 40-48. Thematic repetition of Davidic rule with a more detailed explanation of the covenant theme suggests a later addition to vv. 21-24a.[71] Like 36:27, verse 24b stresses that the people will live in obedience to the Lord's statutes and ordinances. From v. 25 we find promises that run through verse 28. The promises are sealed by an epithet עולם "forever" found five times (vv. 25(2), 26(2), 28). The permanence of the promise is

66 Blenkinsopp, *Ezekiel*, 176.

67 Jacob not Abraham is mentioned here probably because he is the ancestor of the twelve tribes. In 33:23-29, we have Abraham not Jacob as the ancestor of Israel in which land possession is mentioned.

68 Here is a switch to second person. Tooman considers this as a sign of locution form 20:42, which was not syntactically adjusted, to match to the new context. See Tooman, "Covenant and Presence," 169.

69 The MT has ונתתים "I will put them." AV has "I will place them." Here NRSV follows the Targum, which reads, "I will bless them." This makes sense as it is followed by והרביתי "I will multiply."

70 Literally "over/upon them." The preposition עליהם "upon them" instead of the usual בתוכם "in their midst" signifies that the presence of God would inspire and hover upon them.

71 Cf. Zimmerli, *Ezekiel 2*, 276; Millard C. Lind, *Ezekiel* (Scottdale, PA: Herald Press, 1996), 302.

assured by the prefixes עד and ל attached to עולם.[72] The word bears the meaning of duration and nuances of permanence, durability, inviolability, irrevocability and immutability.[73] Ezekiel's emphasis is the final solution of covenant relationship. It is no longer the covenant alone that is described as eternal. Possession of the land, the monarch, the sanctuary and the divine presence are all explicitly permanent.[74]

First, the people will dwell in the land forever (v. 25a) – The land is identified as the land given to "my servant Jacob." This promise echoes Gen 28:13-15; 35:9-15. Ezekiel may use Jacob instead of Abraham as the ancestor of the twelve tribes. Their ancestor (my servant Jacob) or the descendants of Jacob, who are in exile, lost the land in Ezekiel's lifetime. Promise of land to the fathers will be realized with the returning exiles. A land where their ancestors dwelled will be given to them. The returning exiles will possess that land (cf. 36:36). The claim of the non-deported group for possession of the land is negated (Cf. 11:15; 33:24). The land is portrayed as defiled by its inhabitants until Yahweh cleansed the exiles and made the land like the Garden of Eden when the exiles return home (cf. 36:33-37).

Secondly, Davidic rule shall be established forever (v. 25b): David shall be a prince to them forever. If Israel is to be restored, she must be restored to unity as David ruled the territory of the twelve tribes. [75] Unlike v. 22 and v. 24 the term נשׂעי "prince/ruler" is used here. In Ezekiel the term is used several times when speaking of the Davidic head of state.[76] This is the ancient and honorable term for a ruling office in Israel. This designation appears to emphasize a limitation on the powers and activities of the Davidic house.[77] Joyce comments that the use of this term in this text represents a downgrading of royal language.[78] In Ezek 40-48, the prince's chief function is to be the patron of the liturgy, as a religious leader.[79] Vawter and Hoppe comment: "The use of נשׂיא in Ezekiel probably reflects the prophet's hesitancy to endorse the kind of monarchy that produced the abuses

72 In Hebrew Bible the term has two major senses: bygone times and the future. When עד is attached to it, it conveys the meaning of something static or unchangeable, and when ל is attached to it, it conveys a temporal progression of "always" or "perpetual." See further discussion in Preuss, "עולם," *TDOT* Vol. X, 530-545.

73 Cf. Block, *Ezekiel 25-48*, 416.

74 Cf. Tooman, "Covenant and Presence," 170.

75 Cf. Robert W. Jenson, *Ezekiel* (Grand Rapids, Michigan: Brazos Press, 2009), 288.

76 See Ezek 7:27; 12:10, 12; 19:1; 21:30; 34:24.

77 Cf. Ralph W. Klein, *Ezekiel: The Prophet and His Message*, Studies in the Personalities of the Old Testament (Columbia: University of Carolina Press, 1988), 153.

78 Cf. Paul M. Joyce, *Ezekiel: A Commentary* LHB/OTE 482 (New York: T&T Clark, 2007), 211.

79 See 44:3; 45:7-9, 16-17, 22; 46:2,4,8,10,12,16-18; 48:21-22. In Deuteronomy 17:18-20, the נשׂיא is to devote himself entirely to the study of the Law. It may be that the author (Ezekiel) adopts the ideology and political theory of the authors of Deuteronomy. See discussion in Blenkinsopp, *Ezekiel*, 176.

that marred the Davidic dynasty. As used in the Pentateuch, it perhaps designates the monarchy or the human ruler under the aegis of the covenant of Sinai."[80] This term found in v. 25, 26, and 28 is a strong indication that Ezekiel is here thinking not so much of a line of Davidic kings, as he had known them in the past. The new ruler would have "all the qualities of wisdom, endowment with the Spirit, righteousness and peace that were expected of God's anointed ruler."[81] Cooke writes, "He (the *nasi*) is overshadowed by the ministry of worship; his function amounts to little more than providing and attending the sacrifices on Sabbaths and festivals." [82] We find here a little exposition of the Davidic tradition of the messianic advent of the king. In the time of restoration, a Davidic king will have both the role of an administrator and a leader. He will have responsibility for spiritual care preparing Israel to worship God.

Thirdly, Yahweh will make an everlasting covenant with them (v. 26-27a). The covenant formula has two significant qualifiers: ברית שלום "covenant of peace" and ברית עולם "eternal covenant." The promise to the exiles is not only restoration and reunification; it is a covenant making qualified by peace and permanence (Cf. 34:25-31). The covenant of peace and eternal covenant recalls Noachian covenant (Gen 9:12), Abraham (Gen 17:7), Mosaic (Exod 31:16; Lev 24:8), and Davidic (2 Sam 7). The covenant envisions by Ezekiel goes beyond Jeremiah's new covenant (Jer 31:31). Ezekiel looks forward to an everlasting covenant between God and Israel, which is a covenant of wholeness, peace and plenty, a covenant of peace.[83]

The content of the covenant includes a blessing for population increase and the eternal presence of the divine with the establishment of מקדש in the land. First, the covenant is defined by blessing of the population. The MT lacks "blessing" in verse 26 which forces us to read: "I will give them and multiply them." This is missing also in the LXX. Block reads, "I will give to them (the land of Israel)." claiming that "the land of Israel" is inserted to make explicit what is implicit in the verb ונתתים.[84] Greenberg and Allen argue that ונתתים (I will give them) was mistakenly inserted here.[85] NRSV follows the Targum and reads "And I will bless them and multiply them." The Targum reading is an appropriate reading as the sentence is abrupt without the predicate. Blessing with population increase recalls the priestly blessing (Gen 1:22; Gen 22:17 cf. Ezek 36:11).

80 Vawter & Hoppe, *A New Heart*, 204.

81 Cf. Taylor, *Ezekiel: An Introduction and Commentary*, 240.

82 Cooke, *Ezekiel* Vol. II, 403. Cf. Ezek 44:3; 46:1-2, 16-18.

83 For discussion about covenant in the Hebrew Bible and Ezekiel See further discussion in E. Kutsch, "ברית," in *TLOT* Vol. 1, 256-266.

84 Block, *Ezekiel 25-48*, 408.

85 Greenberg, *Ezekiel 21-37*, 757; Allen, *Ezekiel 20-48*, 191.

Secondly, Yahweh will set his sanctuary in the midst of the restored people forever. This promise of covenant goes beyond Jeremiah's restoration.[86] Verses 26-28 contain the eternal presence of Yahweh with three emphases:

ונתתי את־מקדשי בתוכם לעולם	I will put my sanctuary in their midst forever (v. 26)
יהוה משכני עליהם	My tabernacle shall be with them (v. 27)
מקדשי בתוכה לעולם	(when) my sanctuary is in her midst forever (v. 28)

These promises are the most elevated promises of eschatological salvation in Ezekiel's book."[87] Yahweh declares that he will put his own מקדש "sanctuary" in the midst of the people forever. Yahweh commanded Moses to make the sanctuary where he will meet his people (Exo 15:15; 25:8; Lev 16:33; 19:30). In the vision of judgment of God there are several occasions when Yahweh abandons the sanctuary due to the impurities of the inhabitants of Jerusalem. Particularly the vision in chaps 8-11 depicts Yahweh abandoning the Jerusalem temple, and moving to the East. But, Yahweh himself had been מקדש מאט (a little sanctuary) to his people in exile (11:16). He now promises a full restoration of his sanctuary in the land. Yahweh promises that he will set his מקדש in their midst forever. The temple was the sign of God's eternal presence in Israel's midst."[88] Tooman observes that "the subject of divine presence only appears in the diaspora-oriented oracles."[89] This text anticipates hope of restoration of the whole diaspora, not including those who lived in the land.

Here two terms are used of the sanctuary. First, מקדש (sanctuary/temple) is the place where Yahweh dwells in the midst of Israel. This word is related to the verb to sanctify.[90] This is Ezekiel's favorite designation for the sanctuary which refers to the true home of Yahweh, unpolluted by Israel's sin.[91] This recalls the

86 In the prophecy of consolation in Jeremiah (30-33), we find prediction of restoration of the exiles in the same manner as Ezekiel. However, there is no mention of promise of divine dwelling among the exiles and re-establishment of the sanctuary in the land. Tobias Häner argues that vv. 26-28 was added up to link with Lev 26:11 a that announces, "Yahweh will put his dwellings among his people." See Tobias Häner, *Bleibendes Nachwirken des Exils: Eine Untersuchung zur kanonischen Endgestalt des Ezechielbuches*, HBS 78 (Freiburg: Harder, 2014), 455.

87 Cf. Jenson, *Ezekiel*, 288.

88 Vawter & Hoppe, *A New Heart*, 170.

89 Tooman, "Covenant and Promise," 159. See other examples in Ezek 11:14-21; 34:25-31; 43:9.

90 This term occurs 105 times in the book of Ezekiel. It has an implication of 'holy,' 'pure' and 'consecrated.' Being 'holy' emphasizes a condition of cultic and moral purity. The term used as the sanctuary connotes the sacredness of the divine who dwells in it. See further discussion in Tova Ganzel, "The Concept of Holiness in the Book of Ezekiel" (PhD Dissertation: Bar-Ilan University, Ramat-Gan, Israel, 2005).

91 Cf. Steven S. Tuell, "Divine Presence and Absence in Ezekiel's Prophecy," in *The Book of Ezekiel Theological and Anthropological Perspectives*, SBL Symposium Series 9 (Atlanta: SBL, 2000), 114.

divine presence with the exiles in Ezek 11:16. The Lord makes Israel a holy nation with God's sanctuary set in its midst (Ex 19:6). The divine presence is mediated through the temple and the cultic acts carried out in it (Ezek 40-48). Divine presence with the restored community is subsumed in the sanctification of Israel, the visible sign of which is the sanctuary in their midst. The second term for temple is משכן, often translated tabernacle. In Ezekiel, the term is found only here and in 25:4. From a secular usage of human dwelling, this term have come to denote a complex tent sanctuary in the priestly literature.[92] A synonym for tabernacle in the book of Exodus is אהל מועד "tent of meeting" (Exo 29:10), where God meets with the people. This may recall P's tent-shrine, not a temple building.[93] This usage perhaps connected with the ark in the earlier period and would have been used in a later period to refer to divine abode in the Jerusalem temple.[94] It is from the conception of the sanctuary as a משכן that the rabbis derived the notion of the Shekinah, the Lord's indwelling of his people.[95] Thus for Ezekiel, God's action to create a new community is illustrated in the form of establishing the abode of Yahweh among them.

Restoration of the exiles with a divine presence among them will have a great impact (v. 27b-28). This is expressed in the covenant formulas (1) "I will be their God and they shall be my people," and (2) "the nations will know that Yahweh sanctifies Israel." This statement is the climax of the covenant.[96] The ultimate purpose of restoration and purification of the exiles is to restore a relationship between Yahweh and his people. In the context of dispersion among the nations, Israelites will learn that Yahweh calls them to restore the covenant relationship which was made with their ancestors.

Yahweh's sanctification of the exiles and the establishment of the sanctuary in the land have interconnected significance. First, through purification and sanctification of Israel, the nations will know who is Yahweh. Yahweh manifests his

---

92 Ex. 35:15, 18; 36:14, 20, 22; Num 3:23, 25, 26, 29, 35, 36, 38; 4:14. See further discussion in D. Kellermann, "משכן," *TDOT* Vol. IX, 58-64. The roots of the language שכן (dwelling/tabernacling/abide) may have come from theophany of the divine cloud and pillar of fire accompanying Israel during the exodus and desert wanderings. Cf. Hummel, *Ezekiel 25-48*, 1097.

93 Tuell, "Divine Presence and Absence in Ezekiel's Prophecy," 114.

94 Cf. Zimmerli, *Ezekiel 2*, 277. Cf. G. Von Rad, *Old Testament Theology Vol. 1*, trans. D.M.G. Stalker (Louisville: Westminster John Knox Press, 2001), 234-236.

95 Cf. Jenson, *Ezekiel*, 289. Thus, the Targum paraphrases 37:27: "I will make my Shekinah dwell among them." See Samson Levy, *The Targum of Ezekiel*, Aramaic Bible 13 (Collegeville: Liturgical Press, 1990), 104.

96 The covenant formula portrayed in Ezekiel is an exposition of both Davidic tradition and Sinai tradition. We can observe that unlike Jeremiah who separates the tradition, Ezekiel fuses the Sinai tradition and the Davidic tradition. Von Rad expresses that the Sinai covenant tradition dominates Ezekiel's thought that "I their God, they my people," is a dominating theme in the covenant making. See further discussion in G. Von Rad, *Old Testament Theology Vol. II*, trans. D.M.G. Stalker (Louisville: Westminster John Knox Press, 2001), 236-237.

holiness in the sight of the nations (cf. 20:41; 28:25; 36:23). Yahweh owns honor when the covenant profaned by the people living in the land is restored with the arrival of the community of the exiles. Second, establishment of the sanctuary in the midst of Israel is a sign of the sanctification of Israel. The sanctuary "would be a sign to the nations that Israel was being maintained as a people sacred to God."[97] In the earlier chapter of the book, there was an accent on Yahweh's presence as his כבוד. The כבוד יהוה departed Jerusalem and the Temple due to defilements and moved to the land of exile. Yahweh's כבוד will return to Jerusalem in the מקדש when the covenant is restored between Yahweh and the exiles. There is a play on words in the use of the root קדש here. Yahweh says, בתוכה ... אני יהוה מקדשי בתיות מקדש "I am who sanctify... when my sanctuary is in their (her) midst." As discussed earlier, purity and holiness are the prerequisite for the presence of the sanctuary among his people. The presence of Yahweh's sanctuary (מקדש) in the midst of the people is his sanctification (קדש) and election of Israel to be his holy nation, consecrated for his glory.[98] The purpose of Yahweh's restoration of the exiles is the sanctification of Israel so that his divine presence will abide with them forever. When Yahweh restores Israel, the land, the people and the Temple in Jerusalem will be sanctified.

5. Summary and Conclusion

Ezekiel 37:15-28 is one of the sign-act oracles that illustrates restoration and purification of the exiles. As one of restoration oracles (Ezek 33-37), this broadens the concept of restoration by including the whole diaspora community. The oracle shifts its concern from the judgment of God on the inhabitants of the homeland to focus on consolidating the identity of the exiles. With symbolic representations, the prophet predicts that the people scattered by the Assyrian and the Babylonian deportations are to be united under one ruler and one shepherd. The text predicts that the restored community will not defile themselves with idols, as did the inhabitants of the land during the exilic period. Rather, they will be united as one nation with a new ruler in their own land with the dwelling of Yahweh among them. Not only will the people be restored in the land, the sanctuary will also be established in the land. Restoration for Ezekiel is unique in that it involves purification, sanctification, and reestablishment of the sanctuary in the land.

The promised restoration might not be a geographical unity (of north and south kingdoms), but a unity of the diaspora community into one nation under one ruler. The text does not look forward to a military-style monarchy. It rather foresees a prince, a religious leader and shepherd-servant leadership of a new Israel. The text visualizes restoration of the exiles back to their own land

97 Charles R. Biggs, *The Book of Ezekiel* (London: Epworth Press, 1996), 120.

98 Cf. Block, *Ezekiel 25-48*, 421.

and purification of the exiles from their impurities so that the sanctuary and the sheltering presence of Yahweh will be with them forever.

We can infer that oracles of hope of restoration in Ezekiel offer hope to the exilic groups of all diaspora. This oracle pertains to reestablishment of Israel as a nation in the land. Surprisingly, there is no mention of the people living in Judah in relation to restoration. While oracles of judgment condemn those who remained in the land during the time of exile, oracles of restoration focus on the exiles. While the non-deported groups are characterized as defiled and punished, the exiles are characterized as purified, sanctified and restored. The oracles concerning purification and divine presence only occur when the diaspora groups are addressed. Hence, the main thrust of this oracle is restoration of the exiles and rebuilding of a new community out of the returning exiles.

Restored nation in the fullest sense is a dream for the prophet and the disciples of Ezekiel. In this oracle, the redactors recapitulated the original work of Ezekiel in the situation of identity crisis with a new vision of a one nation. Those who did not participate in the refinement of exilic experience were not mentioned as part of the covenanted people in the new community. The returning groups will establish a new Israel, the purified and sanctified community with the divine presence among them. The eternal presence is sealed by the promise that Yahweh will be a משכן to them and he will place his מקדש in their midst forever. The community after restoration of the sanctuary and establishment of the new community is not discussed in this oracle. Who will be in the new community and what defined the identity of the new Israel is explicitly discussed in chapters 40-48.

Chapter 7

The New Temple Community (Ezekiel 44:1-16)

1. Introduction

Ezekiel 40-48 is commonly known as the vision of a new temple and a new community. The chapters are concerned with the temple, the land, and the people in the restored Israel that had already been anticipated in earlier prophecies (1-39). It envisions a new society organized according to a new worldview, which relates to temple, holiness and divine presence. The entire section is presented as a vision of the restored community in which a purified cult stands at the center of a purified community.[1] There are various views concerning the authorship and the history of its composition.[2] We may assume that the final form of the text is

1 Cf. John W. Wevers, *Ezekiel*, The Century Bible (London: Thomas Nelson and Sons, 1969), 295.

2 For much of the twentieth century scholars such as Gustav Holscher, Charles C. Torrey, Harmut Gese, Walter Eichrodt, Ralph W. Klein, Walther Zimmerli and Ronald M. Hals among others, this block of vision (40-48) is either a pseudepigraph or a composite work formed over the course of many years. Other scholars such as Rudolph Smend, Susan Niditch, Jon Douglas Levenson, Kalinda Rose Stevenson, Menahem Haran and Moshe Greenberg, among others argue for literary coherence or unity with a single hand in its composition. See discussion in Paul M. Joyce, "Temple and Worship in Ezekiel 40-48," in *Temple and Worship in Biblical Israel: Proceedings of the Oxford Old Testament Seminar*, LHB/OTS 422 (London: T&T Clark, 2006), 145-163; also see Marvin E. Sweeney, "Form and Coherence in Ezekiel's Temple Vision (Ezekiel 40-48)," in *Reading Prophetic Books: Form, Intertextuality, and Reception in Prophetic and Post-Biblical Literature*, FZAT 89 (Tubingen: Mohr Siebeck, 2014), 233-250. Recent studies emphasizes on a core of Ezekielian material with later redactional layers. See Thilo Alexander Rudnig, *Helig und Profan: Redaktionskritische Studien zu Ez 40-48*, BZAW

built on an authentic vision of Ezekiel chosen by editors as the perfect statement of their society's foundation and end.[3] The link between these chapters and the early chapters (1-39) is suggested by the departure and reentry of כבוד יהוה. The profanation of the temple culminating in the departure of the glory of God (8-11) now returns to the Temple (43:1-9). The regulations in chapters 40-48 are designed to preserve the holiness of the temple and the community, and to prevent future profanation that had caused the exile.[4]

Ezekiel 44 has been a key text for important ventures: first, to discuss the history of Levitical priesthood; second, to examine the relation between Ezekiel and the priestly writings; and third, to study group identification on the basis of boundary constructions. It was Julius Wellhausen who promulgated a foundation for the study of this text in his discussion of the origin of Levitical priesthood.[5] Scholars have challenged Wellhausen's thesis and many critiques abandon his view.[6] Attempts are made to seek the relation between priests and Levites in reconstructing the history of priesthood in the Hebrew Bible; which however, is not my concern. Little concern is paid to the portrayal of the community of the new temple and how the text draws a boundary between the exiles and the non-exilic group by cultivating purity and holiness. An exegesis of 44:1-16 will show how group identity is constructed in the vision by structuring the hierarchical design of the temple community.

---

287 (Berlin: Walter de Gruyter, 2000); also Michael A. Lyons, "Envisioning Restoration: Innovations in Ezekiel 40-48," in *I Lifted my Eyes and Saw: Reading Dream and Vision Reports in the Hebrew Bible*, LHB/OTS 584, eds. Elizabeth R. Hayes and Lena-Sofia Tiemeyer (London: Bloomsbury, 2014), 72-73.

3 Cf. Karl-Friedrich Pohlmann, *Ezechiel: Der Stand Der Theologischen Diskussion* (Darmstadt: Wissenschaftliche Buchgesellschaft, 2008), 132.

4 Cf. D.M.G. Stalker, *Ezekiel: Introduction and Commentary* (London: SCM Press Ltd., 1968), 269.

5 For him, this text prescribes the Levitical priests a subordinate role. The priestly writing of the Pentateuch, which came later than Ezekiel, knew the distinction between the Levites and priests. See Julius Wellhausen, *Prolegomena to the History of Israel* (Atlanta, Georgia: Scholars Press, 1994; reprinted of the edition of 1885), 124.

6 Many scholars have challenged the presentation and view of Wellhausen. For example J. Gordon McConville, Rodney K. Duke, Steven L. Cook and Greenberg among others see the distinction between priests and Levites as pre-exilic. See J. Gordon McConville, "Priests and Levites in Ezekiel: A Crux in the Interpretation of Israel's History," Tyndale Bulletin 34 (1983): 3-31. Rodney K. Duke, "Punishment or Restoration? Another Look at the Levites of Ezekiel 44:6-16," *JSOT* 40 (1988): 61-68. Steven L. Cook, "Innerbiblical Interpretation in Ezekiel 44 and the History of Israel's Priesthood," *JBL* 114, no. 2 (1995): 193-208. Moshe Greenberg, The Design and Themes of Ezekiel's Program of Restoration," *Interpretation* 38 (1984): 181-208. Also see discussion in Merlin D. Rehm, "Levites and Priests," *ABD* Vol. 4, 493-310.

2. Nature and Design

Ezekiel 44 belongs to the larger unit of chapter 40-48 which presents a vision of the new temple. In the previous larger units, we find Yahweh's judgment of Israel (1-24), prophecy against foreign nations (25-32), and vision of restoration of Israel (33-39). Ezekiel asserts that the people had defiled Yahweh's sanctuary and that Yahweh departed Jerusalem and the temple (8-11). Yahweh promised to purify Israel and restore the holy presence of Yahweh to Israel (36-37). From chapter 40, there is a new subject of temple vision with a renovated temple complex and temple services marked by categories of areas, access, and boundaries. With the entry of divine כבוד in the sanctuary (43:4), Ezekiel now turns in 44:1-31 to the statutes and laws of the temple, the community, and temple officials. A new policy provides guidelines for admission to the worshipping community and redraws boundaries to the composition of the priesthood.[7] The whole issue is to safeguard holiness of the temple and purity of Israel. This passage is the finest example of drawing boundaries in Israel's cultural map.

The vast block of materials in 40-48 follows a pattern of vision reports, which are frequently introduced by the narrative framework of visionary guidance formulas.[8] This is also found in Ezekiel 44 where we find visionary guidance formulas in v.1 and v. 4. As vision report, Ezekiel 44 has a lengthy series of ordinances beginning in 41:6 that runs through chapter 47. While the pattern of vision report marks the oracle, it is followed by divine speech of judgment on the house of Israel (vv. 5-9) and on the Levites (vv.10-14). Hence, we may categorize the oracle as both vision reports and prophetic judgment speech. Cultic ordinances in this oracle are concerned with the theme of the persons who will be in the community and who will serve in the temple. Nancy R. Bowen writes: "This chapter defines the Temple's access based on social boundaries...verses 1-16 consider access to the Temple by Yahweh, the prince, foreigners, Levites, and Zadokites."[9] Two classes of temple officials are explicitly mentioned in this text: Levites and priests. The visionary guidance formula "Then he brought me to the north gate to the front of the temple" (v.1) marks the beginning of the unit. The chapter may be cut into two parts: vv. 1-16 and vv. 17-31. The end of divine speech in v. 16 and change of the subject to detailed description of vestments,

7 Nelson argues that "Ezekiel 40-48 (*legislation of a new temple community*) restores and safeguards more strongly than ever the boundaries of Israel's fundamental culture map." See Richard D. Nelson, *Raising Up a Faithful Priest: Community and Priesthood in Biblical Theology* (Louisville, Kentucky: Westminster/John Knox Press, 1993), 112. (Italics mine).

8 Vision reports describes what the prophet sees or hears in an inner perception. There may be three main types of vision reports: (1) presence visions which describes how prophets encounters God, (2) word-symbol visions that led to perception of the word of God (2) event visions – description of events seen by prophets as witnesses. See glossary of genres in Hals, *Ezekiel*, 358. For discussion about the genre of vision reports see Susan Niditch, *The Symbolic Vision in Biblical Tradition*, HSM, 30 (Chico, California: Scholars Press, 1983).

9 Nancy R. Bowen, *Ezekiel*, AOTC (Nashville: Abingdon Press, 2010), 250.

role, and responsibilities of the priests from verse 17 marks this shift.[10] I will treat vv. 1-16 as a separate unit describing the new temple community- its membership, officials and their degrees of access.[11] The unit may be divided into four sections: (1) 44:1-3 – the closure of the east gate and the *Nasi*; (2) 44:4-9 – defilement of the sacred space and exclusion of foreigners; (3) 44:10-14 - subordinate status of Levites; and (4) 44:15-16 – Zadokites the only legitimate priests.

3. Setting

While the overall unity of the book of Ezekiel is observed, thematic differences, prescriptive style of cultic ordinances, and the overall nature of holiness spectrum indicate chapters 40-48 to be a later hand.[12] We observe enormous parallel materials with the priestly writings and the holiness code, yet comparably distinctive in nature. Chapters 40-43 give a totally different atmosphere of the restored temple reflecting on the details of its construction and the entry of the glory of Yahweh into it. From chapter 44 the temple vision turns into giving of new legislation for the returning exiles, in which the priestly ideals of purity and holiness are reflected.

While some believe the whole oracle is an ideal of utopian legislations for the future, some have argued that it was a law code compiled during the Persian period.[13] Many scholars believe that the materials in 44:1-16 are a series of later additions, which reflect the postexilic struggle within the community of the

10 Verses 17-31 have an entirely different sort of issue that reflects the priestly tradition in Leviticus 6. They are stipulations of holiness required for priestly behavior. Hals has three sub-units in this chapter – vv. 1-3, 4-5, and 6-31. He thinks that vv. 4-5 constitute a transitional link between what has preceded (1-3) and what follows (vv. 6-31). See Ronald. M. Hals, *Ezekiel*, FOTL Vol. XIX (Grand Rapids, Michigan: Eerdmans, 1989), 314.

11 Some commentators put vv. 6-31 together as a unit having continuous theme that concerns the persons who have to serve in the temple – Levites and priests. For this see Walther Zimmerli, *Ezekiel 2*: *A Commentary on the Book of the Prophet Ezekiel 25-48*, tran. James D. Martin, eds. Paul D. Hanson and Leonard Jay Greenspoon (Philadelphia: Fortress Press, 1983). But this scheme overlooks the connection between vv. 1-3 (access to the temple area by the *Nasi*), and vv. 4-5 (Yahweh's address of the prophet concerning membership of the temple community) with vv. 6-16 (foreigners, Levites and priests). Hence, the overall unity of vv. 1-16 (1-31) should be maintained. Milgrom, Block, and others take up this schematic composition.

12 For example, detail prescriptions of sacrifice are not found until chapter 40. Yahweh's presence as distancing from the community is not matching with the idea of transformed community and indwelling of Yahweh among them in chapters 34-37.

13 Cook believes that it a utopian whereas Tuell argues that it was prompted by the Persian collection of provincial legal material. See G. A. Cook, *A Critical and Exegetical Commentary on the Book of Ezekiel Vol. 1*, ICC (New York: Charles Scribner's Sons, 1937), 425; Steven S. Tuell, *The Law of the Temple in Ezekiel 40-48*, HSM 49 (Atlanta, Georgia: Scholars Press, 1992), 13-14.

exiles and between Zadokite and other Levitical priests.[14] While the lateness of the vision and possible redaction of the original corpus is maintained by many scholars, there is also support for it being from the hand of the prophet Ezekiel.[15] Certain issues favor a later hand on the original work. A repetition of the entry of Yahweh's כבוד (43:4-5 and 44:4) with supplementary notes of caution added in 44:5 suggests a later hand.[16] The distinctions between Zadokites and the Levites reflect an intense dispute in the priestly ranks. This is not reflected in the early oracles. It is likely beyond what Ezekiel would have said and is to be attributed to a later hand.[17] The materials in this chapter include vision reports with long and extensive elaborations added by a long series of rules and prescriptions for the priesthood. This arrangement suggests a highly and prolonged process of growth of the text. Hence, it is improbable that the prophet himself was responsible for them.[18] Karl-Friedrich Pohlmann thinks the whole vision to be codified in the time of Darius, authored by Zadokite priests for their own *Tora des Tempels*.[19] R. E. Clements dates the whole vision (40-48) between 520-516 BCE when the task of rebuilding the Jerusalem temple was undertaken.[20] We may date the oracle to a late exilic or early postexilic period when formation of a new temple community was in process.

4. Text Analysis and Comments

4.1. The Closure of the East Gate and the *Nasi* (vv. 1-3)

v. 1. Then he brought me back by way of the outer gate of the sanctuary facing east. And it was shut.

---

14 Wevers argues that the statement/passage "that only Zadokite priests were allowed to perform sacrificial duties is one of the latest layer of tradition in this section (40-48). See Wevers, *Ezekiel*, 297.

15 See Menahem Haran, "The Law Code of Ezekiel 40-48 and Its Relation to the Priestly School," in *Hebrew Union College Annual* 50 (Cincinnati: Hebrew Union College, 1979), 45-71; Also Moshe Greenberg, "The Design and Theme of Ezekiel's Program of Restoration," *Interpretation* 38 (1984): 181-208.

16 Walther Eichrodt, *Ezekiel: A Commentary*, trans. Cosslett Quin, OTL (Philadelphia: Westminster Press, 1970), 562; cf. Zimmerli, *Ezekiel 2*, 444-445.

17 Ralph W. Klein, *Ezekiel: The Prophet and His Message*, Studies on the Personalities of the Old Testament (Columbia: University of Carolina Press, 1988), 178.

18 Cf. R. E. Clements, *Ezekiel* (Louisville: Westminster Jon Knox Press, 1996), 177.

19 He writes: "As Darius sought from the priests of Egypt an ancient and authoritative law by which the people would live and the temples be ordered, so the Zadokite clergy of the restored Jerusalem cultus set about the codification "*ihrer eigenen Tora des Tempels*" (their own Torah of the Temple). See Pohlmann, *Ezechiel*, 133.

20 Clements, *Ezekiel*, 177; cf. Joyce, *Ezekiel*, 219.

v. 2. Then Yahweh[21] *said to me, this gate shall remain shut, it shall not be opened; and no one shall enter by it. Because Yahweh the God of Israel has entered by it, it shall remain shut.*
v. 3. But the[22] *prince, as he is the prince*[23] *shall sit in it to eat bread before Yahweh. He shall enter by way of the porch of the gate, and by the same way he shall go out.*

The prophet in his visionary state is conducted back to the eastern gate in the outer wall of the outer court (v. 1). Through this gate he saw Yahweh entered into the sanctuary (43:4). The use of the term מקדש "sanctuary" not בית "house" here suggests that God's glory transformed a house into a sanctuary.[24] The prophet is told that the gate would remain closed (v. 2). The closure of the gate is significant for various reasons. First, it may suggest that never again could the east gate be used in connection with the pagan worship of the sun mentioned earlier in 8:16-18. Second, because Yahweh entered though it, no one else is permitted entry. Third, the east gate was the opening from where the glory of the Lord who departed had returned and that by shutting the door permanently; it indicates that the Lord will never again leave his sanctuary.[25] It illustrates a hope for the restored people that even though by their defilement and profanation, they lost divine presence in Jerusalem, God has returned to them. Now as the exiles return, Yahweh's presence with them will be permanent, as he moved back from the land of exile to the Jerusalem temple.

---

21 LXX [239] omits Yahweh. Following the LXX, Zimmerli and Allen propose that this is a gloss arguing that the celestial guide is the speaker. See Zimmerli, *Ezekiel 2*, 437; also Allen, *Ezekiel 20-48*, 244. Milgrom objects this view that the MT is not ungrammatical since Yahweh is the speaker. See Jacob Milgrom and Daniel I Block (in conversation), *Ezekiel's Hope: A Commentary on Ezekiel 38-48* (Eugene, Oregon: Cascade Books, 2012), 132.

22 The particle את plus nominative occurs twelve times in Ezekiel. It simply means "the" It is suggested to replace with אך meaning "surely" "only" "but" "yet" etc., which has an assertive meaning, often introducing with emphasis the expression of truth or restrictive meaning – in contrast to what precedes. NRSV, REB, NAB read "only." Hence, we take the emendation. See the usage of אך in *BDB*, 36.

23 Most commentators follow LXX and Syriac deleting the repetition as dittograph. But the repetition indicates emphasis, which is good to retain.

24 מקדש (sanctuary) is used in relation to Yahweh's presence among Israel (5:11; 11:16; 24:21; 37:26) and as a term referring to the inner sancta of the temple (44:5,7,8,9,11,15,16; 47:12; 48:21). בית (house/temple) refers to the whole temple area and the building itself in Ezekiel (8:16; 40:5; 41:5; 43:11; 44:11; 45:1946:24;47:1; 48:21). Zimmerli understands that בית in a narrower sense is the temple building and מקדש elsewhere has a theological sense of Yahweh's presence in it. See Zimmerli, *Ezekiel 2*, 440. See also further discussion in Milgrom-Block, *Ezekiel's Hope*, 148-149.

25 Cf. Herbert G. May, "The Book of Ezekiel: Introduction and Exegesis," *The Interpreter's Bible*, Vol. 6, 307; Peter C. Craigie, *Ezekiel*, The Daily Study Bible (OT) (Edinburgh: Saint Andrew Press, 1983), 295; Margaret S. Odell, *Ezekiel*, Smith & Helwys Bible Commentary (Macon, Georgia: Smyth & Helwys Publishing, Inc., 2005), 504-505.

The prophet is also told that only the *Nasi* (prince) is allowed to sit there. He will be there to eat in the presence of Yahweh. This title נשׂיא is the favorite title for Israel's promised new ruler (Cf. 34:24; 37:25; 45:7-9). His role as a guardian of the new community is given in greater detail in vv. 45-56. Here restricted access to the sanctuary is the issue. He is allowed to eat here, i.e. the outer court. What he has to eat is probably a "communal meal" or a "sacrificial meal."[26] The privilege is reminiscent of the place reserved for the king in the pre-exilic temple (cf. 2 kings 11:12; 23:3). He is not allowed to eat in the inner court and in the holiest area.

4.2. Defilement of the Sanctuary and Exclusion of Foreigners (vv. 4-9)

v. 4. And he brought me by way of the gate of the north to the front of the house; and I saw, behold, the glory of Yahweh filled the house of Yahweh; and I fell upon my face.
v. 5. And Yahweh said to me, son of man, note carefully, look closely and listen attentively what I am speaking to you concerning[27] *all the ordinances of the house of Yahweh and all its laws. And pay attention concerning those* ***who may be admitted to the house and all those who are to be excluded***[28] *from the sanctuary.*
v. 6. Say to the rebellious house,[29] *the house of Israel; thus says the Lord Yahweh, enough is all your abominations, O house of Israel.*
v. 7. By admitting foreigners, uncircumcised in heart and flesh in my sanctuary to profane my house;[30] *when you offered my food, the fat and the blood, you broke*[31] *my covenant with all your abominations.*
v. 8. And you have not kept the charge of my holy things, but you have put foreigners to keep my charge in my sanctuary to them.[32]

26 Cf. 46:2. Cooper understands it so. See Lamar E. Cooper Sr., *Ezekiel*, NAC Vol. 17 (United States of America: Broadman & Holman Publishers, 1994), 389.

27 ל is used here and in the next line to mark the topic of a verb of saying. See the use of ל in B. Waltke and M. O'Connor, *Introduction to Biblical Hebrew Syntax* (Winona Lake, Ind: Eisenbrauns, 1990), 210 (11.2.10g).

28 The MT reads "the entry of the house and the exits of the sanctuary." Many translations follow LXX and Syriac proposing to read למבואי – hiphil participle constructs: "those to bring in, i.e., "to be admitted" (for למבוא) and ולמוצאי – "those to let go out," i.e., "to be excluded" (for מוצאי). The next verses discuss about access to the temple, including foreigners. Here the subject is who are to be included and to be excluded in the temple community. Hence, the emendation is retained.

29 The MT lacks "house" here and reads, "Say to the rebels, the house of Israel." This could be an error. LXX emends it "Say to the provoking/rebellious house, even to the house of Israel."

30 את־ביתי "my house" is absent in LXX perhaps to make the reading smooth.

31 The MT is ויפרו – "they have broken" (Hiph. impf. 3 mpl.). As LXX, Syriac, Vulgate read, ותפרו "you broke/have broken" is the more likely reading.

32 LXX reads δια τουτο "therefore" instead of לכן "to them," and connects it with verse 9. But alteration is "probably a harmonious alteration." Cf. Milgrom - Block, *Ezekiel's Hope*, 135.

v. 9. Thus says Yahweh Lord; all foreigners uncircumcised in heart and flesh shall not enter into my sanctuary, (no one) of all the foreigners[33] *who are among Israel.*

With the prophet being led into the inner court through the north gate, Ezekiel was cautioned to mark well the ordinances and laws of the temple and mark those who are to be admitted to or to be excluded from the sanctuary. Ezekiel looks and sees that the Temple is filled with the glory of Yahweh. As in 1:28 and 43:3, he responds by falling on his face. 44:4-5 repeats 43:3-5 and hence a possible sign of a later addition. The repetition could also indicate emphasis on commissioning of Ezekiel for the second time. "The new reference to the return of כבוד יהוה makes it clear that it is the return of God to the temple that serves as a basis for the regulations to follow."[34] The two words – הבית "the house" (5 times) and המקדש "the sanctuary" (3 times) in general refer to the Temple. The former may indicate the temple compound into which there are enclosures and doors. The latter may indicate the grounds where rituals take place. Once Yahweh's glory enters the temple, it is transformed from a house to a sanctuary.

The prophet is asked to note carefully (literally שום לבך – set/put your heart), look closely (lit. וראה בעיניך – and see by/with your eyes), and listen attentively (lit. ובאזניך שמע – and hear by/with your ears), the parallel of which is found in 40:4. The reason for this command is that Yahweh is going to proclaim a series of laws (ordinances/statutes) concerning the temple (v. 5a), in the manner of Moses.[35] Yahweh's appeal is added with a command to pay attention concerning who will be in the new temple community. The MT reads, "be attentive to the entrance and the exits of the sanctuary." (v. 5b). Syriac, Targum and many other translations emend it "be attentive to those who may be admitted to the house and all those to be excluded from the sanctuary." This reading makes more sense as the following lines discuss rejection of a certain community whose abominations defiled the sanctuary. This is the second case of access to the temple after the ayfn in this chapter.

Before explicitly mentioning "foreigners," an accusation of the house of Israel is conveyed with the designation, "the rebellious house" (v. 6). Some commentators presume this verse as a description of the Levites, who allowed

33 Here ל in לכל בן נכר is not a preposition, but emphatic particle corresponding to Arabic *la* "indeed." Cf. Zimmerli, *Ezekiel 2*, 449.

34 Cf. McConville, "Priests and Levites in Ezekiel," 18.

35 Yahweh's instructions mediated through Ezekiel are called חקות "statutes." Commentators observe thematic parallels between Ezekiel and Moses. McKeating identified three themes: (1) Moses and Ezekiel on a high mountain behold a vision of a temple, and encounter the glory of Yahweh (Exo 24-27; Ezek 40:2; 43:1-5) (2) They receive regulations concerning priestly functions (Exo 28-29; Ezek 44:15-31), (3) Moses and Ezekiel creates and recreates a people. See H. McKeating, "Ezekiel the 'Prophet' Like Moses," *JSOT* 61 (1994): 97-109. See also Mark A. Awabdy, "YHWH Exegetes Torah: How Ezekiel 44:7-9 Bars Foreigners from the Sanctuary," *JBL* 131, no. 4 (2012): 701.

foreigners in the temple.[36] But the accusation addresses the house of Israel and the rebellious house. This designation מרי "rebellious house" is used only here in 40-48. But it echoes Ezekiel's initial commissioning when Yahweh sent him to "the people of Israel designated as "nation of rebels" in 2:3 and elsewhere in 2:5-6, 8, 3:9, 26-27; 17:12; 24:3. This indictment is found in the Korah narrative (Num 16:3) and in Moses' reply (Nu 16:7). It is also found in Deut 3:26 (Yahweh's response to Moses) and 1 Kings 12:28 (Jeroboam's indignation about worship at Jerusalem alone). The two terms together imply the common people; who are predicted to face Yahweh's judgment (cf. 2:7; 12:9; 17:1, 12). They are called a rebellious house because they have allowed foreigners in Yahweh's sanctuary.

A strong indictment is their many abominations (verse 6b). The emphatic idiom רב־לכם מכל תועבותיכם "enough is your abomination" echoes the wrath pronounced by Moses to the Levites who revolted against Aaronide priesthood (Num 16:7).[37] Deuteronomy 3:26 also employ this idiom when Yahweh replied to Moses' request to enter the Promised Land. It is an expression of Yahweh's anger. As indicated earlier, abominations refer to cultic and moral defilement.[38] This text speaks about the rebellion of the house of Israel. The reason for Yahweh's anger is the abominations of the house of Israel that defiled the sanctuary, the land and the people.

The next verses (vv. 7-9) articulate the accusation against the Israelites and a rigorous stand on the exclusion of foreigners from the sanctuary. The accusation of Israel's sin is "admitting בני־נכר "sons of foreigners," into the sanctuary (v. 7), and giving them charge of Yahweh's holy things (קדשי) (v. 8). The most rigorous judgment is that foreigners should not enter into the sanctuary (v. 9). The reason behind the exclusion is that they are "uncircumcised in heart and flesh" (vv. 7&9). The description of foreigners as "uncircumcised in flesh and spirit" is unusual in Ezekiel. It is spoken only in connection with the representation of death in the oracles against foreign nations (28:10; 31:18; 32:19-32).[39] Uncircumcised in heart was a sign of stubbornness and rebellion among the people of Israel (Deut 10:16; 30:6; Jer 4:4; 9:26). Ezekiel also indicts unfaithful Israelites, who admitted foreigners to the temple. Allen asserts that "the pagan intrusion cast a cloud of profanation over the central act of altar worship… Israel had neglected its cultic responsibilities as the covenant people by entrusting them to pagans."[40] While בני־נכר (foreigners) are excluded from the sanctuary, גרים (aliens) are included in

---

36 See for example, Milgrom-Block, *Ezekiel's Hope*, 140.

37 Milgrom reads these verses in the light of punishment of the sons of Korah in Numbers 16-18. For him, they are the Levites who are referred to as practicing various kinds of abominations. See Milgrom-Block, *Ezekiel's Hope*, 137.

38 See the discussion in chapter 3.

39 Cf. Zimmerli, *Ezekiel 2*, 454. The concept of circumcision as a sign of purification is found also in Jer 4:4; 9:25; Deut 10:16; 30:6; Lev 26:41.

40 Allen, *Ezekiel 20-48*, WBC Vol. 29, 261.

land allotment in 47:22.[41] Zimmerli rightly concludes that the overall description of the foreigner as "uncircumcised in body and in heart" reflected the beginnings of the exclusive attitude towards all foreigners."[42] The purpose of excluding foreigners is to preserve holiness and purity. This theme is highlighted again in 44:23 where the priestly task is to teach the "difference between the holy (קדש) and the common (חל), the unclean (טמא) and the clean (תהור)."

The house of Israel is charged with another illicit act that pollutes the sanctuary. They profaned the sanctuary when they offered "Yahweh's food, the fat and the blood." (v. 7b). This implies that the admittance of foreigners and their participation in the ritual offerings pollutes the sanctuary.[43] Those improper acts of rituals, including admitting foreigners and sacrifice of the lay people are "breaking of the covenants" (v. 7c). As Zimmerli notes, "As far as Israel is concerned, the question (of foreigners involved in temple service) cannot be answered with certainty. In the description of the temple abominations in chapter 8, Ezekiel himself has given no indication of this offence."[44] However, it is clearly indicated that "the rebellious house, the whole house of Israel" are involved in this cultic offence. This is the frequent theme of admonition of the inhabitants of Jerusalem. Hence, this could point to the non-exilic worshipping community who lived in the land. Their worship was denied in the new temple.

One important concern is to define who are בני־נכר in this text. Why did such a strict rule of exclusion be imposed on them? As illustrated in other biblical records, a general idea is that Ezekiel is thinking of temple-slaves who performed more menial duties, e.g. Gibeonites (Josh 9:23, 27), or the Carites (2 Kings 11:4-8), or the later Nethinim.[45] Foreigners (בן־נכר) are allowed to participate in Yahweh's worship in certain biblical texts.[46] The exclusion of foreigners/aliens became stricter as time went on.[47] This question may be better understood by analyzing the term נכר in relation to other semantic terms זרים (aliens) and גרים (non-indigenous residents) in the book of Ezekiel.

41 There is an inclusive emphasis on allotment of land to aliens who reside with Israelites in 47:22. Joyce argues that 47:22 concern pious proselytes whereas the concern in this chapter is with sinful pagans and admission to the sanctuary. See Paul M. Joyce, *Ezekiel: A Commentary* LHB/OTE 482 (New York: T&T Clark, 2007), 232.

42 Zimmerli, *Ezekiel 2*, 454.

43 Priestly regulations prohibit laypersons to perform sacred functions of the priests and Levites, lest they be killed. See Num 1:51; 3:10, 38; 18:7.

44 Zimmerli, *Ezekiel 2*, 454.

45 Nethinim is an ethnic group included in the list or returning exiles found in both Ezra 2:43-58 and Nehemiah 7:46-60. The name probably reflects the early decades of the post-exilic era. Cf. Allen, *Ezekiel 20-48*, WBC, 260.

46 Isaiah 56:3-8 favors בן־נכר to take part in in the service of the sanctuary Cf. Deut 29:10-13.

47 Haggai (2:14), Ezra (4:3), and Nehemiah (13:7-9, 30) excluded those who had not been in exile and the Samaritans, who claimed Jewish blood. Their worship was termed as "unclean." Their participation in the construction of Jerusalem wall was denied.

In Ezekiel the only time "foreigners" בני־נכר (sons of foreignness) בן־נכר (son of a foreign) occur in any form is in 44:7& 9. The terms נכר found 36 times, and נכרי 45 times in the Hebrew Bible are used of that which is alien and to be excluded.[48] It is used mainly to connote otherness in terms of relationship with the Israelites or as a distinguishing characteristic in opposition to Israel.[49] The term refers to uncircumcised gentiles (Exod 12:43; Ezek 44:7, 9; Gen 17:12); separate seeds against mixed marriage in Ezra-Nehemiah (Neh 9:2; Ezra 9); and foreign gods (Deut 31: 16; Jer 5:19).

Ezekiel employs the plural noun זרים to refer to foreign nations (7:21; 11:9; 16:32; 28:7, 10; 30:12; 31:12). Another term used for foreigners is גרים (nonindigenous residents) who were granted land inheritance (47:22-23). גרים practiced the rite of circumcision (cf. Exo 12:48-49) to become ritually acceptable. This is the only time Ezekiel employs בן־נכר as "foreigner/alien" in the book. It is plausible that Ezekiel speaks about the outside members, whose immorality disqualified them from service in the sanctuary. They are those who are not fit for cultic activities of any sort.[50] They are described as uncircumcised in heart and flesh, which in a literal and figurative sense implies unclean. Thus, in Ezekiel, these two terms refer to the defiled realm. Therefore, Ezekiel denies the impure people who defiled the temple and the land to become members of the Temple community because their presence will pollute the sanctuary.[51]

Who are בן־נכר in this text? They are the house of Israel, the rejected group who are represented as practicing abominations in the land. They are not of other nations, or aliens, but are included in the temple community of Trito-Isaiah (Isa 60:10; 61:5). The text neither refers to non-Israelites (זרים), nor nonindigenous residents (גרים), but those of sons of foreignness (בן־נכר), uncircumcised in heart and flesh – the defiled group of Israelites who lived in the defiled land (Judah). This text is a delegitimization of those who remained in Judah during the exile,

48 The nominative נכר often appears in a construct relationship to indicate which is morally unacceptable. The main usage includes: those outside the covenant (Gen 17:12; xo 12:43), idolatry in terms of foreign gods (Josh 24:20; Jer 5:19), hostile foreign people (Neh 9:2; 13:30) enemies (2 Sam 22:45); נכרי is predominantly used of foreign people (Exod 2:22; Deut 14:21; Isa 2:6); as a metaphor for apostasy of Israel (Jer 2:21); strange action of God (Isa 28:21). Only in Trito-Isaiah are foreigners given a positive relationship and role (56:3,6; 60:10; 61:5). See discussion in A. H. Konkel, "נכר," *NIDOTTE* Vol. 3, 109.

49 In terms of relationship נכר indicates "other/another" (Prov 27:2; Eccl 6:2), unfamilial -outside the family (Gen 31:15), stranger (Exod 21:8), people foreign to Israelites (Deut 17:15; 2 Sam 15:19; Ruth 2:10); strange woman (Prov 2:16; 5:20; 6:24; 7:5). It also represents inanimate objects - foreign land (Exod 2:22), foreign city (Jgs 19:12), and foreign language (Prov. 6:24). See further discussion in Lang, "נכר," *TDOT* Vol. IX, 423-431.

50 Cf. Katheryn Pfisterer Darr, "The Book of Ezekiel: Introduction, Commentary, and Reflections," in *NIB*, Vol. VI, 1574.

51 Awabdy writes, "… any impulse toward integrating eligible foreigners into YHWH worship has been subordinated to restoring and maintaining the purity of YHWH's sacred space. See Awabdy, "YHWH Exegetes Torah," 703.

who were presented as defiling the sanctuary. They could be the same people addressed by Ezra and Nehemiah as the impure with mixed ethnicity of the land (Ezra 9:2, Neh 9). Their presence in the new temple community was barred fearing that the sanctity of the new temple community will be tainted. Hence, access to the sanctuary for them was completely denied.

4.3. Subordinate Status of the Levites (vv. 10-14)

v. 10. But[52] *the Levites who deserted me when Israel went astray from me, when they went astray*[53] *after their idols; they shall bear their punishment.*
v. 11. And they shall serve in my sanctuary having oversight on the gates of the house, serving in the house. They shall slaughter the burnt offering and the sacrifice for the people and they shall attend to them[54] *to serve them.*
v. 12. Because they ministered[55] *to them for idols they became*[56] *stumbling block for the iniquity of the house of Israel. Therefore, I lifted my hand upon them, says the Lord Yahweh. They shall bear their punishment.*[57]
v. 13. And they shall not draw near to me as priests nor come near to any of my sacred things, to the holiest of the holy things. But they shall bear their shame and their abominations, which they committed.
v. 14. And I shall give them to keep the charges of the house for all its services and all what is to be done in it.

Ezekiel 44:10-14 outlines the subordinate role of the Levites. It speaks of the punishment of the Levites and their obligations as the consequence of their iniquity. The Levites are to serve as ministers in the sanctuary, to act as gatekeepers, to kill the sacrificial animals, and to attend to the people in the outer court. The reason for their inferior role is explained as punishment for their sin, particularly of their idol worship.

Verse 10 and 12 offer indictment of the Levites for leading their people towards worshipping idols. These verses echo a popular sin of the inhabitants of Jerusalem known from chapters 1-39. The Levites are reproached as "going astray"

52 כי אם is a strong adverb used to restrict the immediately preceding clause. See Waltke-O'Connor, *Introduction to Biblical Hebrew Syntax*, 671 (39.3.5d).

53 אשר תעו "when they went astray" is deleted in LXX and Syriac perhaps to harmonize the flow of the verse.

54 Literally ועמדו "they shall stand before them." LXX has "people" instead of "them."

55 MT has ישרתו (imperfect form) while perfect is expected. But in some cases a simple imperfect express past actions, actions repeatedly brought to a conclusion in the past or actions which have continued or been repeated in the past. See further discussion in Wilhelm Gesenius, *Gesenius' Hebrew Grammar*, edited and enlarged by E. Kautzsch (Oxford: Clarendon Press, 1978 reprinted), 330-339, no. 112. It may also be a scribal error for שרתו. See Zimmerli, *Ezekiel 2*, 449, Block, *Ezekiel 25-40*, 625.

56 LXX reads και εγενετο "and it came to pass" suggesting to read ויהי.

57 Literally "they shall bear their iniquity/guilt." LXX omits the clause.

and "having gone far away from Yahweh." These strong statements of reproach are dependent on the overall condemnation of the inhabitants of Jerusalem as found in the judgment speeches of chapters 1-24. Verse 11 echoes vv. 10 &12 that because they committed sins, the Levites shall keep the gates of the house (sanctuary) and do menial works in the house of Yahweh. In verse 13, we find a recapitulation of subordinate role of the Levites. There are many interpretations for the punishment of the Levites and their assigned role in the temple. The most important question scholars try to answer is: "Are the Levites punished or restored in Ezekiel 44:10-14?"

Wellhausen argues that these verses reflect punishment of the Levites who officiated at worship at high places during the time of Josiah's reform.[58] Josiah brought all the Levites into Jerusalem and permitted them to serve in the Jerusalem temple. But the priesthood of those Levites from the countryside was rejected (Deut 18:6-8; 2 Kings 23:8-9). From the perspective of Wellhausen, vv. 10-14 are a harsh critique of the Levites. Other critics however, have challenged Wellhausen's hypothesis. Cook argues that since Ezekiel 44 makes reference to the Levites' service before גלולים "idols" not at the "high places" referred to in the Deuteronomic history, this text does not lay out punishment of the Levites.[59] Stevenson and Duke interpret נשׂא עון "bear the iniquity/punishment" in the context of Israel's offence.[60] That is, not the Levites, but the Israelites went astray from Yahweh to worship idols. Margaret S. Odell's interpretation is that "the Israelites took the initiative, with the result that the Levites ended up being far form Yahweh."[61] Milgrom holds a view that "it is not the Levites but the laity who are condemned for allowing foreigners to guard the sancta."[62] In his final work edited by Block, Milgrom posits that Ezekiel is merely applying the Levitical duties ascribed by Numbers 1-3. He argues that ונשׂא עון "they shall bear their iniquity/ punishment" here in v. 10 and v.12 are in the perfect tenses and hence it is not a statement about the future.[63] It means that both Levites and Israel bore their punishment, when they were exiled. Block argues that this text should be understood in the light of Numbers 18. He argues, "While the past sins of the Levites are not undermined, Ezekiel's primary intention is to guarantee the future sanctity of the temple, not

58 Wellhausen, *Prolegomena to the History of Israel*, 121-124.

59 Cook, "Innerbiblical Interpretation in Ezekiel 44," 195.

60 See Kalinda Rose Stevenson, *The Vision of Transformation: The Territorial Rhetoric of Ezekiel 40-48,* SBLDS 154 (Atlanta: Scholars Press, 1996), 73-74; Duke, "Punishment of Restoration," 67.

61 Margaret S. Odell, *Ezekiel*, Smyth & Helwys Bible Commentary (Macon, Georgia: Smyth & Helwys, 2005), 508.

62 See Jacob Milgrom, "The Term "עבדה," in *Studies in Cultural Theology and Terminology* SJLA 36 (Leiden: E.J. Brill, 1983), 42 (18-46).

63 He makes a claim that here the initial ו attached to נשׂא is not consecutive but copulative. See Milgrom-Block, *Ezekiel's Hope*, 152.

to demote the Levites."[64] In spite of these interpretations, NRSV renders this text: "The Levites... shall bear their guilt" (v.10) so also Numbers 18:23 reads: "but the Levites shall perform the service of the tent of the meeting, and they shall bear responsibility for their own offences." Hence, the references "their" (Ezek 44:10) and "their own" (Num 18:23) point to the Levites. Cook reads Ezekiel 44 in the light of Numbers 16-18 as reflections and valuations of Israel's inner history for the restored community.[65] Katheryn Pfisterer Darr rightly argues that the phrase "they shall bear their guilt (iniquity)" carries an accusing finger at the Levites."[66] That Milgrom and others read "their" as "Israelites" not the Levites, contrasts with verse 13. In v. 13, Levitical priesthood is denied priestly functions because of their abominable practices.

The duty of the Levites and the reason for such subordinate status is discussed in verses 11-14. First, the Levites are assigned to guard the gates of the house. They are not in charge of the sacred places, but the whole temple area. In Ezra and Nehemiah the door keepers (שׁערים) are still differentiated from the Levites. P does not mention the doorkeepers and in Chronicles they are reckoned among the Levites.[67] Secondly, their duty also includes slaughtering animals for sacrifice. According to priestly legislation, the slaughtering of the animal for sacrifice was not a priestly function and might be performed by a layman (Lev 1:5, 11). In Ezekiel 44, lay people are barred from the inner court and the Levites slaughter animals and prepare burnt offerings for the laity. Slaughtering and offering of a burnt offering (purification offering) by the Levites separates the priests and the Israelites permanently.[68]

Again in verse 12, the reason for subordinate role of the Levites is recapitulated. "Because they (the Levites) ministered to them (people) for idols, they became a stumbling block for the iniquity of the house of Israel." The expression ישרתו "they ministered/they kept on serving" though an imperfect, functions as actions in the past which has continued or repeated actions.[69] The Levites bore their guilt of serving the idols or serving the Israelites before their idols. Verse 12b takes up v.12a by expressing punishment of the Levites with the

---

64 See Daniel I. Block, *The Book of Ezekiel Chapters 25-48*, NICOT (Grand Rapids: Eerdmans, 1997), 629. Cf. Cook, "Innerbiblical Interpretation in Ezekiel 44," 197-200.

65 Cook sees Ezekiel 44 as a hermeneutical exposition of the Korah Text in Numbers 16-18 by Zodokite priests in their vision of the Temple community. He argues that by their exposition, they maintained "a more rigorous scheme of holiness gradation than other contemporary priestly groups." See Cook, "Innerbiblical Interpretation in Ezekiel 44," 207.

66 Darr, "The Book of Ezekiel," 1576-1577.

67 Cf. Zimmerli, *Ezekiel 2*, 455.

68 Thus Ezekiel transfers ritual slaughter to the Levites from the laity that in effect barred them from the inner gates. Cf. Milgrom-Block, *Ezekiel's Hope*, 159. For discussion on עלה "burnt offering" see Milgrom, *Leviticus 1-16*, AB (New York: Doubleday, 1991), 172-177. Also see, D. Kellermann, "עולה/עלה," *TDOT* Vol. XI, 96-113.

69 See textual note on verse 12 in page 16.

clause אל־כן "therefore," followed by נשׂאתי ידי עליהם "I lifted up my hands unto them." The benevolent oath taking of Ezekiel 20:5f, 28, 42; 47:14 is transformed to punishment. Duke argues that the perfect verb נשׂאתי is rightly understood as a reference to past actions."[70] However, the following line ונשׂאו עונם "they shall bear their iniquity." points to future punishment. Hence, the punishment can be said as already occurred or about to take place.

Verse 13a forbids the Levites from performing priestly duties as does the priestly legislation (Num 18:3). They are denied access to כל־קדשׁי and "my sacred things" and קדשׁדי הקדשׁים "the holy of holies."[71] According to the priestly account, Aaron and his sons alone among the Levites were set apart to serve as priests. Levites are a gift to serve Aaron and his sons (Num 3:2-3; 18:6-7). But they share the same responsibilities of guarding the tabernacle. (Num 3:6-8; 18:5). In Deuteronomy, there is no restriction of priestly service to the Aaronite family alone. It asserts the equivalence of Levites and priests (Deut 18:5).[72] Whether all Levitical families performed priestly function before Ezekiel 44 is a subject of debate.[73] The intention of this line is to exclude the Levites from participating in the cultic acts performed in the inner court of the sanctuary. According to our text, Levites were disqualified as priests, except the Zadokites.

Verses 13b-14 explain two consequences of the Levites' past actions. This also gives the reason for disqualifying the Levites from a priestly status. First, "they shall bear their shame for their actions." Block argues that כלמה "shame" had been used in Ezekiel in the context of salvation. It indicates intense sense of unworthiness in the light of ones' past actions."[74] Secondly, "they shall bear their abominations which they committed." The exact meaning of this punishment is unclear. Some have argued the punishment in terms of reinstatement to an original status.[75] It implies that they shall bear the consequence of shame; that is a

---

70 See Duke, "Punishment or Restoration," 69.

71 קדשׁי and קדשׁי הקדשׁים may refer to sacrifices considered absolutely and irreversibly holy or to the most sacred objects in the innermost part of the sanctuary. See Block, *Ezekiel 25-48*, 631.

72 It says "For the Lord your God has chosen Levi out of all your tribes to stand and minster in the name of the Lord, him and his sons for a all time." (Num 18:5 NSRV). Milgrom argues that Deuteronomy prescribes certain acts of priestly duties to the Levites such as civil administration (cf. Deut 21:5; 10:8; 17:9; 18:5) and diagnosing and treating skin diseases (Deut 24:8). But, there is restriction to offer sacrifices in the sanctuary. See discussion in Milgrom-Block, *Ezekiel's Hope*, 161-162.

73 On popular argument is that the Levites who once were legitimate priests lost their status after Josiah's reform as punishment for their idolatry – that is ministering at shrines other than the temple. Hence Ezekiel innovates a theological reason for the loss of priestly status. P adopts Ezekiel's innovation, but regards the distinction in status between Zadokites and Levites as one that had existed form the beginning. See discussion in Stalker, *Ezekiel*, 296-297.

74 Block, *Ezekiel 25-48*, 632. See Ezek 16:53-54, 60-63; 20:39-44; 36:31-32; 39:25-26; 43:10-11.

75 For example, Block argues that "this text does not represent demotion (of the Levites) from a previous higher rank, this is a reinstatement to their original noble position." See Block, *Ezekiel*

feeling of guilt as well as a subordinate role of priesthood due to their abominable practices. Verse 14 restates the Levites' responsibilities: "They shall keep the charges of all its services and all that is to be done in it." Their duty is to perform all the duties in the outer court of the sanctuary.

What exactly caused a subordinate status for the Levites? In verse 6, Israel is condemned for the abominable practices, as they brought foreigners into Yahweh's temple and went astray for idols. So also the Levites were accused of failing to prevent the people from worshiping idols. Instead of loyalty to Yahweh in the time of Israel's crisis of faith, they too went far away. Hence, they were denied access to the inner sanctuary. There is no direct reference to Levites leading the people into idol worship elsewhere in the book. Rather, the entire priestly house is sinning and excoriated for failure to keep holiness and purity (Ezek 22:26; 44:23). Milgrom proposes that rejection of the Levites is portrayed with the knowledge of the priestly tradition in Numbers 18 and the Deuteronomic understanding of priests and Levites.[76] For Cook, this text is a rereading of Numbers 16-18 in the postexilic community.[77] Both Milgrom and Cook overlook the differences of Ezekiel and Numbers. In Numbers 16, a group of priests including Korah rebelled against Moses and Aaron. Numbers18 blames the whole priesthood for the profanation of the shrine (18:1). But here in Ezekiel, Levites are blamed for serving the laity before idols. This text could be a refinement of priesthood within the restored Israelite temple community. It can be assumed that there was a passion to preserve the sanctity of the whole ritual system when the returning exiles reconstructed the temple in the late sixth century BCE. So, this text could be an ideological reasoning to marginalize certain groups of priests in the context of restoration of the priesthood in the new temple community.[78]

4.4. Zadokites – The Only Legitimate Priests (vv. 15-16)

v. 15. But the priests, the Levites who are the sons of Zadok kept the charges of my sanctuary when Israel went astray from me. They shall come near to me to serve me; and they shall stand before me to being near to me the fat and the blood, says the Lord Yahweh.

v. 16. And they shall enter into my sanctuary and they shall come near to my table to serve me; and they shall keep my charge.

Verses 15-16 emphasize the role of the Zadokites. These verses echo the preceding statements about the Levites (v.15) and offer a prescription for the

---

25-48, 632.

76 See Milgrom-Block, *Ezekiel's Hope*, 151-153.

77 Cook, "Innerbiblical Interpretation in Ezekiel 44," 201-204.

78 Keith W. Carley writes, "The attitude expressed in vv. 10-14 toward the Levites can best be understood as the outcome of a struggle for dominance among rival priestly groups." See Carley, *The Book of the Prophet Ezekiel* (London: Cambridge University Press, 1974), 293-294.

future (v.16). Wellhausen argues that this text is the earliest biblical tradition that distinguishes between priests (the sons of Zadok) and Levites (the former priests of the high places).[79] In contrast to the role of the Levites, Zodokite priests of the Levites will stand before Yahweh and offer to him his food, the offerings of fat and blood (v.16). They shall come to Yahweh's table (altar). While Levites will serve to guard the gate of the house, Zadokite priests are permitted to offer sacrifices (40:46), and participate in the consecration of the altar (43:19). Thus for Ezekiel, Zadokites are cult functionaries from the tribe of Levi, but distinguished from the rest of the Levites by their superior status -כהנים "priests" descended from Zadok. Ezekiel is the only book of the Hebrew Bible in which Zadok appears as the ancestor of legitimate priests of the Jerusalem temple.[80]

The origin of the Zadokites is obscure. They may have been priests in Jerusalem before David captured the city and during the monarchy. Zadok was a priest aligned with David (2 Sam 8:17; 15:24-29; 20:25), who anointed Solomon as king (1 Kings 1:32-46). The Chronicler preserves a genealogy of Zadok that makes him a descendant of Aaron's son Eleazar (1 Chro 6:3-8).[81] The Zadokites claimed to be in the line of Eleazar, an elder son of Aaron (1 Chro 6:3-8; 24:3, 6), while the other priests claimed to be of the line of Ithimar, Aaron's youngest son (1 Chro 24:3). Ezra claimed himself to be the descendant of Zadok (Ezra 7:2). Nehemiah mentions the name of some priests as sons of Zadok (Neh 13:13). We learn that biblical texts that mention Zadokites do not give us sufficient information for the origin of Zadokite priesthood.

Zadokites are appointed as the offerers of sacrifice and guardians of the inner sanctuary. The reason for their approval is that "they kept the charge of my sanctuary when the people of Israel went astray." No other biblical evidence supports this claim.[82] Eichrodt writes: "This reason, which has little connection with historical fact, is an astonishing one, and would have been totally unimaginable from the mouth of Ezekiel."[83] The clause is in contrast with his thought on Ezekiel 7:26, 22:26, which enlists idolatry of the priests. Approval of Zadokites in vv. 15-16 conflicts with Ezekiel's charge against the Jerusalem priests

---

79 Wellhausen, *Prolegomena to the History of Israel*, 123-124. He interprets this text as Ezekiel's invention of moral grounds to justify the distinction between Zadokites and Levites.

80 Bruce Vawter and Leslie J. Hoppe, *A New Heart: A Commentary on the Book of Ezekiel*, ITC (Grand Rapids: Eerdmans, 1991), 199. See Ezek 40:46; 43:19; 44:15; 48:11.

81 Cf. Num 25:6-13. It was Eleazar's son Phineas to whom God promised the covenant of a perpetual priesthood because of the fidelity he showed in a time of Israel's rebellion.

82 Some have argued the connection of this text with apostasy of Israel found in Exodus 32. Some other connect it with the rebellion of sons of Korah in Numbers 16:1-19. M. E. Andrew writes, "Indeed it could be assumed from chapters 8-11 that the Zadokites, the Jerusalemite priests, were the ones primarily implicated in the abominations described there. See M. E. Andrew, *Responsibility and Restoration: The Course of the Book of Ezekiel* (Dunedin, New Zealand: University of Otago Press, 1985), 211.

83 Eichrodt, *Ezekiel*, 565.

in 8:16. This text might reflect the reality of priestly conflicts in the post-exilic period."[84] It is regarded as later Zadokite propaganda.[85] In the early post-exilic age, the Zadokites were the official priests wherein very few Levites returned from Babylon according to the list in Ezra 2. Ezekiel himself was probably a Zadokite (cf. Ezek 1:3), as was Ezra (Ezra 7:1-7). Carley writes, "It was under the influence of 44:6-31 that a note of the exclusive rights of the Zadokites who 'may come near to serve the Lord' was added in 40:46; 43:19 and 48:11.[86] It is highly probable that after the exile, the struggle for supremacy among the priests was resolved by giving those who traced their descent from Aaron, the brother of Moses, the privilege of serving in the sanctuary. The authors of this passage are firm in their partiality for the Zadokites, "because the regulations for the sanctity of the priesthood which follow (44:17-31) apply to them only, with no further attention being paid to the Levites at all."[87] Stevenson contends that the characterization of the temple and the priests in control of the territory of the house of Yahweh reflects the worldview of the elite social group, and "there is no question that the book of Ezekiel is the work of an elite social class."[88] Ezekiel's hierarchical paradigm is evidence in this chapter. Whether the separation of priests and Levites is an Ezekielian innovation is challenged by many critiques.[89] What we know from this text is that Ezekiel's author in the late sixth century endorsed supremacy of the Zadokites with their exclusive perspective.

5. Summary and Conclusion

The above study shows that Ezekiel 44 is a vision of restored community defined by the law of the temple. The oracle maintains holiness of the temple and purity of the temple community. The new temple is a visible sign of the eternal presence of Yahweh among his people. Since the כבוד יהוה returned to the new temple, the sanctity of the temple has to be preserved so that it might not be profaned and defiled in the future. The east gate from where Yahweh's כבוד entered the

84 Cf. Charles R. Biggs, *The Book of Ezekiel* (London: Epworth Press, 1996), 136.

85 Bowen, *Ezekiel*, 252.

86 Carley, *Ezekiel*, 296.

87 Cf. Andrew, *Responsibility and Restoration*, 211.

88 Stevenson, *Vision of Transformation*, 158.

89 For Wellhausen, the distinction between priests and Levites is a postexilic innovation. However, many critics have challenged this thesis. One ground of argument is linguistic critique of Hurvitz. Other studies focus on competition between the lines of Abiathar and Zadok in the monarchic Israel, and separate roles of Levites and priests in the preexilic Israel. However, these studies do not deny the anti-Levite polemic of Ezekiel 44. For discussion on linguistic notes see Avi Hurvitz, *A Linguistic Study of the Relationship between the Priestly Source and the Book of Ezekiel: A New Approach to an Old Problem* (Paris: J. Gabalda, 1982). McConville, "Priests and Levites in Ezekiel;" Raymond Abba, "Priests and Levites in Ezekiel, *VT* XXVIII, no. 1 (Jan 1978): 1-9, also M. D. Rehm, "Levites and Priests," 297-310, Block, *Ezekiel 28-48*, 634-637; Milgrom-Block, *Ezekiel's Hope*, 141-148.

sanctuary is shut permanently so that no one enters the way Yahweh the God of Israel entered in it. The sanctity of temple chambers and its spatial access as well as participation in the worship was enforced with strict boundaries.

First, the *Nasi* (ruler) has a limited authority over the new temple community. He is a guardian of the temple with limited access. He is responsible to overlook the east gate, which shall be shut at all times so that Yahweh's temple will never be profaned again. The limited authority and access to the temple area illustrates the centrality of the cultic center in the new temple community.

Secondly, the house of Israel, the defiled nation was condemned for her past failures to preserve the sanctity of the sanctuary. A new item of their abomination added to their punishment. It was their admittance of בן־נכר (sons of foreignness) in the sanctuary that defiled the land. A very rigorous rule of prohibiting בן־נכר entrance into the temple is a new feature of the community. The בן־נכר could be identified as the non-exilic group who engaged in various abominations. For them, access to the sanctuary is impossible. They were denied group membership.

Thirdly, the Levites were assigned a subordinate role and status. While their role in the cult was not denied, their status was subsidiary compared to the priests. Their role includes serving the laity and keeping the gates of the temple. They were also assigned the duty of slaughtering animals that for the priestly legislation was the task of common people. The subordinate status of the Levites according to our text is due to their infidelity and impurity in the past. There are certain allusions to the punishment of the Levites due to their iniquities in the priestly writings. However, these do not provide sufficient evidence to support this claim. They are categorized as non-legitimate priests.

Finally, the Zadokites alone are legitimate priests. They alone offer sacrifices and serve at the altar of Yahweh. There are many questions concerning the origin of the priesthood of the Zadokites. The reason for the superior status of the Zadokites referred to in this text "because they served Yahweh during Israel's apostasy" gains no support outside the book of Ezekiel. Some have argued this claim as the self-categorization of the Zadokite priests.

Ezekiel 40-48 seeks to structure a new society in which divine holiness cannot be violated. Ezekiel 44 prescribes a temple community with new access and boundaries. As we set this chapter in the late sixth century BCE, it appears that Ezekiel's school, the Zadokites endeavored to maintain purity of the new cultic community so that no defilement and profanation would drive the holy presence of Yahweh away from the sanctuary. By doing this, a priestly worldview of a society is maintained by restricting the cultic community, functionaries and temple's spatial boundaries.

Social identity maintains that identity formation and boundary construction are intertwined. When identity is threatened, boundaries defining identity are narrowly defined. I have mentioned earlier that in a situation where identity of a group is threatened, radical ideology develops as its response. Zadokite priests of the late exilic period responded their exile and struggle with a more stringent legislations. In the process of reinstating a new temple community, disputes about access, privileges and duties in relation to the temple services arise. In that situation, a rationale for deliberate cultic legislations was inevitable. The framework of holiness and purity provided a rationale for excluding various persons from the community.[90]

Ezekiel 44:1-16 could have come from the time when Israel reinstated the priesthood in the new temple community where a concern for holiness of the sanctuary and purity of its officials and the community was at its highest point.[91] This text is a well-composed work and a mechanism for maintaining the social system of the new temple community. While envisioning a new temple community, Ezekiel and his successors (the Zadokites) continued the policy of exclusivism, which is already found in the previous chapters. By doing so, they reject certain groups of people from membership in the community. They deny priestly status of certain groups of the Levites, who perhaps, had equal status with the priests in monarchic Israel, and claimed the legitimacy of the Zadokite priesthood. The rationale for this exclusiveness lies in the inevitability of holiness of the sanctuary and purity of Israel. The new temple community thus excludes and undermines certain groups who were viewed as failing to maintain purity when they were in the land by practicing religious and viral actions that were viewed negatively by those writing and editing these texts.

90 Cf. Bowen, *Ezekiel*, 254.

91 Cf. Clements, *Ezekiel*, 195-196.

Conclusion

This study on Ezekiel has shown that purity is used significantly in the definition of Israelite identity to differentiate the exiles from those who remained in Judah during the exilic period. The following remarks summarize the outcomes of this research.

First, this study has demonstrated that identity construction and the use of purity are connected in the book of Ezekiel. Purity as a group norm and a symbolic system plays a decisive role in defining who is in and who is out of the community of Israel. In the situation of exilic catastrophe, Ezekiel and his successors, known as Ezekiel's school reviewed the current situation, and envisioned a society, providing a rationale for defining the true Israel. By maintaining purity as a criterion for Israel's society, those who remained in Judah are viewed as the defiled, and those in exile are viewed as being purified for the future community.

Second, as shown in chapter 2, intergroup relationship between the Israelites in the sixth century BCE was marked by conflicts, competition and differentiation. This was caused primarily by deportations and difference of socio-historical settings in the exilic age. As found in literatures of the exilic period, the main contenders of this conflict were the exiles of Babylonia and those who remained in Judah. In such a situation of crisis of identity, literatures of the exilic age developed the idea of ingroup and outgroup within Israelite community. Boundaries that defined identity were narrowly conceived. The exiles of Babylonia, who were most threatened by the loss of identity, innovated new ideas and revised traditions of the past. They also developed ideologies in which the idea of purity was a great concern. This can be found significantly in the book of Ezekiel, one of the exilic literatures.

Next, the priestly concept of purity has a new meaning in the book of Ezekiel as it was interpreted in the context of group relationship. It transcends a constricted meaning of ritual symbol. It is a condition required for Israel in her relationship to Yahweh and the community. Impurity is a failure to comply with the norms of living as the people of God. Various types of impurity such as menstruation, contact with corpse, food impurity, bloodshed, child sacrifice, idolatry, and sexual misconduct defile the land (Israel), the people (community), and the sanctuary. Hence, failure to keep purity means detaching from Israel. Using purity as a group norm, Ezekiel distinguishes the people living in the homeland from the exiles. Those who lived in Judah and Jerusalem during the exile were accused of transgressing purity regulations. On the contrary, the exiles received divine favor as his כבוד and his משכן dwelt with them.

My exegetical studies of Chapters 4-7 also contribute to the understanding of Ezekiel's oracle in relation to purity and group identity. The exegetical studies show how purity is used in relation to condemnation of the homelanders by the Babylonian exiles. They also illustrate the biased view of the authors of Ezekiel, who categorize the exiles as the ingroup. The comparison of the two groups in Ezekiel 11:14-21 and 33:21-29 in chapter 4 demonstrates ingroup favoritism and outgroup disgust. In these passages, the presence of divine כבוד with the exiles, and promise of future possession of the land to the exiles mark ingroup preference. On the other hand, the passages reject the homelanders in their claim of land ownership because they commit different kinds of abomination and social crimes. In chapter 5 (22:1-31), I have pointed out that the sin of the inhabitants of Jerusalem and Judah is explicated in the form of abominations, bloodshed, sexual misconduct, idolatry, and profanation of Sabbath and the holy things. The veracity of these cultic sins and impurities are far from reality. Therefore, they serve as sociological tools for rejection of the homelanders. In chapter 6 (Ezekiel 37:15-28), I have demonstrated that the book of Ezekiel focuses on the restoration of the exiles, strategically ignoring discussion on the fate of the inhabitants of Jerusalem and Judah. I also have shown that restoration and purification are concurrent in the prophecies of restoration. Restoration and purification will begin with the returning exiles, although the fate of those who remain in the land is not mentioned. In my final chapter (44:1-16), I have shown that the law of the temple (chapters 40-48) envisions an exclusive new temple community. The non-exilic group was portrayed as foreigners and Levites, the perpetrators of Yahweh's worship. The self-categorization of Zadokite priesthood is evidently portrayed in this vision.

The application of theories of group identity in this study reveals that social organization and relationship determines group identification. The Social Identity Theory offered by Tajfel and others explains how a particular community, such as the exiles of Israel, defines themselves and others in the context of conflicts and intergroup relationship. Extreme denigration of the homelanders could be understood in the light of Sherif's conflict theory. Bar-Tal's idea of group beliefs/norms as conscious act and Walzer's theory of radical politics/ideology as a response to experience of exile added to explain the development of such ideologies. As Emile Durkheim, Mary Douglas, and others maintain, boundaries, including purity, define who are in and who are out of the community. There was a boundary marker between the contesting groups of the Israelites in the exilic period. As Mary Douglas and others theorize, purity is a symbolic cultural and social mechanism that draws a line between the exiles and the non-exilic group as defined in Ezekiel. The Social Identity Theory and its related concepts such as boundary mechanisms and purity in group relationships explain the social dynamics of the exilic age and group identification in the exilic literature. The use of social science in general, and the application of social (group) identity and related concepts in particular, are highly commendable for a study of group dynamics in the development of biblical tradition.

Finally, it is clearly shown that bias view in group identification is necessitated by circumstances. It can be a conscious act in response to certain situations. The period of the exile of the sixth century BCE is recognized as a creative age. During this period, traditions were redacted and transformed into new meaning. The history of the period shows the traumatic experiences of the exile. Israelites were in a situation of loss of land and loss of their identity as the people of God. It is plausible that Ezekiel sought a rationale for explaining the exilic catastrophe and a vision for the new Israel. At the dawn of the restoration, when the exiles and the homelanders were in intergroup relationships, priestly author(s) of Ezekiel maintained a more stringent view on group membership. For them, maintaining purity is an imperative to regulate the worship of Yahweh. A rationale for deliberate cultic legislation was inevitable. For the exiles, it is not surprising to identify the non-exiles as the outgroup as they were strangers, who lived in other land, and who had already mixed with people of other nations. It is likely that the authors of Ezekiel, in their attempt to maintain the identity of Israel enforced a rigorous purity legislation that excludes some members of the community of Israel, who did not experience the exile.

Bibliography

Abba, Raymond. "Priests and Levites in Ezekiel." *Vetus Testamentum* XXVIII, no. 1 (Jan. 1978): 1-9.

Abrams, Dominic and Michael A. Hogg (eds.), *Social Identity and Social Cognition* Oxford: Blackwell, 1999.

Abrams, Dominic and Michael Hogg. "An Introduction to the Social Identity Approach." Pages 1-9 in *Social Identity Theory: Constructive and Critical Advances*. Edited by Dominic Abrams and Michael Hogg. New York: Springer-Verlag, 1990.

Abramson, Harold J. "Migrants and Cultural Diversity: On Ethnicity and Religion in Society." *Social Compass* 25, no. 5 (1979): 5-29.

Ackroyd, Peter R. *Exile and Restoration: A Study of Hebrew Thought of the Sixth Century.* London: SCM Press Ltd., 1968.

Ahn, John J. *Exile as Forged Migrations: A Sociological, Literary, and Theological Appropriation on the Displacement and Resettlement of the Southern Kingdom of Judah*. BZAW 147. Berlin: De Gruyter, 2011.

Albertz, Rainer. "More or Less than a Myth: Reality and Significance of Exile for the Political, Social, and Religious History of Judah." Pages 20-33 in *By the Irrigation Canals of Babylon: Approaches to the Study of the Exile*, LHB/OTE 526. Edited by John J. Ahn and Jill Middlemas New York: T&T Clark, 2012.

Albertz, Rainer. *Israel in Exile: The History and Literature of the Sixth Century BCE.* Translated by David Green. *Atlanta: Society of Biblical Literature*, 2003.

Albright, William F. *The Archaeology of Palestine*. Harmondsworth, Middlesex: Penguin Books, 1949.

Allen, Leslie C. *Ezekiel 1-19*, WBC Vol. 28. Waco, Texas: Word Books, 1994.

________. *Ezekiel 20-48*, WBC Vol. 29. Dallas, Texas: Word Books, 1990.

Amit Yarah, "Epoch and Genre: The Sixth Century and the Growth of Hidden Polemic." Pages 135-151 in *Judah and the Judeans in the Neo-Babylonian Period.* Edited by Oded Lipschits and Joseph Blenkinsopp. Winona Lake, Ind: Eisenbrauns, 2003.

Ammerman, Nancy T. "Religious Identities and Religious Institutions." Pages 217-224 in *Handbook of the Sociology of Religion.* Edited by Michele Dillon. Cambridge: Cambridge University Press, 2003.

Amorim, Nilton Dutra. "Desecration and Defilement in the Old Testament." PhD Dissertation: Andrews University, 1986.

Andre. "טמא." Pages 330-342 in *TDOT* Vol. V. Edited by G. Johannes Botterwek and Helmer Ringgren. Translated by David E. Green. Grand Rapids, Michigan: Eerdmans, 1980.

Andrew, Herbert T. "The Letter of Aristeas." Pages 83-122 in *The Apocrypha and Pseudepigrapha of the Old Testament in English with Introductions and Critical and Explanatory Notes to the Several Books.* Edited by R. H. Charles. Oxford: Clarendon Press, 1913.

Andrew, M. E. *Responsibility and Restoration: The Course of the Book of Ezekiel.* Dunedin, New Zealand: University of Otago Press, 1985.

Ashmore, Richard D. Lee Jussim and David Wilder (eds.) *Social Identity, Intergroup Conflict, and Conflict Reduction.* Oxford: Oxford University Press, 2001.

Averbeck, Richard E. "טהר." Pages 365-353 in *NIDOTTE* Vol. 2. Edited by Willem A. Van Gemeren, et.al. Grand Rapids, Michigan: Zondervan, 1997.

________. "טמא." Pages 338-353 in *NIDOTTE* Vol. 2. Edited by Willem A. Van Gemeren, et.al. Grand Rapids, Michigan: Zondervan, 1997.

Awabdy, Mark A. "YHWH Exegetes Torah: How Ezekiel 44:7-9 Bars Foreigners from the Sanctuary," *JBL* 131, no. 4 (2012): 685-703.

Baker, Coleman A. "Social Identity Theory and Biblical Interpretation." *Biblical Theology Bulletin* 42, no. 3 (August 2012): 129-136.

Bar-Tal, Daniel. "Delegitimization: The Extreme Case of Stereotyping and Prejudice," Pages 169-182 in *Stereotyping and Prejudice: Changing Conceptions.* SSSP. Edited by Daniel Bar-Tal, Carl F. Graumann, Arie W. Kruglanski and Wolfgang Stroebe. New York: Springer-Verlag, 1989.

________. "Causes and Consequences of Delegitimization: Models of Conflict and Ethnocentrism," *Journal of Social Issues* 46, no. 1 (1990): 65-81.

________. *Group Beliefs: A Conception for Analyzing Group Structure, Processes, and Behavior* SSSP. New York: Springer-Verlag, 1990.

Barstad, Hans M. *The Myth of the Empty Land: A Study in the History and Archaeology of Judah During the "Exilic" Period.* Oslo: Scandinavian University Press, 1996.

________. "After the Myth of the Empty Land:" Major Challenges in the Study of Neo-Babylonian Judah." Pages 3-20 in *Judah and the Judeans in the Neo-Babylonian Period.* Edited by Oded Lipschits and Joseph Blenkinsopp. Winona Lake, Ind: Eisenbrauns, 2003.

________. *History and the Hebrew Bible: Studies in Ancient Israelite and Ancient Near Eastern Historiography.* Tubingen: Mohr Siebeck, 2008.

Barton, John. "The Prophets and the Cult." Pages 11-22 in *Temple and Worship in Biblical Israel.* Edited by John Day, LHB/OTE 422. London: T&T Clark, 2005.

Becker, Penny Edgell. *Congregations in Conflict: Cultural Models of Local Religious Life.* Cambridge: Cambridge University Press, 1999.

Becking, Bob. "On the Identity of the 'Foreign Women in Ezra 9-10." Pages 31-49 in *Exile and Restoration Revisited: Essays on the Babylonian and Persian Periods in Memory of Peter R. Ackroyd.* LSTS 73. Edited by Gary N. Knoppers and Lester L. Grabbe with Deirdre N. Fulton. New York: T&T Clark, 2009.

________. "Yehudite Identity in Elephantine." Pages 403-419 in *Judah and the Judeans in the Achaemenid Period: Negotiating Identity in an International Context.* Edited by Oded Lipschits and Joseph Blenkinsopp. Winona Lake, Ind: Eisenbrauns, 2011.

Begg, Christopher T. and Paul Pillsbury. *Judean Antiquities 8-10, Flavius Josephus: Translation and Commentary Vol. 5.* Edited by Steve Mason. Leiden/Boston: Brill, 2005.

Benite, Zvi Ben-dor. *The Ten Lost Tribes: A World History.* Oxford: Oxford University Press, 2009.

Biggs, Charles R. *The Book of Ezekiel.* London: Epworth Press, 1996.

Blenkinsopp, Joseph· *Ezekiel: Interpretation A Bible Commentary for Teaching and Preaching.* Louisville: John Knox Press, 1990.

________. *A History of Prophecy in Israel.* Revised and enlarged. Louisville, Kentucky: Westminster John Knox Press, 1996.

________. "Bethel in the Neo-Babylonian Period." Pages 93-105 in *Judah and the Judeans in the Neo-Babylonian Period.* Edited by Oded Lipschits and Joseph Blenkinsopp. Winona Lake, Ind: Eisenbrauns, 2003.

________. Isaiah 56-66: A New Translation with Introduction and Commentary. AB Vol. 19B. New York: Doubleday, 2003.

________. "Judean, Jews, Children of Abraham." Pages 461-482 in *Judah and the Judeans in the Achaemenid Period: Negotiating Identity in an International Context.* Edited by Oded Lipschits and Joseph Blenkinsopp. Winona Lake, Ind: Eisenbrauns, 2011.

Block, Daniel I. "Ezekiel's Boling Cauldron: A Form Critical Solution to Ezekiel XXIV: 1-14." *Vetus Testamentum* 41 (1991): 12-37.

________. *The Book of Ezekiel Chapters 1-24.* NICOT. Grand Rapids: Eerdmans, 1997.

________. *The Book of Ezekiel Chapters 25-48* NICOT. Grand Rapids: Eerdmans, 1998.

Boadt, Lawrence. "Book of Ezekiel." Pages 711-722 in *Anchor Bible Dictionary* Vol. 2. Edited by D. N. Freedman, et al., New York: Doubleday, 1992.

Bourdieu, Pierre. *Distinction: A Social Critique of the Judgment of Taste.* Translated by Richard Nice. Cambridge, MA: Harvard Univ. Press 1984 (French 1979).

Bowen, Nancy R. *Ezekiel.* AOTC. Nashville: Abingdon Press, 2010.

Bowie, Fiona. *The Anthropology of Religion: An Introduction.* Oxford: Blackwell Publishers, 2000.

Brewer, Marilynn B. "Intergroup Identification and Intergroup Conflict: When Does Ingroup Love Becomes Outgroup Hate?" Pages 17-30 in *Social Identity, Intergroup Conflict, and Conflict Reduction.* Edited by Richard D. Ashmore, Lee Jussim and David Wilder. Oxford: Oxford University Press, 2000.

Brown, F., S. Driver and C. Briggs, *The Brown-Driver-Briggs Hebrew and English Lexicon.* Peabody, Massachusetts: Hendrickson Publishers, 2004 (fifth printing).

Brown, Roger. *Social Psychology.* New York: The Free Press, 1986.

Brown, Rupert and Dora Caprozza. "Motivational, Emotional, and Cultural Influences in Social Identity Processes." Pages 3-30 in *Social Identities: Motivational, Emotional and Cultural Influences.* Edited by Rupert Brown and Dora Capozza. Hove, East Sussex: Psychology Press, 2006.

Brownlee, William H. *Ezekiel 1-19,* WBC Vol. 28. Waco, Texas: Word Books Publisher, 1986.

Brubaker, Rogers and Frederick Cooper. "Beyond "Identity." *Theory and Society* 29, no. 1 (Feb. 2000): 1-47.

Brueggemann, Walter. *Hopeful Imagination: Prophetic Voices in Exile*. Philadelphia: Fortress Press, 1986.

Carley, Keith W. *The Book of the Prophet Ezekiel.* London: Cambridge University Press, 1974.

Carroll, Robert P. "The Myth of the Empty Land." *Semeia* 59 (1992): 79-93.

________. "Exile! What Exile? Deportations and the Discourse of Diaspora." Pages 62-79 in *Leading Captivity Captive: "The Exile" as History and Ideology.* Edited by L. L. Grabbe. JSOTSup 278. Sheffield: Sheffield Academic Press, 1998.

Carter, Charles E. *The Emergence of Yehud in the Persian Period: A Social and Demographic Study.* JSOTSup. 294. Sheffield: Sheffield Academic Press, 1999.

________. "Ideology and Archaeology in the Neo-Babylonian Period." Pages 301-322 in *Judah and the Judeans in the Neo-Babylonian Period.* Edited by Oded Lipschits and Joseph Blenkinsopp. Winona Lake, Ind: Eisenbrauns, 2003.

Chaves, Mark. *Congregations in America.* Cambridge, MA: Harvard University Press, 2004.

Clements, R. E. "Chronology of Redaction in Ezekiel 1-24." Pages 283-294 in *Ezekiel and His Book: Textual and Literary Criticism and their Interrelation,* edited by J. Lust (Leuven: Leuven University Press, 1986.

________. *Ezekiel.* Louisville: Westminster Jon Knox Press, 1996.

Codrington, R. H. *The Melanesians: Studies in their Anthropology and Folklore.* New Haven: Hraf Press, 1957; first edition 1891.

Cohen, Anthony P. *The Symbolic Construction of Community.* London/New York: Tavistock Publications, 1985.

Coogan, Michael David. *West Semitic Personal Names in the Murasu Documents.* Missoula, Montana: Scholars Press, 1976.

Cook, Steven L. "Innerbiblical Interpretation in Ezekiel 44 and the History of Israel's Priesthood." *JBL* 114, no. 2 (1995): 193-208.

Cooke, G. A. *A Critical and Exegetical Commentary on the Book of Ezekiel Vol. 1.* ICC. New York: Charles Scribner's Sons, 1937.

________. *A Critical and Exegetical Commentary on The Book of Ezekiel Vol. II.* ICC. New York: Charles Scribner's Sons, 1937.

Cooper, Sr., Lamar Eugene. *Ezekiel.* NAC Vol. 17. USA: Broadman & Holman Publishers, 1994.

Coser, Lewis. *The Functions of Social Conflict.* New York: The Free Press, 1956.

Craigie, Peter. *Ezekiel.* Philadelphia: Westminster Press, 1983.

Crane, Ashley. *Israel's Restoration: A Textual-Comparative Exploration of Ezekiel 36-39.* VTSup 122. Leiden/Boston: Brill, 2008.

Daguid, Ian M. *Ezekiel and the Leaders of Israel.* VTSup 56. Leiden: E. J. Brill, 1994.

Darr, Katheryn Pfisterer. "The Book of Ezekiel: Introduction, Commentary, and Reflections." In *The New Interpreter's Bible: A Commentary in Twelve Volumes*, Vol. VI. Nashville: Abingdon Press, 2001.

Davidson, Steed Vernyl. *Empire and Exile: Postcolonial Readings of the Book of Jeremiah.* New York: T&T Clark, 2011.

Derett, J. Duncan M. "Impurity and Idolatry: John 13:11; Ezekiel 36:25." *Bibbia e Oriente* 172, XXXIV no. 2 (April-May 1992): 87-92.

Deutsch, Nathaniel. "The Proximate Other: The Nation of Islam and Judaism." Pages 91-117 in *Black Zion: African American Religious Encounters with Judaism.* Edited by Yvonne Chireau and Nathaniel Deutsch. New York: Oxford University Press, 2000.

Dever, William G. *What Did the Biblical Writers Know and When Did They Know it? What Archaeology Cal Tell Us about the Reality of Ancient Israel.* Grand Rapids, Michigan: Eerdmans, 2002.

Dijkstra, Meindert. "The Valley of Dry Bones: Coping with the Reality of the Exile in the Book of Ezekiel." Pages 114-133 in *The Crisis of Israelite Religion: Transformation of Religious Tradition in Exilic and Post-Exilic Times.* Edited by Bob Becking and Marjo C. A. Korpel. Leiden: Brill, 1999.

Domeris, William R. "The Land Claim of Jeremiah-Was Max Weber Right?" Pages 136-149 in *Jeremiah (Dis)placed: New Directions in Writing/Reading Jeremiah.* Edited by A. R. Pete Diamond and Louis Stulman. New York: T&T Clark, 2011.

Douglas, Mary. *Purity and Danger: An Analysis of Concepts of Pollution and Taboo.* New York: Oxford University Press Inc., 1966.

________. *Natural Symbols: Explorations in Cosmology.* New York: Pantheon Books, 1970.

________. *Jacob's Tears: The Priestly Work of Reconciliation.* Oxford: Oxford University Press, 2004.

Duhm, Bernhard. *Das Buch Jesaja, Handkommentar zum Alten Testamentum.* Gottingen: Vandenhoeck & Rupreckt, 1892.

Duke, Rodney K. "Punishment or Restoration? Another Look at the Levites of Ezekiel 44:6-16." *JSOT* 40 (1988): 61-68.

Durham, John I. *Exodus.* WBC Vol. 3. Nashville: Thomas Nelson Publishers, 1987.

Durkheim, Emile. *The Elementary Forms of Religious Life.* Translated by Karen E. Fields. New York, NY: The Free Press, 1995; French 1912.

Durslesser, James A. *The Metaphorical Narratives in the Book of Ezekiel.* Lewiston, New York: Edwin Mellen Press, 2006.

Edelman, Diana. "Settlement Patterns in Persian-Era Yehud." Pages 52-62 in *A Time of Change: Judah and its Neighbours in the Persian and Early Hellenistic Periods*. LSTS 65. Edited by Yigal Levin. London: T&T Clark, 2007.

Eichrodt, Walter. *Ezekiel: A Commentary*. Translated by Cosslett Quin. OTL. Philadelphia: Westminster Press, 1970.

Eisenstat, Yedida. "Sanctification and Shame: Balik's In the City of Slaughter in Light of Leviticus and Ezekiel." Pages 263-282 in *Purity, Holiness, and Identity in Judaism and Christianity: Essays in Memory of Susan Haber*. Edited by Carl S. Ehrlich, Anders Runesson and Eileen Schuller. Tubingen: Mohr Siebeck, 2013.

Eliade, Mircea. *Man and the Sacred*. New York: Harper & Row, 1974.

Ellemers, Naomi, Russel Spears, and Bertijan Doosje (eds). *Social Identity Context, Commitment, Content*. Oxford: Blackwell, 1999.

Erikson, Kai T. *Wayward Puritans: A Study in the Sociology of Deviance*. New York: John Wiley & Sons, 1966.

Esler, Philip E. *Conflict and Identity in Romans: The Social Setting of Paul's Letter*. Minneapolis: Fortress Press, 2003.

________. "Ezra-Nehemiah as a Narrative of (Re-Invented) Israelite Identity." *Biblical Interpretation* 11 (2003): 413-426.

Faust, Avraham. "Settlement Dynamics and Demographic Fluctuations in Judah from the Late Iron Age to the Hellenistic Period and the Archaeology of Persian-Period Yehud." Pages 23-64 in *A Time of Change: Judah and its Neighbours in the Persian and Early Hellenistic Periods*. LSTS 65. Edited by Yigal Levin. London: T&T Clark, 2007.

________. *Judah in the Neo-Babylonian Period: Archaeology of Desolation*, SBL ABSS 18. Atlanta, Georgia: SBL, 2012.

________. "The Shephelah in the Iron Age: A New look on the Settlement of Judah." *Palestine Exploration Quarterly* 143, no. 3 (2013): 203-219.

Feinstein, Eve Levavi. "Sexual Pollution in the Hebrew Bible: A New Perspective." Pages 114-145 in *Bodies, Embodiment, and Theology of the Hebrew Bible*. Edited by S. Tamar Kamionskowski and Wonil Kim, LBH/OTE 465. New York: T&T Clark, 2010.

Finkel, Irving. "The Cyrus Cylinder: the Babylonian Perspective." Pages 4-34 in *The Cyrus Cylinder: The King of Persia's Proclamation from Ancient Babylon*. Edited by Irving Finkel. London: I. B. Tauris & Co. Ltd., 2013.

Finkelstein, Israel. "Migration of Israelites into Judah after 720 BCE: An Answer and an Update." *ZAW* 127, no. 2 (2015): 188-206.

Fisch, S. *Ezekiel: Hebrew Text & English Translation with an Introduction and Commentary*. London: The Soncino Press, 1950.

Fohrer, Gerhard. *Die Hauptprobleme des Buches Ezechiel*, BZAW 72. Berlin: Topelmann, 1952. 130.

Fonrobert, Charlotte Elisheva. *Menstrual Purity: Rabbinic and Christian Reconstructions of Biblical Gender*. Stanford, California: Stanford University Press, 2000.

Frazer, James G. *The Golden Bough A Study in Magic and Religion*. Old Saybrook, CT: Konecky & Konecky, 1922; first published in1890.

Frymer-Kensky. "Pollution, Purification, and Purgation in Biblical Israel." Pages 399-414 in *The Word of the Lord Shall Go Forth, Essays in honor of David Noel Freeman in Celebration of his Sixtieth Birthday*. Edited by Carol L. Meyers and M. O'Connor. Winona Lake, Ind: Eisenbrauns, 1983.

Galambush, Julie. *Jerusalem in the Book of Ezekiel: The City as Yahweh's Wife*, SBL Dissertation Series 130. Atlanta, Georgia: SBL, 1992.

Ganz, Herbert J. "Preface." Pages vii-xv in *Cultivating Symbolic Boundaries Differences and the Making of Inequality*. Edited by Michele Lamont and Marcel Courier. Chicago: The University of Chicago Press, 1992.

Ganzel, Tova. "The Concept of Holiness in the Book of Ezekiel." PhD Dissertation: Bar-Ilan University, Ramat-Gan, Israel, 2005.

________. "The Defilement and Desecration of the Temple in Ezekiel." *Biblica* 89, no. 3 (2008): 369-379.

________. "Description of the Restorations of Israel in Ezekiel," *Vestamentum* 60 (2010): 197-211.

Geertz, Clifford. *The Interpretation of Cultures: Selected Essays*. New York: Basic Books, 1974.

Gesenius, Wilhelm. *Gesenius' Hebrew Grammar*. Edited and enlarged by E. Kautzsch. Oxford: Clarendon Press, 1978 reprinted.

Godbey, Allen H. *The Lost Tribes A Myth: Suggestions Towards Rewriting Hebrew History*, Library of Biblical Studies. New York: KTAV Pub. House, 1974.

Goldstein, E.W. "By the Blood that You Shed You are Guilty:" Perspectives on Female Blood in Leviticus and Ezekiel." Pages 57-69 in *Jewish Blood: Reality and Metaphor in History, Religion, and Culture*. Edited by Mitchell B Hart, RJSS. London: Routledge, 2009.

Gorman Jr., Frank H. *The Ideology of Ritual: Space, Time and Status in the Priestly Torah*. JSOT Sup 91. Sheffield: Sheffield Academic Press, 1990.

Grabbe, Lester L. "They Shall Come Rejoicing to Zion' or Did They? The Settlement of Yehud in the Early Persian Period." Pages 116-127 in *Exile and Restoration Revisited: Essays on the Babylonian and Persian Periods in Memory of Peter R. Ackroyd*. LSTS 73. Edited by Gary N. Knoppers and Grebbe, Lester L.) with Deirdre N. Fulton. New York: T&T Clark, 2009.

Graffy, Adrian. *A Prophet Confronts His People: The Disputation Speech in the Prophets*. AnBib 104. Rome: Biblical Institute, 1984.

Grayson, A. K. Assyrian and Babylonian Chronicles. Vol 5 of Texts from Cuneiform Sources. Locust Valley, NY: J. J. Augustin, 1975.

Greenberg, Moshe. *Ezekiel 1-20* AB Vol. 22. Garden city, New York: Doubleday & Company Inc., 1983.

________. "The Design and Theme of Ezekiel's Program of Restoration," *Interpretation* 38 (1984): 181-208.

________. "The Etymology of hdn (Menstrual Impurity)." Pages 69-77 in *Solving Riddles and Untying Knots: Biblical, Epigraphic, and Semitic Studies in honor of Jonas C. Greenfield*. Edited by Ziony Zevit, Seymour Gitin, and Michael Sokoloff. Winona Lake, Ind.: Eisenbrauns, 1995.

________. *Ezekiel 21-37*, AB. Garden City, New York: Doubleday, 1997.

Hall, John R. "The Capital(s) of Cultures: A Nonholistic Approach to Status, Situations, Gender, and Ethnicity." Pages 257-285 in *Cultivating Symbolic Boundaries Differences and the Making of Inequality*. Edited by Michele Lamont and Marcel Fournier. Chicago: University of Chicago Press, 1992.

Halperin, David J. *Seeking Ezekiel: Text and Psychology*. University Park, Pennsylvania: The Pennsylvania University Press, 1993.

Hals, Ronald. M. *Ezekiel*, FOTL Vol. XIX. Grand Rapids, Michigan: Eerdmans. 1989.

Häner, Tobias. *Bleibendes Nachwirken des Exils: Eine Untersuchung zur kanonischen Endgestalt des Ezechielbuches*. Herders Bliblische Studien 78. Freiburg: Harder, 2014.

Harrington, Hannah K. *The Purity Texts*, Companion to the Qumran Scrolls, 5. London/New York: T&T Clark, 2004.

________. "Clean and Unclean." Pages 681-689 in *The New Interpreter's Dictionary of the Bible*. Vol. 1. Edited by Katherine Doob Snakenfeld, et al., Nashville: Abingdon Press, 2006.

Haran, Menahem. "The Law Code of Ezekiel 40-48 and Its Relation to the Priestly School." Pages 45-71 in *Hebrew Union College Annual* 50. Cincinnati: Hebrew Union College, 1980.

Hendel, Ronald. "Remembering Mary Douglas: Kashrut, Culture, and Thought-Styles." *Jewish Studies* 45 (2008): 3-15.

________. "Away from Ritual: The Prophetic Critique." Pages 60-79 in *Social Theory and the Israelite Religion: Essays in Retrospect and Prospect.* Edited by Saul M. Olyan. Atlanta: SBL, 2012.

Herion, Gary A. "Elephantine Papyri." Pages 445-455 in *Anchor Bible Dictionary* Vol. 2. Edited by David Noel Freedman. New York: Doubleday, 1992.

Hermann, Siefgried. *A History of Israel in the Old Testament Times*. London: SCM Press Ltd., 1975.

Hinkle, Steve and Rupert Brown. "Intergroup Comparisons and Social Identity: Some Links and Lacunae." Pages 48-70 in *Social Identity Theory: Constructive and Critical Advances.* Edited by Dominic Abrams and Michael Hogg. New York: Springer-Verlag, 1990.

Hogg, Michael A. "Intragroup Processes, Group Structure and Social Identity." Pages 65-93 in *Social Groups and Identities: Developing the Legacy of Henri Tajfel.* Edited by W. Peter Robinson. Oxford: Butterworth-Heinemann, 1996.

Hogg, Michael and Dominic Abrams (eds), *Intergroup Relations.* Philadelphia, PA: Psychology Press, 2001.

Houston, Walter. *Purity and Monotheism: Clean and Unclean Animals in Biblical Law*, JSOTSup 140. Sheffield: Sheffield Academic Press, 1993.

Hummel, Horace D. *Ezekiel 1-20*. St. Louis: Concordia Pub. House, 2005.

________. *Ezekiel 21-48*. Saint Louis: Concordia Pub. House, 2007.

Hurvitz, Avi. *A Linguistic Study of the Relationship between the Priestly Source and the Book of Ezekiel: A New Approach to an Old Problem*. Paris: J. Gabalda, 1982.

Jackson, Lynne M. and Bruce Hunsberger. "An Intergroup Perspective on Religion and Prejudice." *Journal for the Scientific Study of Religion* 38 no. 1 (March 1999): 509-523.

Japhet, Sara. "The Concept of the "Remnant" in the Restoration Period: On the Vocabulary of Self-Definition." Pages 432-449 in *From the Rivers of Babylon to the Highlands of Judah: Collected Studies on the Restoration Period. Edited by Sara Japhet.* Winona Lake, Ind.: Eisenbrauns, 2006.

Jenson, Philip Peter. *Graded Holiness: A Key to the Priestly Conception of the World.* JSOT Sup 106. Sheffield: Sheffield Academic Press, 1992.

Jenson, Robert W. *Ezekiel. Brazos Theological Commentary on the Bible*. Grand Rapids, Michigan: Brazos Press, 2009.

Jokiranta, Juha. *Social Identity and Sectarianism in the Qumran Movement. Studies on the Texts of the Desert of Judah.* Leiden: Brill, 2013.

Jost, John R. and Kimberly D. Elsbach. "How Status and Power Differences Erode Personal and Social Identities at Work: A System Justification Critique of Organizational Applications of Organizational Applications of Social Identity Theory." Pages 181-196 in *Social Identity Processes in Organizational Contexts.* Edited by Michael A. Hogg and Deborah J. Terry. Philadelphia, PA: Psychology Press, 2001.

Joyce, Paul M. "Temple and Worship in Ezekiel 40-48." Pages 145-163 in *Temple and Worship in Biblical Israel: Proceedings of the Oxford Old Testament Seminar.* LHB/OTS 422. London: T&T Clark, 2006.

________. *Ezekiel: A Commentary* LHB/OTE 482. New York: T&T Clark, 2007.

Kamiowskowski, S. Tamar. *Gender Reversal and Cosmic Chaos: A Study on the Book of Ezekiel.* JSOT Sup 368. London: Sheffield Academic Press, 2003.

Karpov, Vyacheslav, Elena Lisovkaya, and David Barry. "Ethnodoxy: How popular Ideologies Fuse Religious and Ethnic Identities." *Journal for the Scientific Study of Religion* 51, no. 4 (2012): 638-655.

Kelle, Brad E. "Dealing with the Trauma of Defeat: The Rhetoric of the Devastation and Rejuvenation of Nature in Ezekiel." *JBL* 128, no. 3 (2009): 469-490.

Kellermann, D. "משכן." Pages 58-64 in *TDOT* Vol. IX. Edited by G. Johannes Botterweck, Helmer Ringgren, and Heinz-Josef Fabry. Translated by David E. Green. Grand Rapids, Michigan: Eerdmans, 1998.

________. "עולה/עלה." Pages 96-113 in *TDOT* Vol. XI, Edited by G. Johannes Botterweck and Helmer Ringgren and Heinz-Josef Fabry. Translated by David E. Green. Grand Rapids, Michigan: Eerdmans, 2001.

Kelly, Page H. *Biblical Hebrew: An Introductory Grammar.* Grand Rapids, Michigan: Eerdmans, 1991.

Kessler, John. "Diaspora and Homeland in Early Achaemenid Period: Community, Geography and Demography in Zechariah 1-8." Pages 137-166 in *Approaching Yehud: New Approaches to the Study of the Persian Period.* Semeia Studies 50. Edited by Jon L. Berquist. Atlanta: Society of Biblical Literature, 2007.

________. "Images of Exile: Representations of the "Exile" and "Empty Land" in Sixth to Fourth Century BCE Yehudite Literature." Pages 309-351 in *The Concept of Exile in Ancient Israel and Its Historical Contexts. BZAW* 104. Edited by Ehud Ben Zvi and Christoph Levin. Berlin: De Gruyter, 2010.

Kiefer, Jorn. *Exil und Diaspora: Begrifflichkeit und Deutungen im Antiken Judentum und in der Hebraischen Bibel.* Leipzig: Evangeische Verlagsanstalt, 2005.

Klawans, Jonathan. *Impurity and Sin in Ancient Judaism.* Oxford: Oxford University Press, 2000.

________. "Pure, Violence: Sacrifice and Defilement in Ancient Israel." *Harvard Theological Review* 94, no. 2 (April 2001): 133-155.

________. "Concepts of Purity in the Bible." Pages 2045-2046 in *The Jewish Study Bible*. Edited by Adele Berlin and Marc Zvi Brettler. Oxford: Oxford University Press, 2004.

________. *Purity, Sacrifice, and the Temple: Symbolism and Supersessionism in the Study of Ancient Judaism*. Oxford: Oxford University Press, 2006.

Klein, Ralph W. *Israel in Exile: A Theological Interpretation*. Philadelphia: Fortress Press, 1979.

________. *Ezekiel the Prophet and His Message*. Studies in the Personalities of the Old Testament. Columbia, South Carolina: University of South Carolina Press, 1988.

Knoppers, Gary N. *1 Chronicles 1-9: A New Translation and Commentary*. AB Vol. 12. New York: Doubleday, 2003.

Koehler, Ludwig and Walter Baumgartner. *Hebrew and Aramaic Lexicon of the Old Testament* Vol. 2. Translated by M. E. J. Richardson. Leiden: E. J. Brill, 1995.

Koet, Bart J. "Purity and Impurity of the Body in Luke-Acts." Pages 81-95 in *Dreams and Scripture in Luke-Acts Collected Essays*. Leuven: Peeters 2006.

Kohn, Risa Levit. "As Though You Yourself Came Out of Egypt:" The Ethos of Exile in Ezekiel." *Hebrew Bible and Ancient Israel* 3 no. 2 (2014): 185-203.

________. *A New Heart and a New Soul; Ezekiel, the Exile and the Torah*, JSOTSupp 358. Sheffield: Sheffield Academic Press, 2000.

Konkel, A. H. "rkn." Pages 108-109 in *NIDOTTE* Vol. 3. Edited by Willem A. Van Gemeren, et. al., Grand Rapids, Michigan: Zondervan,1997.

Kooij, Van der. "The Septuagint of Ezekiel and Hasmonean Leadership." Pages 437-446 in *Interpreting Translation: Studies on the LXX and Ezekiel in Honour of Johan Lust*. Edited by F. Garcia Martizes and M Vervenne, BETL 192. Leuven: Peeters, 2005.

Kornfeld. "קדשׁ." Pages 521-527 in *TDOT* Vol. XII. Edited by G. Johannes Botterweck, Helmer Ringgren and Heiz-Joseph Fabry. Translated by David E. Green. Grand Rapids, Michigan: Eerdmans, 2003.

Kutsch, E. "ברית." Pages 256-266 in *TLOT* Vol. 1. Edited by Ernst Jenni and Claus Westermann. Translated by Mark E. Biddle. Peabody, Massachusetts: Hendrickson, 1997.

Kutsko, John F. *Between Heaven and Earth: Divine Presence and Absence in the Book of Ezekiel*. BJS 7. Winona Lake, Ind: Eisenbrauns, 2000.

Lamont, Michele and Marcel Fourier. "Introduction." Pages 1-17 in *Cultivating Symbolic Boundaries Differences and the Making of Inequality*. Edited by Michele Lamont and Marcel Courier. Chicago: The University of Chicago Press, 1992.

Lang. "נכר." Pages 423-431 in *TDOT* Vol. IX. Edited by G. Johannes Botterweck, Helmer Ringgren and Heinz-Josef Fabry. Translated by David E. Green. Grand Rapids, Michigan: Eerdmans, 1998.

Lapsey, Jacqueline E. *Can These Bones Live? The Problem of Moral Self in the Book of Ezekiel.* BZAW 301, Berlin: Walter de Gruyter, 2000.

Lemche, Niels Peter. *Biblical Studies and the Failure of History: Changing Perspectives 3.* Sheffield: Equinox Publishing Ltd., 2013.

Lemke, Werner E. "Life in the Present and Hope for the Future." Pages 200-214 in *Interpreting the Prophets*. Edited by James Luther Mays and Paul J. Achtemeier. Philadelphia: Fortress Press, 1987.

Leuchter, Mark. "Coming to Terms with Ezra's many Identities in Era-Nehemiah." Pages 41- 63 in *Historiography and Identity (Re)formulation in Second Temple Historiographical Literature*. LHB/OTE 534. Edited by Louis Jonker. New York: T&T Clark, 2010.

Levenson, Jon D. "The Temple and the World." *Journal of Religion* 64 no. 3 (1984): 275-298.

Levine, Baruch. "Late Language in the Priestly Source: Some Literary and Historical Observations" Pages 69-82 in *Proceedings of the Eighth World Congress of Jewish Studies*. Jerusalem: World Union of Jewish Studies, 1983.

Levy, Samson. *The Targum of Ezekiel*, Aramaic Bible 13. Collegeville: Liturgical Press, 1990.

Lind, Millard C. *Ezekiel.* Scottdale, Pa: Herald Press, 1996.

Lipka, Hilary. "Profaning the Body" חלל and the Conception of Loss of Personal Holiness in H." Pages 90-113 in *Bodies, Embodiment, and Theology of the Hebrew Bible*. Edited by S. Tamar Kaionkowski and Wonil Kim, LHB/OTE 465. New York: T&T Clark, 2010.

Lipschits, Oded. "Demographic Changes in Judah between the Seventh and the Fifth Centuries B.C.E." Pages 323-376 in *Judah and the Judeans in the Neo-Babylonian Period.* Edited by Oded Lipschits and Joseph Blenkinsopp. Winona Lake, Ind: Eisenbrauns, 2003.

________. *The Fall and Rise of Jerusalem: Judah Under Babylonian Rule.* Winona Lake, Ind: Eisenbrauns, 2005.

Lust, Johan. "Messianism in LXX-Ezekiel: Towards a Synthesis." Pages 417-430 in *The Septuagint and Messianism*. Edited by M. K. Knibb, BETL 195. Leuven: Peeters, 2006.

Lyons, Michael A. *From Law to Prophecy: Ezekiel's Use of the Holiness Code*. LHB/OTS 507. London/New Work: T&T Clark, 2009.

________. "Envisioning Restoration: Innovations in Ezekiel 40-48." Pages 71-63 in *I Lifted my Eyes and Saw: Reading Dream and Vision Reports in the Hebrew Bible*, LHB/OTS 584. Edited by Elizabeth R. Hayes and Lena-Sofia Tiemeyer. London: Bloomsbury, 2014.

Mackenzie, Stephen L. "Deuteronomistic History." Pages 160-168 in *Anchor Bible Dictionary* Vol. 2. Edited by D. N. Freedman, et al., New York: Doubleday, 1992.

Mackie, Timothy P. *Expanding Ezekiel: The Hermeneutics of Scribal Addition in the Ancient Text Witnesses of the Book of Ezekiel*. FRLANT 257. Gottingen: Vandelhoeck & Ruprecht, 2015.

Maier, Gerhard. *Des Prophet Hesekiel Kapitel 25 bis 48*. Wuppertal: R. Brockhaus Verlag, 2000.

Matties, Gordon H. *Ezekiel 18 and the Rhetoric of Discourse*. SBL Dissertation Series 126. Atlanta, Georgia: SBL 1989.

May, Herbert G. "The Book of Ezekiel: Introduction and Exegesis." *The Interpreter's Bible*. Vol. 6. Edited by George Arthur Buttrick et. al., New York: Abingdon Press, 1956.

Mayfield, Tyler D. *Literary Structure and Setting in Ezekiel*. Tubingen: Mohr Siebeck, 2010.

McConville, J. Gordon. "Priests and Levites in Ezekiel: A Crux in the Interpretation of Israel's History." *Tyndale Bulletin* 34 (1983): 3-31.

McKeating, Henry. *Ezekiel*, Old Testament Guides. Sheffield: Sheffield Academic Press, 1993.

________. "Ezekiel the 'Prophet' Like Moses." *JSOT* 61 (1994): 97-109.

Mein, Andrew. *Ezekiel and the Ethics of Exile*. Oxford: Oxford University Press, 2001.

Meyers, Jacob M. *Ezra-Nehemiah: Introduction*, Translation, and Notes. AB. Garden City, New York: Doubleday, 1965.

Middlemas, Jill Annie. *The Templeless Age: An Introduction to the History, Literature, and Theology of the Exile*. Louisville: Westminster John Knox Press, 2007.

________. "Divine Presence and Absence: Aniconism and Multiple Imaging in the Prophets." Pages 183-212 in *Divine Presence and Absence in Exilic and Post Exilic Judaism*. Edited by Nathan Macdonald and Izaak J. De Hulster, FAT 61. Tubingen, Germany: Mohr Siebeck, 2013.

Milgrom, Jacob. *Cult and Conscience: The Asham and The Priestly Doctrine of Repentance*. SJLA 18. Leiden: Brill, 1976.

________. *Studies in Cultural Theology and Terminology*. SJLA 36. Leiden: E. J. Brill, 1983.

________. *Leviticus 1-16*. AB. Doubleday: New York, 1991.

Milgrom, Jacob and Daniel I Block (in conversation). *Ezekiel's Hope: A Commentary on Ezekiel 38-48*. Eugene, Oregon: Cascade Books, 2012.

Milgrom-Wright, "נדה." Pages 232-234 in *TDOT* Vol. IX. Edited by G. Johannes Botterweck, Helmer Ringgren and Heinz-Josef Fabry. Translated by David E. Green. Grand Rapids, Michigan: Eerdmans, 1998.

Moore, Megan Bishop and Brad E. Kelle. *Biblical History and Israel's Past: The Changing Study of the Bible and History*. Grand Rapids, Michigan: Eerdmans, 2011.

Neiman, D. "פגר: A Cananite Cult-Object in the Old Testament." *JBL* 67 (1948): 55-60.

Nelson, Richard D. *Raising Up a Faithful Priest: Community and Priesthood in Biblical Theology*. Louisville, Kentucky: Westminster/John Knox Press, 1993.

Neusner, Jacob. *The Idea of Purity in Ancient Judaism*. SJLA 1. Leiden: Brill, 1973.

________. *Purity in Rabbinic Judaism A Systematic Account: The Sources, Media, Effects, and Removal of Uncleanness*. Atlanta, Georgia: Scholars Press, 1994.

Neyrey, Jerome H. "The Idea of Purity in Mark's Gospel." *Semeia* 35 (1986): 91-128.

________. "The Symbolic Universe of Luke-Acts: They Turn the World Upside Down." Pages 271-304 in *The Social World of Luke-Acts*. Edited by Jerome H. Neyrey. Peabody, MA: Hendrickson Publishers, 1991.

Niditch, Susan. *The Symbolic Vision in Biblical Tradition*. HSM 30. Chico, California: Scholars Press, 1983.

Noth, Martin. *The Deuteronomistic History*. Sheffield: JSOT, 1981.

O'Connor, Robert H. "חלל." Pages 145-153 in *NIDOTTE* Vol. 2. Edited by Willem A. Van Gemeren, et.al. Grand Rapids, Michigan: Zondervan, 1997.

Oakes, P. J. and S. A. Haslam (eds). *Stereotyping and Social Reality*. Oxford: Blackwell, 1994.

Obinwa, Ignatius M. C. *The Shepherd Motif in Ezekiel 34: Its Theological Import and Socio-Political Implications*. FZB 125. Wurzburg: Echter Verlag GmbH, 2012.

Oddie, Morgan. "The Relationship o f Religion and Ethnic Nationalism in Boznia-Hergovina." *Religion in Eastern Europe* XXXII, no. 1 (February, 2012): 34-42.

Oded, B. "Where Is the "Myth of the Empty Land" To be Found? History versus Myth." Pages 55-74 in *Judah and the Judeans in the Neo-Babylonian Period.* Edited by Oded Lipschits and Joseph Blenkinsopp. Winona Lake, Ind: Eisenbrauns, 2003.

Odell, Margaret S. "You are What You Eat: Ezekiel and the Scroll." *JBL* 117 (1998): 229-248.

________. *Ezekiel.* Smith & Helwys Bible Commentary. Macon, Georgia: Smyth & Helwys Publishing, Inc., 2005.

Olley, John W. *Ezekiel: A Commentary Based on Iezekiel in Codex Vaticanus.* Septuagint Commentary Series. Leiden: Brill, 2009.

Pakkala, Juha. "The Exile and Exiles in the Ezra Tradition." Pages 91-101 in *The Concept of Exile in Ancient Israel and Its Historical Contexts.* BZAW 104. Edited by *Ehud Ben Zvi and Christoph Levin.* Berlin/New York: De Gruyter, 2010.

Pandian, Jacob. *Culture, Religion, and the Sacred Self: A Critical Introduction to the Anthropological Study of Religion.* Englewood Cliffs, New Jersey: Prentice Hall, 1991.

Parfitt, Tudor. *The Lost Tribes of Israel: The History of a Myth.* London: Weidenfeld & Nicholson, 2002.

Parker, Robert. *Miasma: Pollution and Purification in Early Greek Religion.* Oxford: Oxford University Press, 1983, (reprint, 2001).

Peterson, Brian Neil. *Ezekiel In Context: Ezekiel's Message Understood in Its Historical Setting of Covenant Curses and Ancient Near Eastern Mythological Motifs,* Princeton Theological Monograph Series 182. Eugene, OR: Pickwick Publications, 2012.

Pfeiffer, Charles F. *Exile and Return.* Grand Rapids, Michigan: Baker Book House, 1962.

Philip, Tarja S. "Gender Matters: Priestly Writing on Impurity." Pages 40-60 in *Embroidered Garments: Priests and Gender in Biblical Israel.* HBM 25. Edited by Deborah W. Rooke. Sheffield: Sheffield Phoenix Press, 2009.

________. *Menstruation and Childbirth in the Bible: Fertility and Impurity.* Studies in Biblical Literature 88. New York: Peter Lang, 2006.

Pierce, Laurie E. "New Evidence for Judeans in Babylon." Pages 399-411 in *Judah and Judeans in the Persian Period.* Edited by Oded Lipschichts and Manfred Oeming. Winona Lake, Ind: Eisenbrauns, 2006.

________. "Judean" A Special Status Babylonia?" Pages 267-277 in Judah and the Judeans in the Achaemenid Period: *Negotiating Identity in an International Context.* Edited by Oded Lipschits, Gary Knoppers, and Manfred Oeming. Winona Lake, Ind: Eisenbrauns, 2011.

Pohlmann, Karl-Friedrich. *Ezechiel: Der Stand Der Theologischen Diskussion.* Darmstadt: Wissenschaftliche Buchgesellschaft, 2008.

Poorthuis, Marcel and Joshua Schwartz. "Purity an Holiness: An Introductory Survey." Pages 1-26 in *Purity and Holiness: The Heritage of Leviticus.* Edited by M. J. H. M. Poorthuis and J. Schwartz. Leiden: Brill, 2000.

Porten, Bezalel. *The Elephantine Papyri in English: Three Millenia of Cross-Cultural Continuity and Change.* Leiden: E. J. Brill, 1996.

________. "Settlement of the Jews at Elephantine and the Arameans at Syne." Pages 451- 470 in *Judah and the Judeans in the Neo-Babylonian Period.* Edited by Oded Lipschits and Joseph Blenkinsopp. Winona Lake, Ind: Eisenbrauns, 2003.

Power, E. "The Shepherd's Two Rods in Modern Palestine and in Some Passages of the Old Testament." *Biblica* 9 (1928): 434-442.

Preuss. "גלולים." Pages 1-5 in *TDOT* Vol. III. Edited by G. Johannes Botterweck and Helmer Ringgren. Translated by David E. Green. Grand Rapids, Michigan: Eerdmans, 1978.

________. "עולם." Pages 530-545 in *TDOT* Vol. X. Edited by G. Johannes Botterweck, Helmer Ringgren and Heinz-Josef Fabry. Translated by David E. Green. Grand Rapids, Michigan: Eerdmans, 1999.

Pritchard, James S. *Ancient Near Eastern Texts Relating to the Old Testament.* Translated by A. Leo Openheim. Princeton: Princeton Univ. Press, 1955.

Propp, William H. C. "The Priestly Source Recovered Intact?" *Vetus Testamentum* XLVI (1996): 458-478.

Rabie, J. M. J. C. Schot, and L. Visser. "Social Identity Theory: A Conceptual and Empirical Critique from the Perspective of a Behavioural Interaction Model." In *European Journal of Social Psychology* 19 (1989): 171-202.

Rad, G. Von. *Studies in Deuteronomy.* Translated by David Stalker. Chicago: Henry Regnery Company, 1953.

________. *Old Testament Theology Vol. I.* Translated by D. M. G. Stalker. Louisville: Westminster John Knox Press, 2001.

________. *Old Testament Theology Vol. II.* Translated by D. M. G. Stalker. Louisville: Westminster John Knox Press, 2001.

Regev, Eyal. "Non-Priestly Purity and its Religious Aspect According to Historical Sources and Archaeological Findings." Pages 223-244 in *Purity and Holiness: The Heritage of Leviticus.* Edited by M. J. H. M. Poorthuis & J. Schwartz. Leiden: Brill, 2000.

Rehm, Merlin D. "Levites and Priests." Pages 297-310 in *ABD* Vol. 4. Edited by Noel Freedman, et. al., New York: Doubleday, 1992.

Renz, Thomas. *The Rhetorical Function of the Book of Ezekiel.* VTSup 78. Leiden: Brill, 1999.

Ringgren. "טהר." Pages 287-296 in TDOT Vol. V. Edited by G. Johannes Botterweck and Helmer Ringgren. Translated by David E. Green. Grand Rapids, Michigan: Eerdmans, 1986.

Robinson, H. Wheeler. *The Religious Ideas of the Old Testament.* London: Gerald Duckworth & Co. Ltd., 1956.

Robinson, W. Peter (ed.). *Social Groups and Identities: Developing the Legacy of Henri Tajfel.* Oxford: Butterworth-Heinemann, 1996.

Rom-Shiloni, Dalit. "Ezekiel as the Voice of the Exiles and Constructor of Exilic Ideology." Pages 1-45 in *Hebrew Union College Annual LXXVI.* Cincinnati: Hebrew Union College-Jewish Institute of Religion, 2006.

________. "Form Ezekiel to Ezra-Nehemiah: Shifts of Group Identities within Babylonian Exilic Ideology." Pages 127-151 in *Judah and Judeans in the Achaemenid Period: Negotiating Identity in an International Context.* Edited by Oded Lipschits, Gary N, Knoppers, and Manfred Oeming. Winona Lake, Ind: Eisenbrauns, 2011.

________. *Exclusive Inclusivity: Identity Conflict Between the Exiles and the People who Remained (6th-5th century BCE).* New York: Bloomsbury, 2013.

Rosenau, William. "Ezekiel 37:15-28: What Happened to the Ten Tribes." Pages 79-88 in *Hebrew Union College Annual* 1925, Special Issue. Cincinnati: Hebrew Union College, 1925.

Rudnig, Thilo Alexander. *Helig und Profan: Redaktionskritische Studien zu Ez 40-48.* BZAW 287. Berlin: Walter de Gruyter, 2000.

Sandgren, Leo Dupree. *Vines Intertwined: A History of Jews and Christians from the Babylonian Exile to the Advent of Islam.* Peabody, Massachusetts: Hendrickson Publishers, 2010.

Schellenberg, Annette. "More than Spirit: On the Physical Dimension in the Priestly Understanding of Holiness." *ZAW* 126 no. 2 (2014): 163-179.

Schneider. "rabdoj." Pages 966-971 in *TDNT* Vol. VI. Edited by Gerhard Friedrich. Translated by Geoffrey W. Bromiley. Grand Rapids, Michigan: Eerdmans, 1968.

Schwartz, Baruch J. "A Priest out of Place: Reconsidering Ezekiel's Role in the History of the Israelite Priesthood." Pages 61-71 in *Ezekiel's Hierarchical World Wrestling with a Tired Reality.* Edited by Stephen L. Cook and Corrine L. Patton. Atlanta: SBL, 2004.

________. "Israel's Holiness: The Torah Traditions." Pages 48-59 in *Purity and Holiness: The Legacy of Leviticus.* Edited by M. J. H. M. Poorthuis and Baruch J. Shwartz. Leiden: Brill, 2000.

Sherif, Muzfer. *In Common Predicament: Social Psychology of Intergroup Conflict and Cooperation*. Boston: Houghton Mifflin Company, 1966.

________. *Group Conflict and Co-operation: Their Social Psychology*. London: Routledge & Kegan Paul Ltd., 1966.

Siedlecki, Armin. "Purity and Power: A Rhetorical Study of the Ideology of Purity and Defilement in the book of Ezekiel." MA Thesis. Wilfrid Laurier University, 1991.

Sklar, Jay. "Sin and Impurity: Atoned or Purified? Yes!." Pages 19-31 in *Perspectives on Purity and Purification in the Bible*. Edited by Baruch J. Schwartz, David P. Wright, Jeffrey Stackert, and Natphtali S. Meshel LBH/OTS 474. New York: T&T Clark, 2008.

Smith-Christopher, Daniel L. *A Biblical Theology of Exile*. Minneapolis: Fortress Press, 2002.

Smith, Daniel L. *The Religion of the Landless: The Social Context of the Babylonian Exile*. Bloomington, Ind: Meyer Stone, 1989.

Smith, Jonathan Z. "What a Difference a Difference Makes." Pages 3-48 in *To See Ourselves as Others See Us, Christians, Jews, "Others" in Late Antiquity*. Edited by Jacob Neusner and Ernest Frerichs. Chico, California: Scholars Press, 1985.

Smith, William Robertson. *Lectures on the Religions of the Semites: The Fundamental Institutions* (with an introduction and additional notes by Stanley A. Cook). United States: KTAV Publishing House, Inc., 1969. Third edition, first pub. 1927.

Stalker, D. M. G. *Ezekiel: Introduction and Commentary*. London: SCM Press Ltd., 1968.

Staub, Ervin. "Individual and Group Identities in Genocide and Mass Killing." Pages 159-184 in *Social Identity, Intergroup Conflict, and Conflict Reduction*. Edited by Richard D. Ashmore, Lee Jussim and David Wilder. Oxford: Oxford University Press, 2001.

Stavrakopoulou, Francesca. "Gog's Grave and the Use and Abuse of Corpses in Ezekiel 39:11-20." *JBL* 129 no. 1 (2010): 67-84.

Stein, Ephraim. Archaeology of the Land of the Bible Vol. II: *The Assyrian, Babylonian, and Persian Periods 732-332 BCE*. New York: Doubleday, 2001.

Stevenson, Kalinda Rose. *The Vision of Transformation: The Territorial Rhetoric of Ezekiel 40-48,* SBLDS 154. Atlanta: Scholars Press, 1996.

Strong, John T. "God's Kabod: The Presence and Absence of Yahweh in the Book of Ezekiel." Pages 69-95 in *The Book of Ezekiel: Theological and Anthropological Perspectives,* SBL Symposium Series 9. Edited by Margaret S. Odell & John T. Strong. Atlanta: SBL, 2000.

Stulman, Louis. "Ezekiel as Disaster/Survival Literature: Speaking on behalf of the Losers." Pages 133-159 in *The Prophets Speak on Forced Migration*. Ancient Israel and Its Literature 21. Atlanta: SBL Press, 2015.

Sumner, William Graham. *Folkways: A Study of the Sociological Importance of Usages, Manners, Customs, Mores, and Morals*. Boston: Ginn & Company, 1906.

Sweeney, Marveen. A. *TANAK: A Theological and Critical Introduction to the Jewish Bible* (Minneapolis: Fortress Press, 2012.

Sweeney, Marvin E. *Reading Prophetic Books: Form, Intertextuality, and Reception in Prophetic and Post-Biblical Literature.* FAT 89. Tubingen: Mohr Siebeck, 2014.

Swidler, Ann. *Talk of Love: How Culture Matters*. Chicago: The University of Chicago Press, 2001.

Tajfel, Henri. *Differentiation Between Social Groups: Studies in Social Psychology of Intergroup Relations.* London: Academic Press, 1978.

________. "Social Stereotypes and Social Groups." Pages 143-156 in *Intergroup Behaviour*. Edited by J. C. Turner and Howard Giles. Philadelphia, PA: Psychology Press, 1981.

________. "Introduction." Page 1-11 in *Social Identity and Intergroup Relations.* Edited by Henri Tajfel. Cambridge: Cambridge University Press, 1982.

________ (ed). *Social Identity and Intergroup Relations*. Cambridge: Cambridge University Press, 1982.

Tajfel, Henri and John C. Turner. "The Social Identity Theory of Intergroup Behavior." Pages 7-24 in *Psychology of Intergroup Relation*. Edited by William G. Austin and Stephen Worchel. Monterey, CA: Brooks/Cole, 1986.

________. "An Integrative Theory of Intergroup Conflict." Pages 94-109 in *Intergroup Relations*. Edited by Michael Hogg and Dominic Abrams. Philadelphia, PA: Psychology Press, 2001.

Taylor, John B. *Ezekiel: An Introduction and Commentary*. Downers Grove, Ill., InterVarsity Press, 1969.

Thompson, Kenneth. "Durkheim and Sacred Identity." Pages 94-104 in *On Durkheim's Elementary Forms of Religious Life*. Edited by N. J. Allen, W. S. F. Pickering and W. Watts Miller. Routledge Studies in Social and Political Thought. London: Routledge, 1998.

Tooman, William A. "Covenant and Presence in the Composition and Theology of Ezekiel." Pages 161-182 in *Divine Presence and Absence in Exilic and Post-Exilic Judaism*, Forschungen zum Alten Testament 61. Edited by Nathan MacDonald and Izaak D. de Hulster. Tubingen: Mohr Siebeck, 2013.

Tuell, Steven Shawn. *The Law of the Temple in Ezekiel 40-48. HSM 49. Atlanta,* Georgia: Scholars Press, 1992.

________. "Divine Presence and Absence in Ezekiel's Prophecy." Pages 97-116 in *The Book of Ezekiel Theological and Anthropological Perspectives*, SBL Symposium Series 9. Atlanta: SBL, 2000.

________. *Ezekiel: New International Biblical Commentary* (Peabody, Massachusetts: Hendrickson Publishers, 2009.

Turner, J. C., M. A. Hogg, P. J. Oakes, S. D. Reicher, and M. S. Wetherell (eds), *Rediscovering Social Group: A Self-Categorization Theory*. Oxford: Blackwell, 1987.

Turner, John C. "Towards a Cognitive Redefinition of the Social Group." Pages 15-40 in *Social Identity and Intergroup Relations.* Edited by Henri Tajfel. Cambridge: Cambridge University Press, 1982.

________. "Some Current Issues in Research on Social Identity and Self-Categorization Theories." Pages 6-34 in *Social Identity Context, Commitment, Content.* Edited by Naomi Ellemers, Russel Spears and Bertijan Doosje. Malden, Massachusetts: Blackwell Publishers, 1999.

Turner, Victor. *The Forest of Symbols: Aspects of Ndembu Ritual.* Ithaca, New York: Cornell University Press, 1967.

Van Seters, John. "The Tent of the Meeting in the Yahwist and the Origin of the Synagogue." *SJOT* 29/1 (2015): 1-10.

Vawter, Bruce and Leslie J. Hoppe. *A New Heart: A Commentary on the Book of Ezekiel*, ITC. Grand Rapids: Eerdmans, 1991.

Velazquez II, Efrain. "The Persian Period and the Origins of Israel: Beyond the "Myths." Pages 61-78 in *Critical Issues in early Israelite History.* Edited by Richard S. Hess, Gerald A. Klingbeil, and Paul J. Ray Jr. Winona Lake, Ind: Eisenbrauns, 2008.

Walkte, Bruce K. and M.O 'Connor. *An Introduction to Biblical Hebrew Syntax.* Winona Lake, Ind: Eisenbrauns, 1990.

Walzer, Michael. *The Revolution of the Saints: A Study in the Origins of Radical Politics.* Cambridge, Massachusetts: Harvard University Press, 1965.

________. "Puritanism as a Revolutionary Ideology." Pages 19-41 in *Puritan New England.* Edited by Alden T. Vaughan and Francis J. Bremer. New York: St Martin's Press, 1977.

Warren, Nathanael James. "A Cannibal Feast in Ezekiel." *JSOT* 38 no. 4 (2014): 501-512.

Weinberg, Joel. *The Citizen-temple Community.* JSOTSup 151. Translated by Daniel L. Smith-Christopher. Sheffield: Sheffield Academic Press, 1992.

Weinfeld, Moshe. "Social and Cultic Institutions in the Priestly Source Against their Ancient Near Eastern Background." Pages 95-129 in *Proceedings of the Eighth World Congress of Jewish Studies*. Jerusalem: World Union of Jewish Studies, 1983.

Weisberg, David B. "A "Dinner at the Palace" During Nebuchadnezzar's Reign." Pages 261-167 in *Homeland and Exile: Biblical and Ancient Near Eastern Studies in honour of Bustenay Oded*. Edited by Gershon Galil, Mark Geller and Alan Millard. Leiden: Brill, 2009.

Wellhausen, Julius. *Prolegomena to the History of Israel*. Atlanta, Georgia: Scholars Press, 1994; reprinted of the edition of 1885.

Wevers, John W. *Ezekiel*. The Century Bible. London: Thomas Nelson and Sons Ltd., 1969.

Whiteley, Charles Francis. *The Exilic Age*. Philadelphia: Westminster Press, 1957.

Wilson, E. Jan. *"Holiness" and "Purity" in Mesopotamia*. Neukirchen, Vluyn: Neukirchener Verlag-des Erziehungsvereins GambH, 1994.

Wilson, Robert R. "Forced Migration and the Formation of the Prophetic Literature." Pages 125-138 in *By the Irrigation Canals of Babylon: Approaches to the Study of the Exile*, LHB/OTS 526. Edited by John J. Ahn and Jill Middlemas. New York: T&T Clark, 2012.

Wolde, Ellen van. "A Cognitive Linguistic Study of the Concept of Defilement in Ezekiel 22:1-16." Pages 257-271 in *Biblical Interpretation and Method: Essays in Honour of John Barton*. Edited by Katharine J. Dell and Paul M. Joyce. Oxford: Oxford University Press, 2013.

Wong Ka Leung. *The Idea of Retribution in the Book of Ezekiel*. VTSup LXXXVII. Leiden: Brill, 2001.

________. "Profanation/Sanctification and the Past Present and Future of Israel in the Book of Ezekiel." *JSOT* 28, no. 2 (2003): 210-239.

Worchel, Stephen, J. Francois Morales, Dario Paez and Jean-Claude Deschamps (eds). *Social Identity: International Perspective*. London: Sage Publications, 1998.

Wright – Milgrom. "hdn." Pages 232-234 in *TDOT* Vol. IX. Edited by G. Johannes Botterwek, Helmer Ringgren and Heinz-Joseph Fabry. Translated by David E. Green. Grand Rapids, Michigan: Eerdmans, 1980.

Wright, Christopher J. H. *The Message of Ezekiel: a New Heart and a New Spirit*. Downers Grove, Ill.: Inter Varsity Press, 2001.

Wright, David P. *The Disposal of Impurity in the Priestly Writings of the Bible with Reference to Similar Phenomena in Hittite and Mesopotamian Cultures*, Facsimile printed by Microfilm, PhD Dissertation Submitted to University of California, Berkeley, 1984. Ann Arbor, MI: University Microfilms International, 1984.

________. "The Spectrum of Priestly Impurity." Pages 150-181 in *Priesthood and Cult in Ancient Israel.* Edited by Gary A. Anderson and Saul M. Olyan. Sheffield: JSOT Press, 1991.

________. "Unclean and Clean (OT)." Pages 729-742 in *ABD* Vol. 6. Edited by David Noel Freedman, et.al. New York: Doubleday, 1992.

Zaithanchhungi. *Mizo-Israel Identity.* Aizawl, Mizoram: L. N. Tluanga, 2008.

Zadok, Ran. *The Jews in Babylonia During the Chaldean and Achaemenian Periods According to the Babylonian Sources.* Haifa: University of Haifa, 1978.

Zimmerli, Walther. *Ezekiel 1: A Commentary on the Book of the Prophet Ezekiel 1-24.* Translated by Ronald E. Clements. Edited by Frank Moore Cross, Klaus Blatzer and Leonard Jay Greenspoon. Philadelphia: Fortress Press, 1979.

________. *Ezekiel 2: A Commentary on the Book of the Prophet Ezekiel 25-48.* Translated by James D. Martin. Edited by Paul D. Hanson and Leonard Jay Greenspoon. Philadelphia: Fortress Press, 1983.

Zorn, Jeffrey R. "Tell-en-Nasbeh and the Problem of the Material Culture of the Sixth Century." Pages 413-447 in *Judah and the Judeans in the Neo-Babylonian Period.* Edited by Oded Lipschits and Joseph Blenkinsopp. Winona Lake, Ind: Eisenbrauns, 2003.

Index of Authors